GOD, UNIVERSE, AND I: PART II, III, AND IV

Criminal Psychotronic Weapons, NanoMicroMagnetic Weapons, Targeted Individuals, Mind Control, Untouched Torture, Directed Energy

PHIEM NGUYEN

Order this book online at www.trafford.com
or email orders@trafford.com

Most Trafford titles are also available at major online book retailers.

Print information available on the last page.

ISBN: 978-1-4669-2205-1 (sc)
ISBN: 978-1-4669-2204-4 (e)

Library of Congress Control Number: 2012906059

Trafford rev. 01/27/2016

www.trafford.com

North America & international
toll-free: 1 888 232 4444 (USA & Canada)
fax: 812 355 4082

Criminal Psychotronic Weapons

Dear reader,

Kept Fighting for Human Dignity

Non-lethal weapons, Criminal Psychotronic Weapons since I was 18 year old until today this trend spread over this planet. This is totally amoral science was perfectly developed which carried out secretly by governments to torture citizens in its countries. The victims without knowledge high-technology was using on them, it was described to them as wonder weapons. Reader please visits this site Raven1.net to understand completely this ill science.
They are so powerful to do everything they wanted and zipped it and do not want it to be known by others, by public. This is so terrible!!!!
For my whole life I thought I could be a Hitler's daughter, I just accidently have known there are a lot of victims as I am few months ago, after August 2010.

In 2003 I wrote my books to describe all the things have happened in my life and I said that was my part and I needed they have to reveal their part to public to complete the whole picture, the whole story. I did it because I have learned that they wanted to continue what was they were doing, I could not believe that was happened in these civilization societies.
Victims are powerless, defend less and were driven into same situations, rape, murder, abuse, humiliate human dignity, harm, and deprive human rights. Citizens have lived under oppression by Governments; Authorities without voices have been heard. That seems no one can stop this tendency, the atrocious holocaust murder, humiliate human dignity and enslave human, the horrible inhumanity sciences, the tyrannies are eager to make reborn colonialism in this 21st Century.
Citizens have lived in this civilization, how you define for your rights?
Scholars, Doctors and Scientists you have your consciences where you place them?
I thought our Ancestors believe in God so we inherited the harmony societies, moral, and happy lives. We are proud of we are men, women but now you tried to destroyed all in just lesser than one century.
I have learned: God with man, man's safe, man's happy but man is God, man kill man, man destroy the whole world, man destroy the earth, man destroy the whole universe if man could.
To soften the political tension and to avert the notion party that was described: you are friends or you are enemies, we are in circle attacking process to caste out the distrust seeds into the societies that made citizens have doubted minds toward government; this created the complexion and the riot.
To fight for Independence which we should drive away the invasion by influences and by forces on this nation and on the world today.

America citizens we have the Constitution emphasized the protection Rights.

We sent letter to UN, to the UN Disarmament, to the World Court, to The Rule of Law, to President, to the Senators, to the Congress, to the FBI, Home Land Security, NSA and Civil Court but without the result.

How and what we should do to stop, to end this amoral Non-lethal weapons/Criminal Psychotronic Weapons in United State of America and around the globe?

We needed the REVOLUTION but that will not be Communism.

We hope that we can change it.

Phiem Nguyen
October 30, 2010

I did not keep the diary since I published my Non-lethal Weapons DVD. Recently, it was early than November 12, 2010 they stole entire digital memo cards which have all the evidences on it but only one picture can prove the Criminal Psychotropic Weapons exist and executed on me.

The following facts are telling the story of harassment, humiliate, abuse, murder and so on.

The day when I was sitting at my computer, I do not know what this was called, cyber attack, they pressed my neck, they speared to my heart then my lung then they twisted my head. I immediately turned off my computer and left the computer table.

Another day it was not too far from now November 2, 2010 they twisted my vain, at this time I could not leave my computer because I could not walk, I immediately turned off my computer and closed the lip and took things to cover my body. For about 15 minutes later I left my computer but I could not walk normally, it was still pain.

One morning around of September I woke up I felt that they implanted chips at the end of my tongue; I had an experience coughing activated from that chip implanted the day after. I thought they could produce the bad breath whichever kind they wanted.

Otober 20. 2010

This morning I went to grocery store then during the time I went back my house from grocery store, I saw 3 electrical service trucks parked at the street under the highway (overpass) when I was waiting for crossing the street at the red light intersection, they made the snooze to my female that meant they activated or executed or monitored the chips that they implanted inside my female(I thought they were doing that during the time I was sleeping because I just felt the sandy and hurt to that place when I took shower as they did it to my female the same process I was described it in my book God Universe and I, it effected like Nano working inside that and destroy the tissues and the cells to make damage and deform my female.)
I walked home after I crossed the street I did not know who attacked Directed Energy to me, just about 10 or 15 minutes walking from the intersection, I felt tire I tried to reach to my house, I was terrible weak, do not have energy left to do anything. I had this experience 2 times in New Orleans in front of my house then another time in Irving I walked home from the store.

Few days later one evening I was sitting in my dinning room I saw the plane past by my window house they executed the snooze to my female, few days before that day the plane past by my window attacked to my female, that made sensation and itchy for several hours until I saw the satellite or police plane past by my window house for a while it was went off.

October 24, 2010 7:41 & 7:42 P.M.

October 27, 2010 8:33 P.M.

October 30, 2010 8:34 P.M.

October 27, 2010 8:29 P.M.

November 03, 2010 1:43P.M.

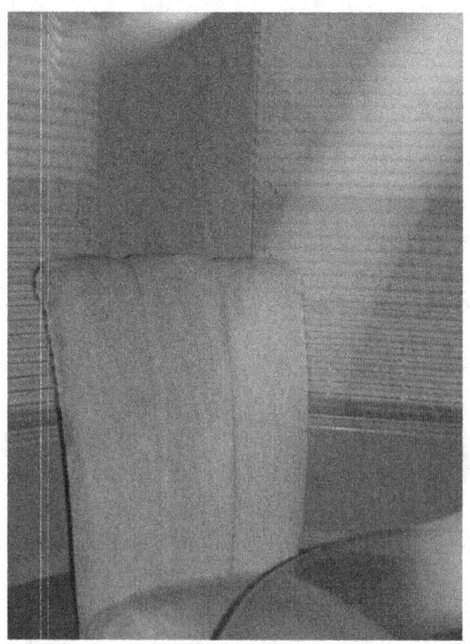

November 03, 2010 1:46 P.M.

November 03, 2010 1:45 P.M.

I indicated the plane because I usually saw the plane made several tours over my house for long period of time, I thought that the plane might carry out their broadcasting services until I was curious to count how long the plane made the tour. I counted 3', 2', 1'.30" and the plane made 12, 11, 9, 8 tours at least.

The plane attacked to my neck, my face I took the pictures to prove. The plane might attack me before that but I did not know that I thought it was from the cars, houses or satellite.

November 01, 2010

(Every night I go to bed they always attack me to my head, my ears, my chest, my macron born, my organs, my stomach, my lover abdomen, my female, my rectum, my legs, my toes, my toes nails, my finger nails, entire my body from head to toes, from inside to out side, from subconscious to conscious.

Every day I take shower, they attacked to my liver, my intestine, my stomach, my lungs, my back bone, my buttocks, my legs, my female and my head.

Everyday I do dishes or prepare for food at my kitchen they attack to my ears, my head, my face, my lip, my mouth, my nose, my stomach, my hang, my female, my rectum, my legs, my feet, my lungs, my back and my kidneys.

Every time I brush my teeth, they attacked to my female, my hang, my rectum, my kidney, my back bone, my chest and my head.

Every time I was sitting at my computer they attack to my head, my forefront, my ears, my face, my nose, my upper lip, my lower lip was damage normal form from their nano chips implanted or tissues, or cells implanted to damage my lower lip as I described it in God Universe and I book, my mouth, my cheeks, my cheek bones, my eyes (my face was sabotage turned to aging, wrinkle, saggy and swoopy eyes), my back, my two side of stomach, and my chest,

Last night October 31, 2010 I went to bed, I used the sheet of aluminum and 3 thick pieces of sponges to cover my female then I placed a heavy fake leather winter coat over my body, they tried to break through it day by day to executed the microwave gun to my female.
I went outside my bed room then I tried to be awakening until 7:30 a.m. November 01, 2010. They did sabotage, harm, deform, and transform my female, my breasts, and my woman body. My head they Pressed in my head to form the different head, they cut, they shot, they attacked by Microwave, they implanted. They create the sound during I am sleeping to turn to man, to turn to snake, to turn animal sounds and they woke me up enough to hear that sound to humiliate me when I awake since 2006 in Irving. They created gay, lesbian, they wanted to transform me into man, they abuse which they pat, tape it into my brain and they made everything on me. They are so terrible sick, terrible evils.
My eyes they used Micromagnetic wave or Nano shot to my eye I took that picture I saw the red microwave shot to my eye but when I upload my pictures to my computer, they hacked in to take off that picture.
Another night I was under their attack when I was in my bed so I went out my bed room I took the picture at my bedroom wall, the picture was shown the several laser circle outside my bedroom wall, that picture was taken off also.

I saw the result of my breast which they destroyed the support cells and tissues and destroyed my normal cells and tissues of my breast and my female also.
I saw that they destroyed the support tissues to hold my eye balls at my both eye havocs.)

Why they intended to do that, to abuse me, to humiliate my human dignity, to show me that they are God, they want to do what they want to do. They are evils.
What they expect me to say, to pray, to wish for the evils. As I said, I am not hypocrite so I pray God, Universe and people destroy all of the evils. Be aware of Stockholm syndrome.

I can say they attack to my entire body from head to toes from inside to outside, day and night from conscious to subconscious 24 hours a day, seven days a week, for 365 days a years constantly since 2004,

I realized they did do the things to harm my life, my dignity, my body, my health and my family since 1962 until today and it will be continue.
They might do the things to harm me before that time but I was too young to understand it.

Why they use Mind Control to enslave people in the system of colonialism? They kill all and they only keep who they want to keep as the organic robot under their commands. Why I said that? I saw their actions doing these things on me, my whole life, I could believe that.

They have to confess to the world what they tried to do to my body, to my brain, to my female, they are eager to produce sex organic robot with Mind Control.

November 01, 2010

They tried to attack to my stomach key hole during the time I was placing ices to the pain they created to my organs so I placed plastic bags and my hand to cover, it made my hand felt soar, hurt and tire muscles.

November 2, 2010

They tried to attacked my stomach key hole when I was in kitchen I had to cover it, I am usually have to cover my female, my head, my stomach and my entire body when I was in my kitchen.
They shot to my right breast at the lunch time, it made my already deform breast (they sabotaged it) more deform, more saggy, another day they shot to my left breast when I took shower I took these pictures but I do not want to show it here, it deserve for only investigation so it has the date on it, it made the tissue die, damage, They are seriously ambitious to get what they wanted.

October 29, 2010 7:29 P.M.

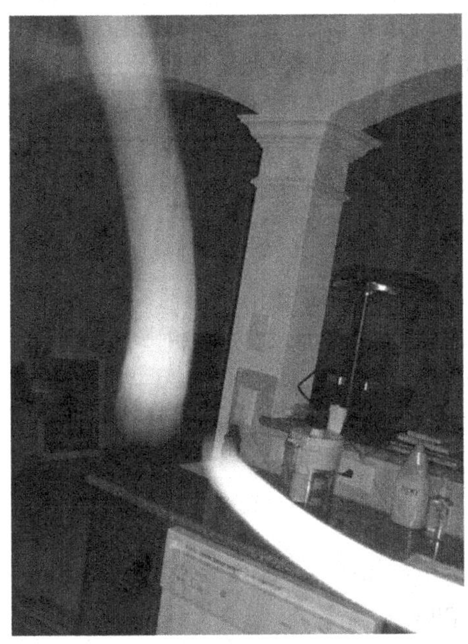

November 02, 2010 5:51 P.M.

November 4, 2010

Yesterday I stood at the stove in the kitchen for doing cooking, they attacked to my chest it effected to my heart like a kind of feeling dried out then I felt tired, I took metal to cover my chest, in the kitchen I usually have pot cover lids.

October 5, 2010

Last night I went to bed, they attacked to my female at the place they implanted chips or Nanotechnology In 2006, 2007 I wrote it in my book God Universe and Me book, I did not know what they tried to do, I covered my body with 3 pieces of sponges, my heavy fake leather jacket and my blanket but they burned my flesh with Micromagnetic, I felt hot then hurt then smelt like flesh burning.

I do not know what they tried to do to my body, they sabotaged my body in the shape they wanted, they created and they wanted to transform me into the gay, the lesbian and man. Why they have to do it? They torture, abuse and humiliate me.
Because they are Tyrannies, they have powers, they are riches and they do what they want to do to me and to this mankind on this planet.

I wrote the Quan Am Buddha story in my book that I compared the innocent in the story to me the victims of Criminal Psychotronic Weapons. They had their intelligent enough to understand that meaning I emphasized in my book. That why the reason they wanted to transform me into the man to cover up their sins.

Now the whole world knew what is the Criminal Psychotronics Weapons was using to whom and from whom. It is not a ghost or unknown reason or wonder weapons which destroyed our lives and it is blooming rapidly over the globe.
Awaken Mankind solves this problem or let God or let Universe solve it for us.
Everyone of us has to ask our selves if we are under Mind Control, be aware of controlling behavior, they created that we do not want to do anything, we are inferior, we are worthless, we fear to do and so on.

November 6, 2010

Last evening when I had dinner the plane past by my window house I counted 2 tours they executed their attacking to my ear, my neck. I took these pictures.
I saw the plane and I noticed the attacking but I did not know it was right for the mission of torture like that or the game they set up to make me feel as I thought so.
I saw the plane was not circulated above my house for last few days it flew over on the other side of 45 Interstate High Way; I asked myself if they did harass some one over there.
In the day time I saw the small plane, it is big enough for technology equipment and crewmembers too.

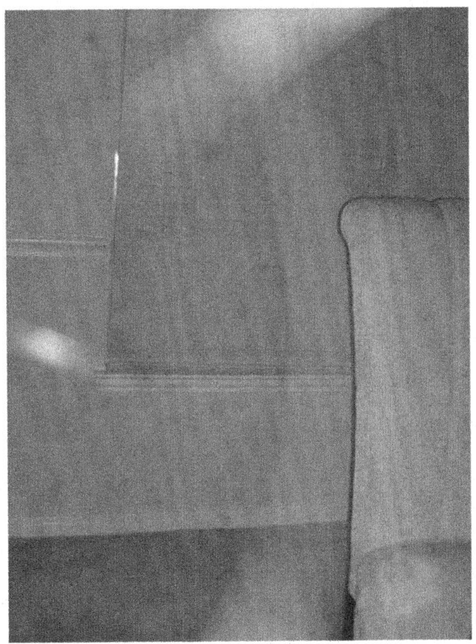

November 5, 2010 9:03 P.M.

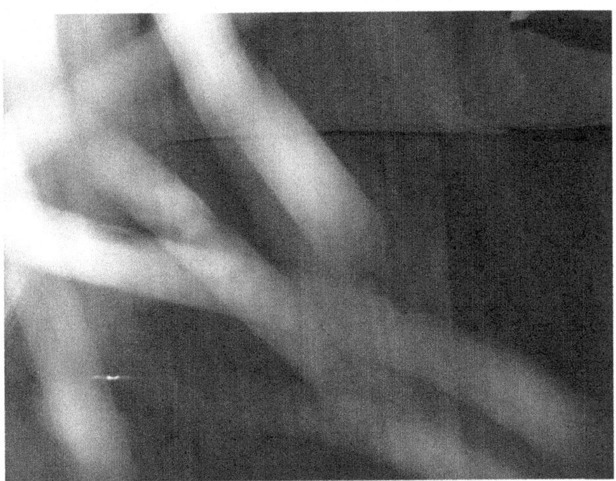

November 5, 2010 9:03 P.M.

However this evening when I was in my dinning-room it had no plane flew circle on this sky neighborhood I took these pictures to prove the attacking to my ear, my neck. They might be here or they are far away haft of the world.

November 6, 2010 8:30 P.M.

November 6, 2010 8:45 P.M.

They continue attacking to Phiem ear when she was sitting at her computer.

November 6, 2010 11:47 P.M.

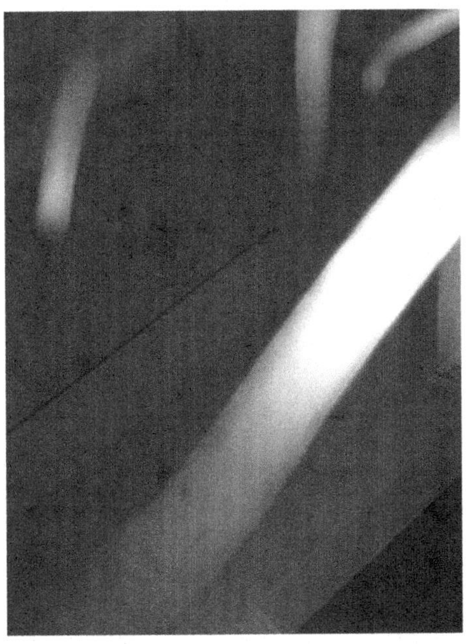

November 06, 2010 11:47 P.M.

Phiem was afraid of going to bed she tried to be awakening all night this night, do you see they still working day and night in order to attack her, this picture prove the date and time.

November 7, 2010 4:02 A.M.

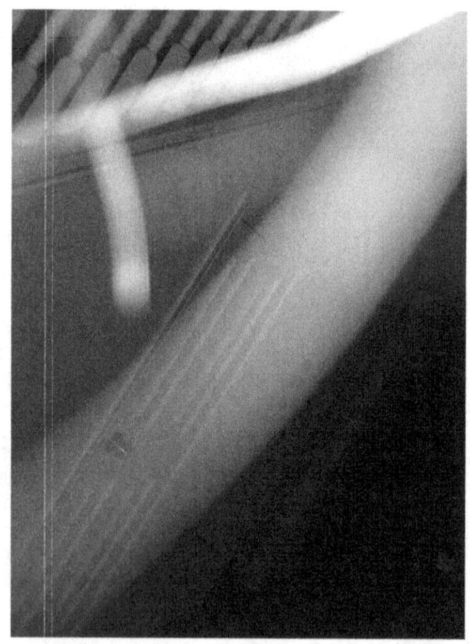

November 7, 2010 7:03 P.M.

The whole house was set to attack to Phiem wherever she went when they activated, those Nanotechnology, Electromagnetic, Micromagnetic were captured on these pictures.

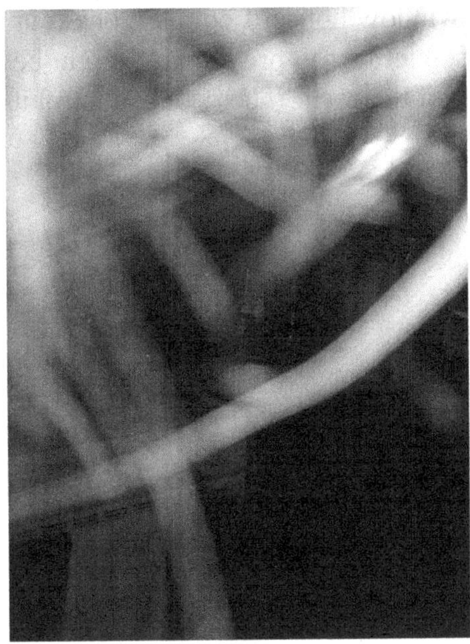

November 7, 2010 7:03 P.M.

The whole house was set to attack to Phiem wherever she went when they activated, those Nanotechnology, Electromagnetic, Micromagnetic were captured on these pictures.

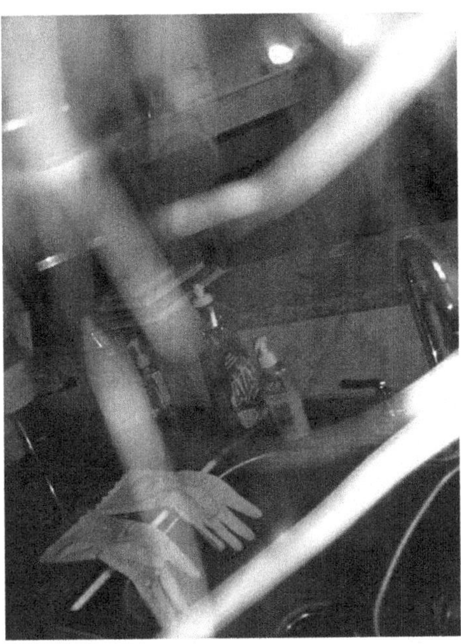

November 7, 2010 7:04 P.M.

The whole house was set to attack to Phiem wherever she went when they activated, those Nanotechnology, Electromagnetic, Micromagnetic were captured on these pictures

This evening I saw the familiar small plane past by my window house, I counted one tour this evening then I notice the shot to my head I took these pictures to prove but it might be the game, they might be here and they might be a half way of the earth. They could control it by satellite but their team should be here guiding and report.

November 7, 2010 7:55 P.M.

They attacked to Phiem head when she was in her dinning room, the circle on her hairs and Microwave heat color.

November 7, 2010 7:53 P.M.

They attacked to Phiem head when she was in her dinning room, the bunch of Nanotechnology on her hairs and Microwave heat color.

November 7, 2010 7:55 P.M.

Weapons attacked to Phiem head was captured in this picture, this was cutting, and the point drilling to Phiem head and she could feel it by her finger at her head.

November 8, 2010 6:56 A.M.

Phiem was afraid of going to bed at night so she tried to be awake for whole night but she was fallen in sleeping at her computer table because she wanted to wait to turn off the porch light before she went to bed. They attacked to her ear and neck, she took these pictures.

November 8, 2010 6:59 A.M.

Phiem was afraid of going to bed at night so she tried to be awakening for whole night but she was fallen in sleeping at her computer table because she wanted to wait to turn off the porch light before she went to bed. They attacked to her ear and neck, she took these pictures.

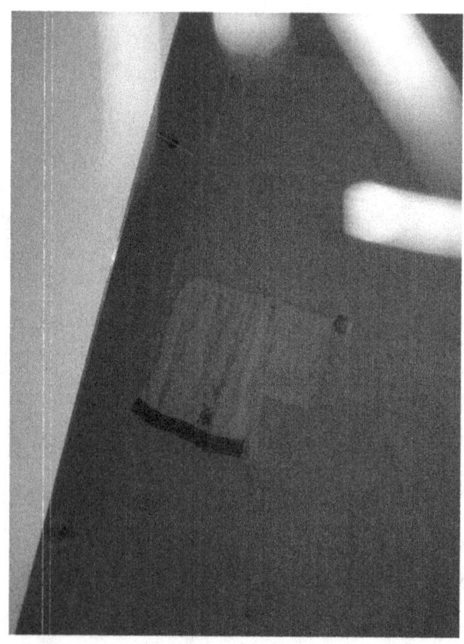

November 8, 2010 2:39 P.M.

Phiem was in her kitchen they attacked to her ear and neck then she went upstairs to take her camera, this is the first shot at her bathroom, they set up the whole house was affected when they activated to each executed to the victim. Victim has no place to hide.

This is the series of pictures was taken in Phiem kitchen that prove the Nanotechnology and electromagnetic to murder, to harm, to deform, to abuse, to humiliate to the victim body with no centimeter left free on her body, from top to toes, from inside to outside, from conscious to subconscious in her house day and night 24/7 for 365 days a year constantly since 2004, this is mention about Nanotechnology and Directed Energy, Electromagnetic, Micromagnetic, Criminal Psychotropic Weapons only.

November 8, 2010 2:40 P.M. (1)

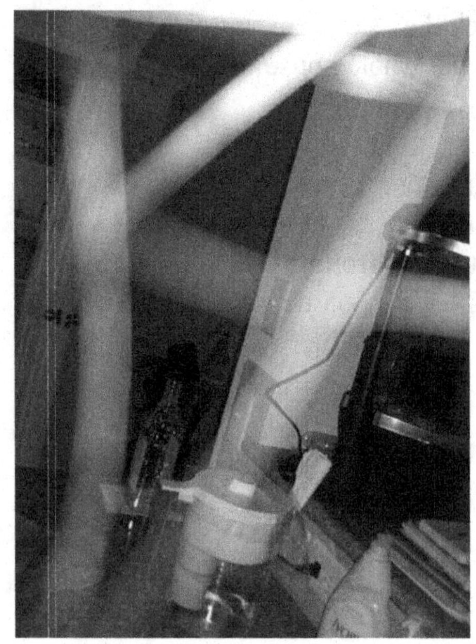

November 8, 2010 2:40 P.M. (2)

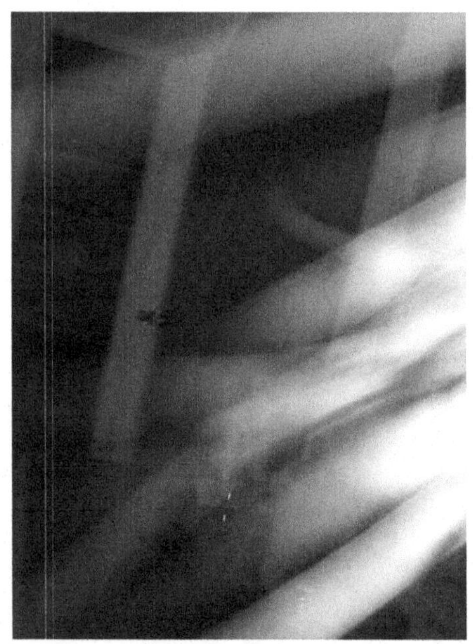

November 8, 2010 2:40 P.M. (3)

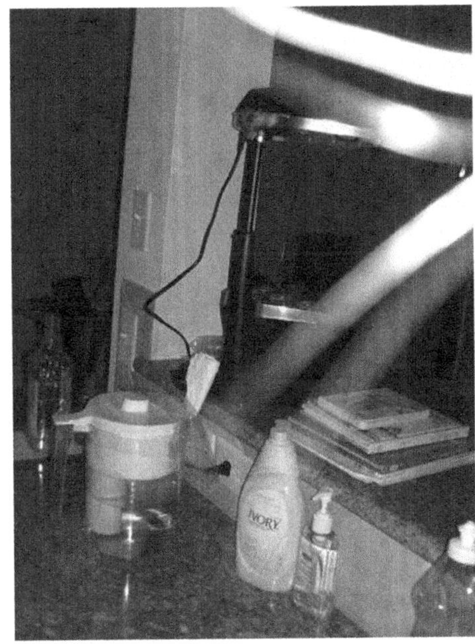

November 8, 2010 2:43 P.M. (4)

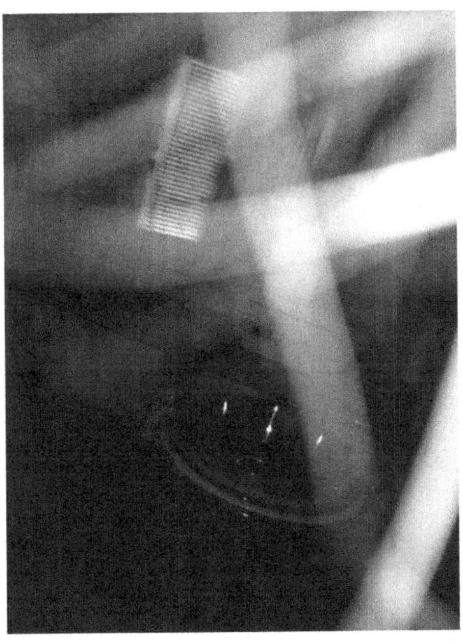

November 9, 2010 1:58 P.M.

Phiem walking around doing exercise they attacked to abuse her, drover her in the difficult and angry situation. Preventing for everything.

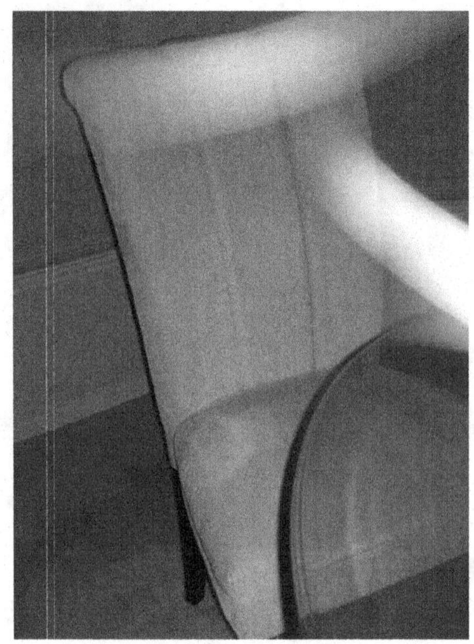

November 9, 2010 9:01 P.M.

Phiem sat at her table for having dinner, she cover her body with pot lid, she saw the plane flew on the sky several tours this evening, she could feel the attacking then she took these pictures but she could not determined that was from the plane, she did not know.

November 9, 2010 9:02 P.M.

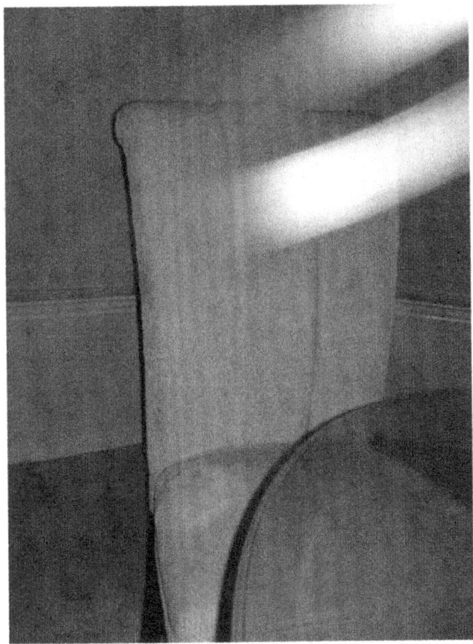

November 9, 2010 9:16 P.M.

Phiem sat at her table for having dinner, she cover her body with pot lid, she saw the plane flew on the sky several tours this evening, she could feel the attacking then she took these pictures but she could not determined that was from the plane, she did not know.

November 9, 2010 9:26 P.M.

They attacked to Phiem back and neck when she was in her dinning room.

November 9, 2010 9:26 P.M.

They attacked to Phiem back and neck when she was in her dinning room.

November 10, 2010 9:32 P.M.

They attacked to Phiem head when she was sitting in her dinning room.

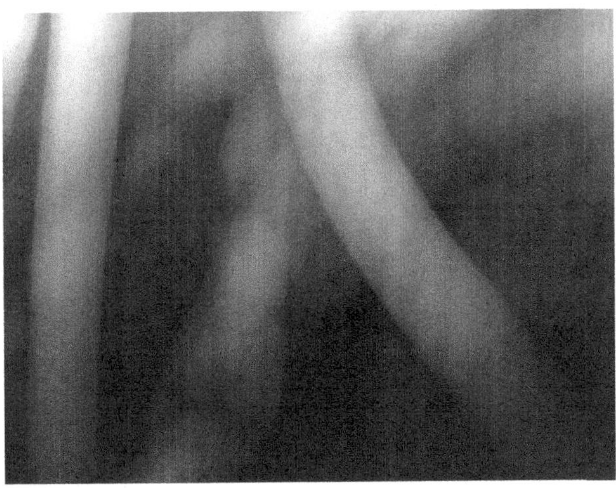

November 10, 2010 9:32 P.M.

They attacked to Phiem head when she was sitting in her dinning room.

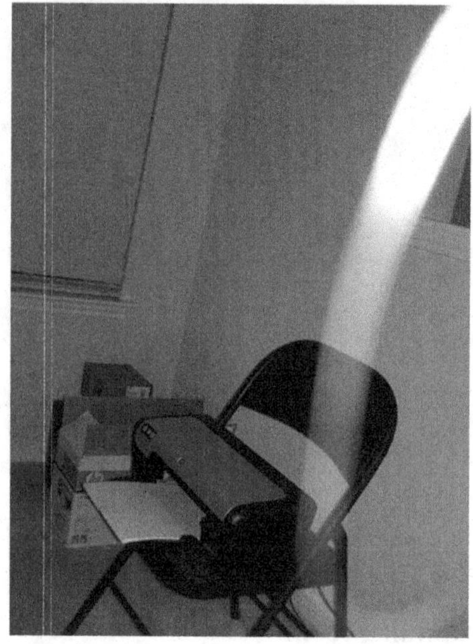

November 9, 2010 9:49 P.M.

They attacked to Phiem ear when she was sitting at her computer.

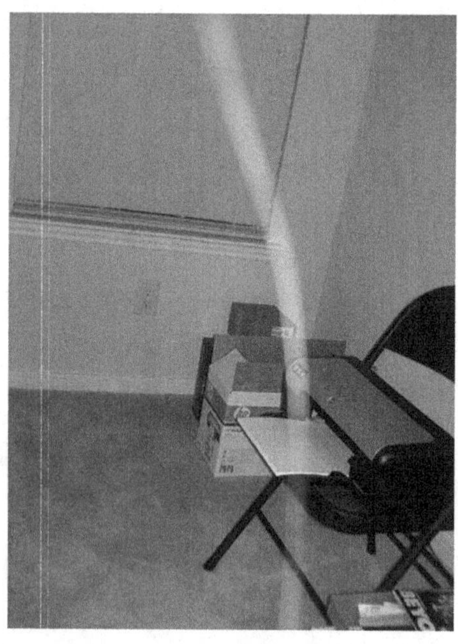

November 9, 2010 9:49 P.M.

They attacked to Phiem ear when she was sitting at her computer.

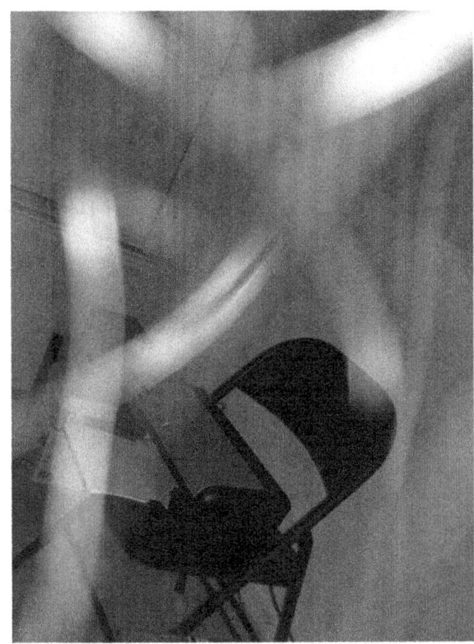

November 9, 2010 10:54 P.M.

They attacked to Phiem ear when she was sitting at her computer.

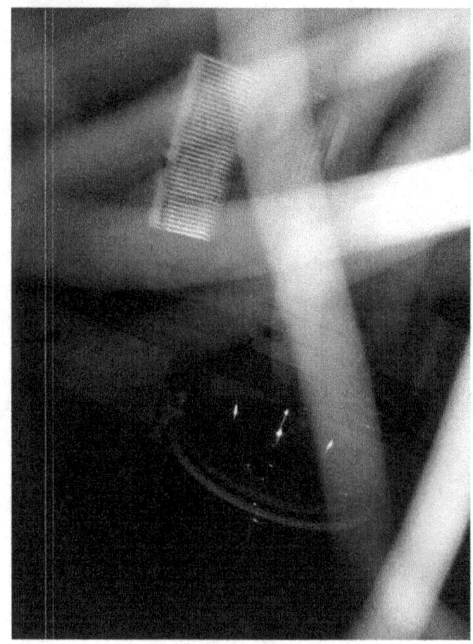

November 9, 2010 1:58 P.M.

Phiem walking around doing exercise they attacked to abuse her, drover her in the difficult and angry situation. They controlled for preventing for everything.

November 10, 2010 9:32 P.M.

They attacked to Phiem head when she was sitting in her dinning room.

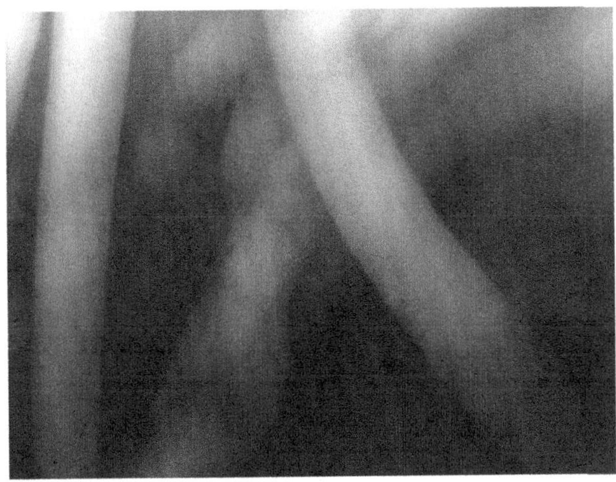

November 10, 2010 9:32 P.M.

They attacked to Phiem head when she was sitting in her dinning room.

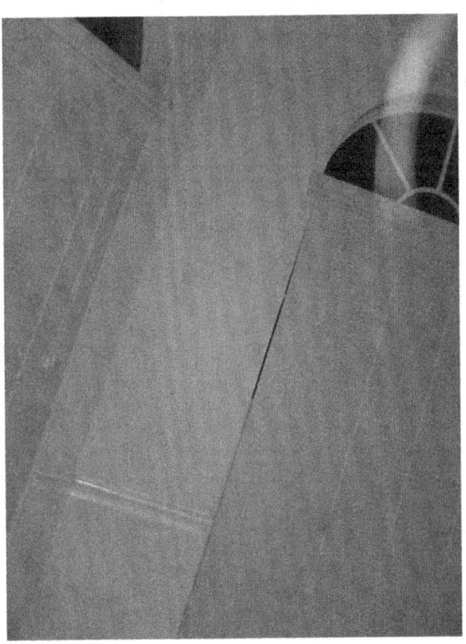

November 10, 2010 9:32 P.M.

They used Nanotechnology to attack to Phiem ear, neck, and head and face when she was at her dinning room.

This show how rich the 80 Billions Spying to torture, rape, abuse and murder me.

November 10, 2010 9:35 P.M.

They used Nanotechnology to attack to Phiem ear, neck, and head and face when she was at her dinning room.
This show how rich the 80 Billions Spying to torture, rape, abuse and murder me.

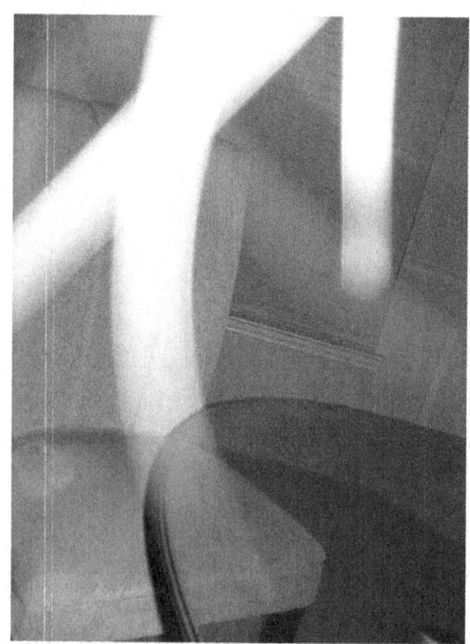

November 10, 2010 9:35 P.M.

They used Nanotechnology to attack to Phiem ear, neck, and head and face when she was at her dinning room.

This show how rich the 80 Billions Spying to torture, rape, abuse and murder me and others.

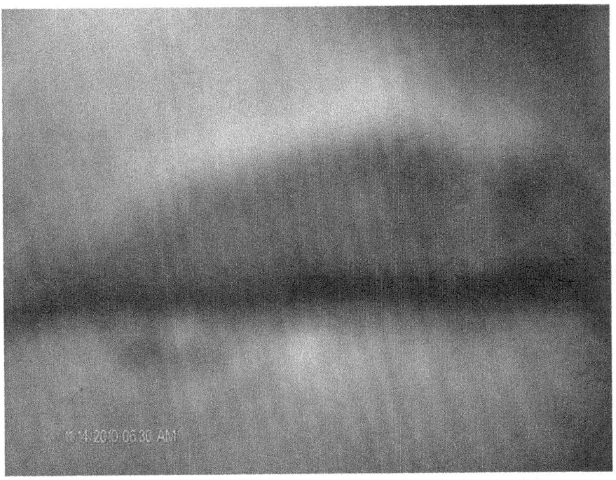

November 14, 2010 6:30 A.M.

They implanted Nanotechnology chips into Phiem's upper lip during the time she was sleeping, this morning when she woke up she saw it then she took these pictures. They used spy camouflage technique to sabotage Phiem lower lip in 2006 in Irving, Texas, that she wrote in her God Universe and Me book.

Her lower lip was completely changing shape; it grew bigger, erased my lip liner. How rude they are? How tyranny they are? I looked to my dictionary to find the vocabulary to fit with their actions but I could not find so I used this savage govern.

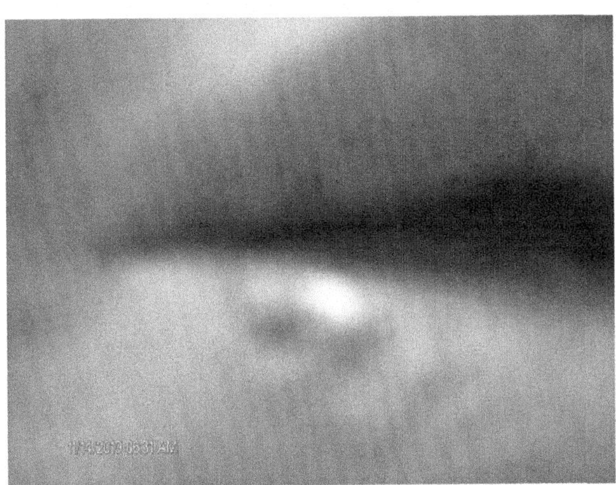

November 14, 2010 6:31 A.M.

They implanted both my upper lip and my lower lip too; I did not know what they tried to do to sabotage my lips, to damage my lips.

This is 80 billions projects?

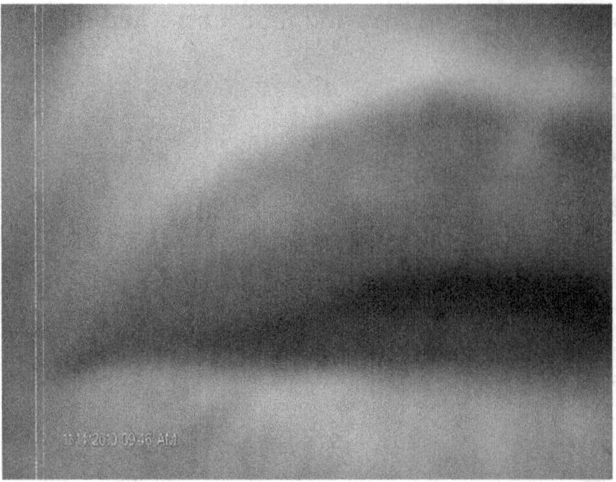

November 14, 2010 9:46 A.M.

After Phiem brushed teeth and washed her face for few hours later, her lips began heated and she could feel soar then it was swollen as in these pictures.

November 14, 2010 9:47 A.M.

Phiem (My lips) were swollen in this picture.

I do not know how they enter into my house, they use spy technique to open any door or from the roof or from underground. They might use hi-tech, Nanotechnology to shot, to implanted the Nanochips into my body.
How ambitious they are and how they want to control and conquer this planet and how much money they desire?
I wanted them to answer me these questions.

November 14, 2010 2:36 P.M. (1)

November 14, 2010 10:19 P.M.

They attacked to Phiem ear when she was sitting at her computer table, computer was not turned on.

They attacked to Phiem'ears when she was in her kitchen, they attacked to her whole body too. These pictures below she took in her kitchen, she wanted to share to reader.

November 15, 2010 1:35 P.M.

November 15, 2010 6:35 P.M.

November 15, 2010 6:36 P.M.

November 15, 2010 6:36 P.M.

November 15, 2010 6:38 P.M.

And

This is the series of pictures were taken at her computer.
They attacked to Phiem's ear, and face when she was sitting at her computer.

November 15, 2010 9:37 P.M.

November 15, 2010 9:38 P.M.

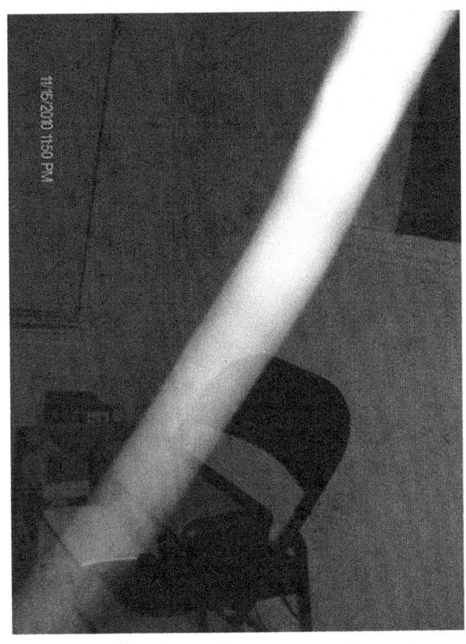

November 15, 2010 11:50 P.M.

November 15, 2010 1:34 P.M.

They attacked to Phiem ear when she was in her kitchen.

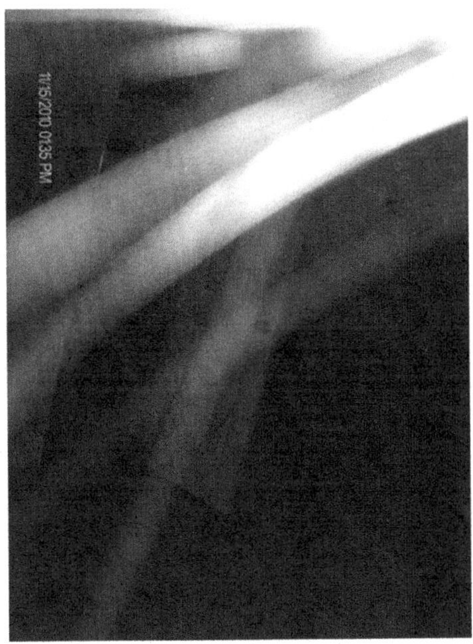

November 15, 2010 1:35 P.M.

And

These pictures below are the extra pictures were taken in my bedroom, reader will see how they get inside my house and in my bedroom on the roof or underground or high-tech!!!

This series of images were captured in Phiem bedroom, this day she was woken up or they deprived her sleeping because do not have the tag caption.
Reader could see the secure room but the high-tech they do not need to get inside the house to attack me (Phiem).

October 6, 2010 5:50 A.M.

October 6, 2010 5:49 A.M.

October 6, 2010 5:48 A.M.

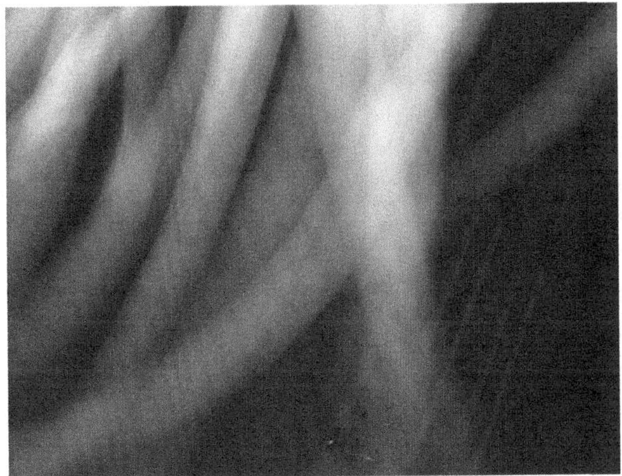

October 6, 2010 5:46 A.M.

October 6, 2010 5:44 A.M.

October 6, 2010 5:39 A.M.

This picture was captured on my ceiling bedroom and the circle is my ceiling bedroom light.

October 6, 2010 5:38 A.M.

October 6, 2010 5:36 A.M.

October 6, 2010 5:35 A.M.

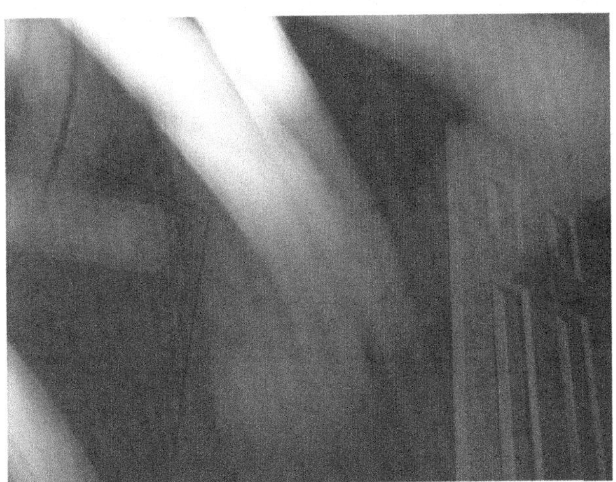

October 6, 2010 5:34 A.M.

October 6, 2010 5:33 A.M.

XXX

After the extra pictures it seems never end so I am continuing upload my pictures to my computer then I want to share my some selective pictures to my readers and to the world.

November 17, 2010 8:22 P.M.

Phiem was at her dinning room they attacked to Phiem's ear, head and neck.

November 18, 2010 12:18 P.M.

They attacked to Phiem'ear when she was sitting at her computer.

November 18, 2010 12:34 P.M.

They attacked to Phiem's ear when she was sitting at her computer.

November 18, 2010 12:56 P.M.

They attacked to Phiem's ear when she was sitting at her computer.

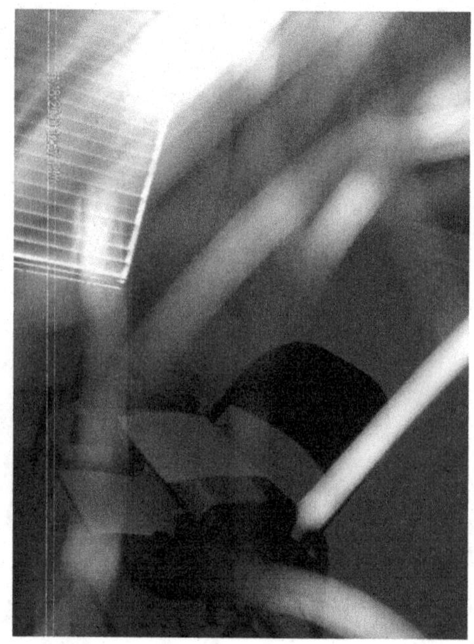

November 18, 2010 12:57 P.M.

They attacked to Phiem's ear when she was sitting at her computer.

November 18, 2010 12:59 P.M.

They attacked to Phiem's body when she sat at her computer desk.

November 18, 2010 12:59 P.M.

They attacked to Phiem's body when she was sitting at her computer table.

November 19, 2010 2:24 A.M.

They attacked to Phiem's ear when she was in her bed to deprive her sleeping since she went to bed at midnight.

November 19, 2010 3:35 A.M

They attacked to Phiem flower when she was in her bed; they tried to do something harm, sabotage, and transform and something else she did not know to her flower. At that time she took this picture to prove that they were using pink or red laser to beam to her flower as it was captured in this picture.

November 19, 2010 3:41 A.M.

This is the first time I captured this light technique was using to attacked, to beam to my flower when I was in bed, they tried to sabotage, harm, transform my flower since I was in bed. I thought it was light technique because it was in image of the light.
They did it to my flower, to my body, my head, my legs, entire my body day and night, I usually took pictures at my computer, dinning room and in my bedroom because I have my hands free to take pictures.

November 19, 2010 3:49 A.M.

They attacked to Phiem's head when she was in her bed since midnight, they deprived her sleeping for not working in the morning when she wake up that she planted to vacuum her floor.

November 19, 2010 3:14 P.M.

They used the red laser beamed to Phiem body when she was in her dinning room having lunch after she finished vacuum her floor. This is the different shape of nanotechnology was presented in this picture.

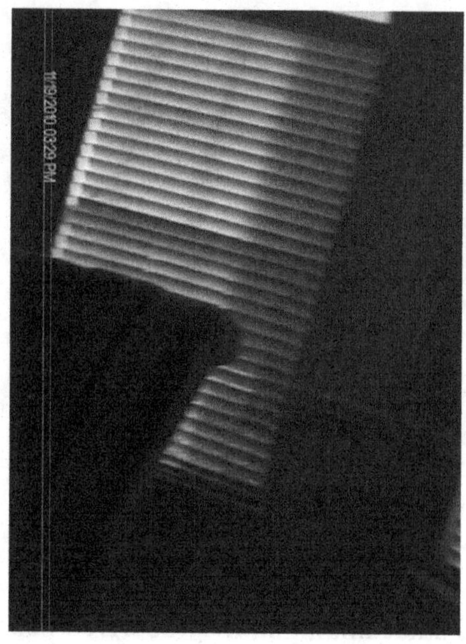

November 19, 2010 3:29 P.M.

They used Nanotechnology to attacked to Phiem entire body, this was shown in this pictured that professional will recognize it.

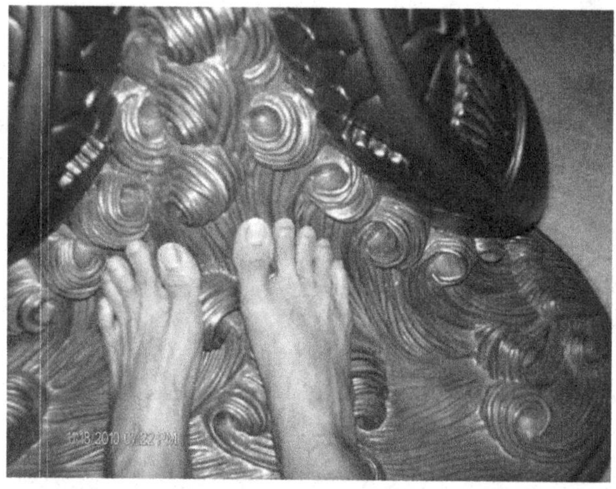

November 18, 2010 7:22 P.M. (1)

They implanted chip inside Phiem's feet they activated soar pain to her feet to her toe-nails.

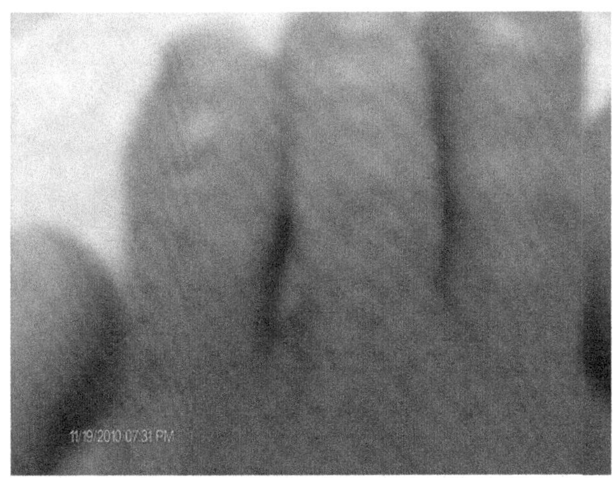

November 19, 2010 7:31 P.M. (2)

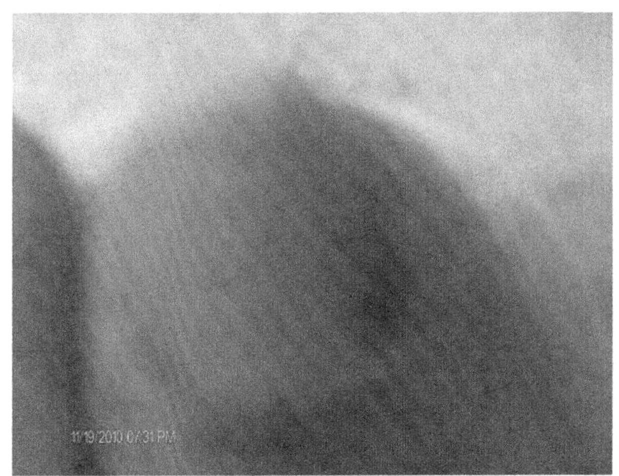

November 19, 2010 7:31 P.M. (3)

November 19, 2010 7:31 P.M. (4)

November 20, 2010 8:48 P.M.

They attacked to Phiem's ear when she was sitting at her computer.

November 20, 2010 9:01 P.M. (1)

They attacked to Phiem's back, neck and back head.

November 20, 2010 9:01 P.M. (2)

November 20, 2010 (3)

November 20, 2010 9:04 P.M. (4)

November 21, 2010 8:54 P.M. (1)

They attacked to Phiem's back head and neck when she was sitting at her dinning room.

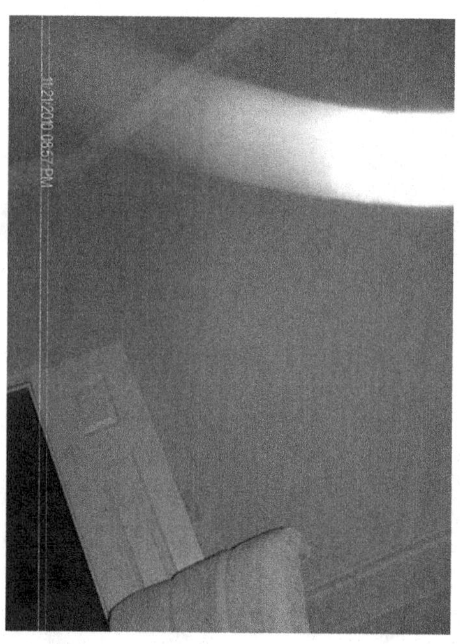

November 21, 2010 8:57 P.M. (2)

They attacked to Phiem's back head and neck when she was sitting at her dinning room.

November 21, 2010 9:00 P.M.

They attacked to Phiem's face when she was having dinner at her dinning room.

November 22, 2010 9:07 A.M.

They attacked to Phiem's ear when she was sitting at her computer.

November 22, 2010 12:10 P.M.

They attacked to Phiem's ear and body when she went downstairs from her computer desk the attacking was following her to the kitchen.

November 22, 2010 12:12 P.M.

Phiem went back upstairs the Nanotechnology attacking was following her upstairs too, it was captured in this picture.

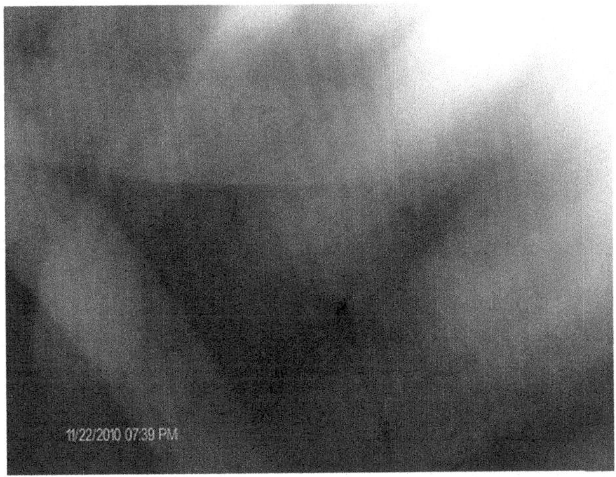

November 22, 2010 7:39 P.M.

They attacked to Phiem's head when she was sitting at her living room.

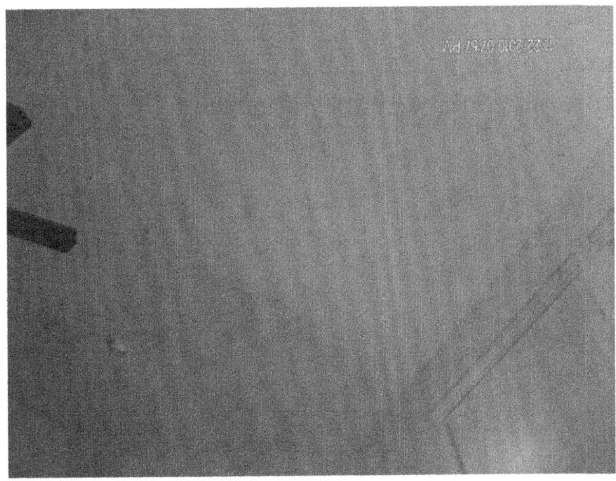

November 22, 2010 7:57 P.M.

They attacked to Phiem's face, neck, chest and stomach sides when she was sitting at her living room. The 2 laser circles were reflected on the ceiling but the colors was formed by light at the ceiling, wall and window.

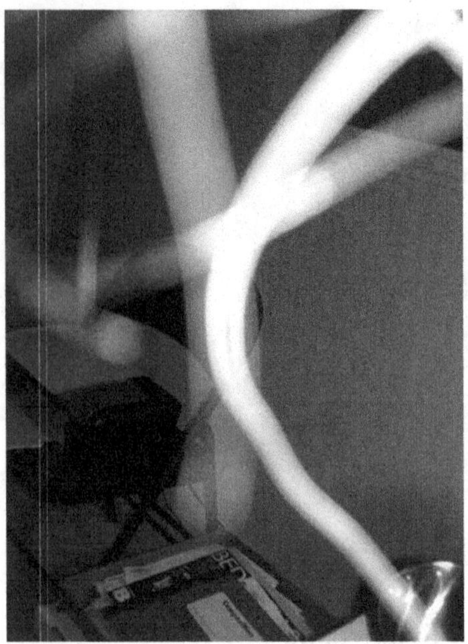

November 23, 2010 5:30 A.M.

Phiem was awakening for the whole night because she had to publish her DVD Criminal Psychotropic Weapons on LuLu.com, this picture she took when they attacked to her ear she was at her computer at that time.

November 23, 2010 5:38 A.M.

They attacked to Phiem's ear when she was sitting at her computer.

November 23, 2010 5:14 P.M. (1)

They attacked to Phiem's flower when she was in her bed to take rest after she was doing her lawn, they attacked to prevent her rest to drive her into mad, and got more tire to attempt murder her.
She just found out the date was turn off mystery so readers can not figure out where was the bright light in this picture.

November 23, 2010 5:23 P.M. (2)

They attacked to Phiem's flower when she was in her bed to take rest after she was doing her lawn.

November 23, 2010 5:39 P.M. (3)

They used Nanotechnology knife to sabotage her flower, she could feel the force into her flower then it pain like cutting. They tried to deform, change shape and now they wanted to transform into man.

They preventing her for taking rest after she was tire working her lawn, they tried to kill her by driving her mad and got more tire for heart attack and stroke.

November 23, 2010 5:39 P.M. (4)

November 23, 2010 5:40 P.M. (4)

November 23, 2010 5:40 P.M. (5)

November 23, 2010 5:40 P.M. (5)

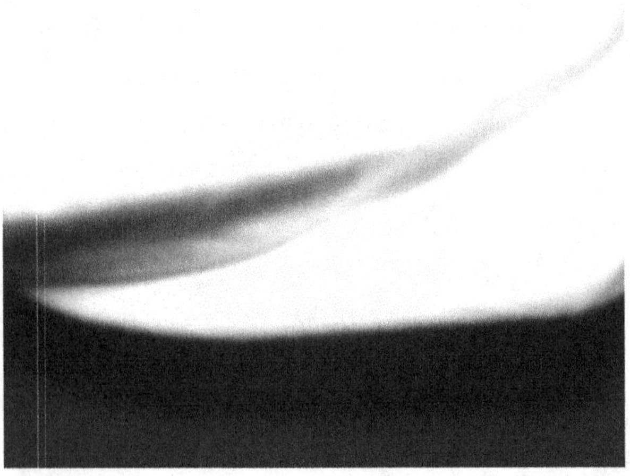

November 23, 2010 5:40 P.M. (6)

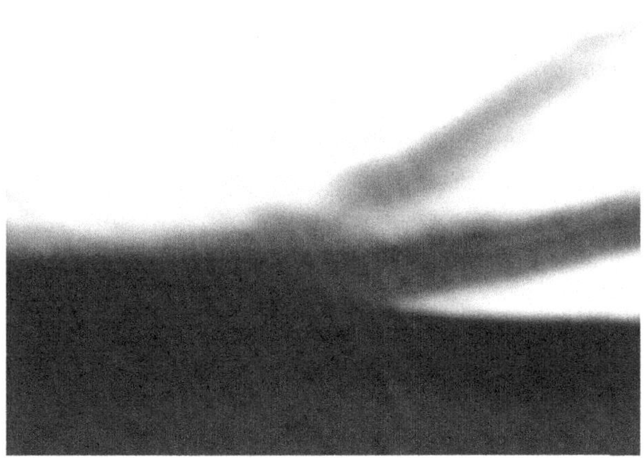

November 23, 2010 5:40 P.M. (7)

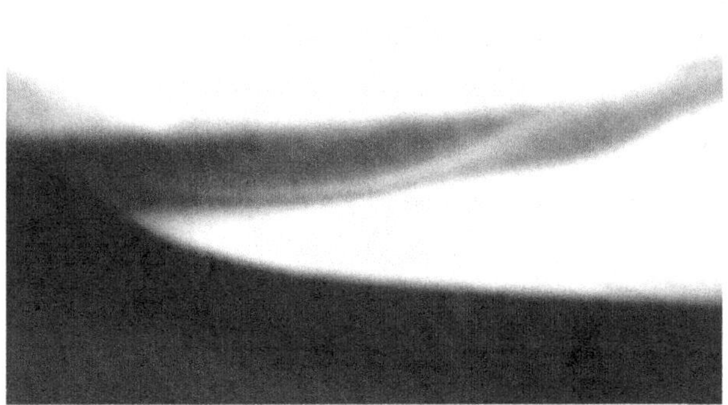

November 23, 2010 5:40 P.M. (7)

November 23, 2010 5:40 P.M. (8)

November 23, 2010 5:40 P.M. (9)

November 23, 2010 5:40 P.M. (10)

November 23, 2010 5:40 P.M. (11)

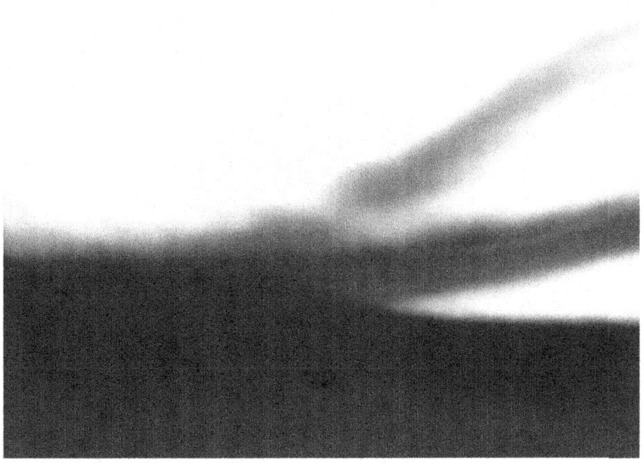

November 23, 2010 5:41 P.M. (12)

November 23, 2010 5:41 P.M. (13)

November 23, 2010 5:41 P.M. (14)

November 23, 2010 5:41 P.M. (15)

November 23, 2010 5:41 P.M. (16)

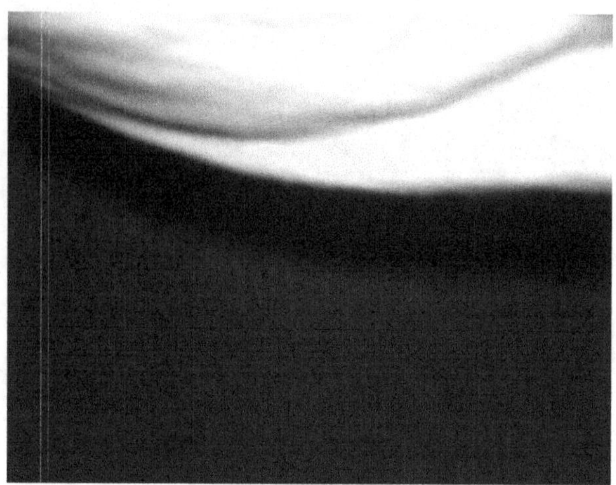

November 23, 2010 5:42 (17)

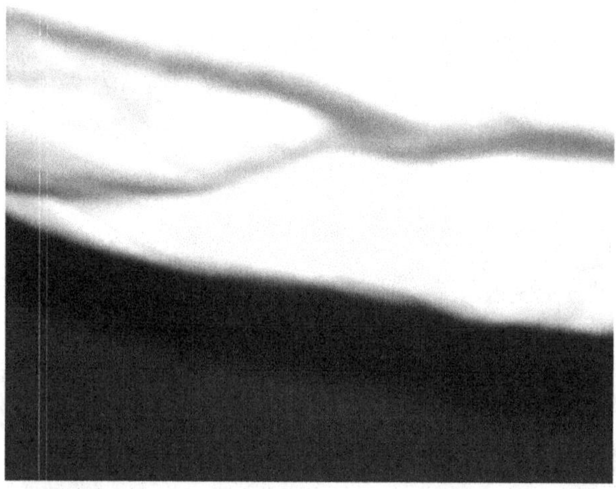

November 23, 2010 5:44 (18)

November 23, 2010 5:44 (19)

November 23, 2010 5:47 (1)

They attacked to Phiem' female when she was in her bed to rest after she's done her lawn, they abuse by creating resent and preventing her to take rest or sleeping, they murder her so often with this method was using, they intended heart attack and stroke.

On the day November 24, 2010 Phiem felt something was strange and bigger at the place they created the strange thing to my female (I could not remember the date but it after I took pictures my female to prove that they did something to my female, they changed shape and smaller). Then they narrower my both hips and they made my buttocks smaller like male body shape.
They implanted cells that were grown the male part on my female at the place when my child was delivery it was torn and it has been sewn. I did not know what they did to my female on November 23, 2010 as I described with pictures manifested above then the evening I felt strange but I was not touch it until I take shower, it was bigger, after I took shower I took those pictures to prove for the investigation only, I do not want to present it here.

November 23, 2010 5:47 (2)

November 23, 2010 5:47 (3)

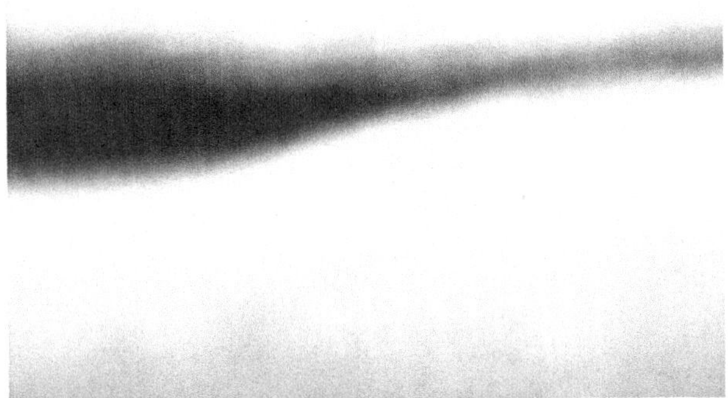

November 23, 2010 5:47 (4)

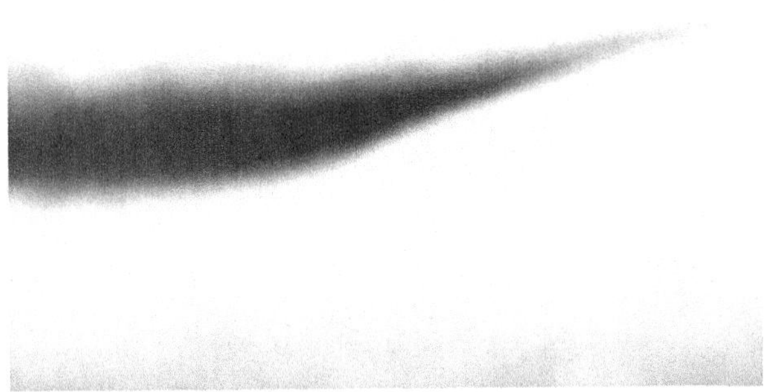

November 23, 2010 5:48 (5)

November 24, 2010 10:26 P.M.

They attacked to Phiem's ear when she was sitting at her computer.

They attacked to Phiem's ear when she was sitting at her computer.

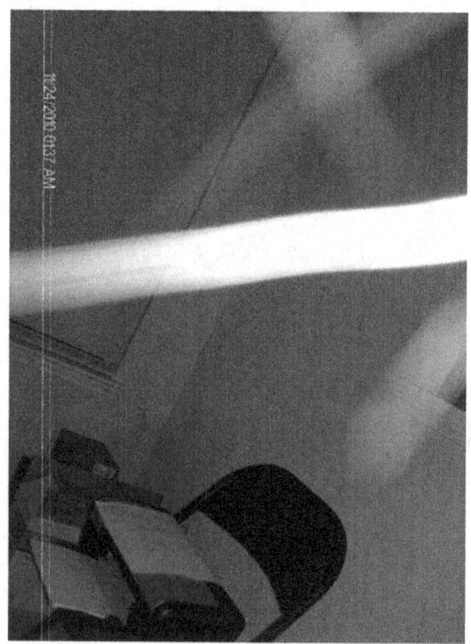

November 24, 2010 1:37 A.M.

They attacked to Phiem's ear when she was sitting at her computer.

November 24, 2010 2:45 A.M. (1)

They attacked to Phiem when she was in her bed room. This color expertise knew what it was.

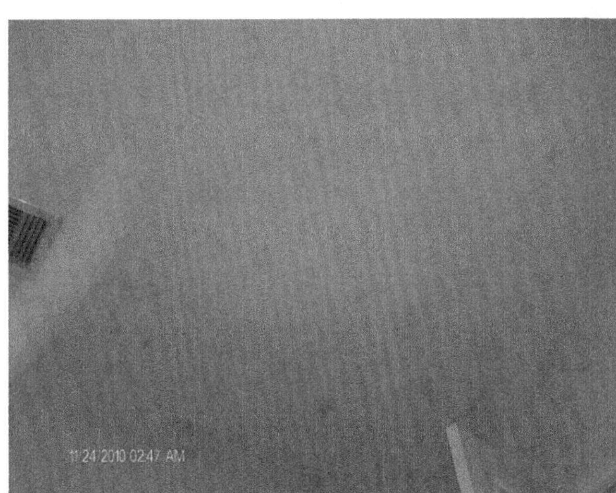

November 24, 2010 2:47 A.M. (2)

November 24, 2010 7:43 P.M. (1)

They attacked to Phiem's ear when she was sitting at her computer.

November 24, 2010 7:43 P.M. (2)

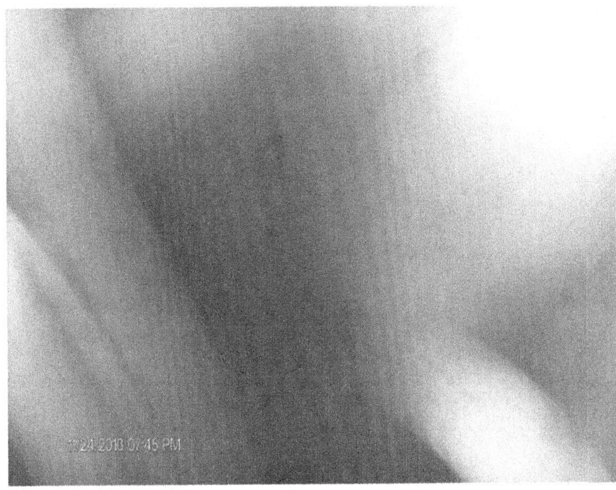

November 24, 2010 7:45 P.M.

They attacked to Phiem's neck when she was sitting at her computer.

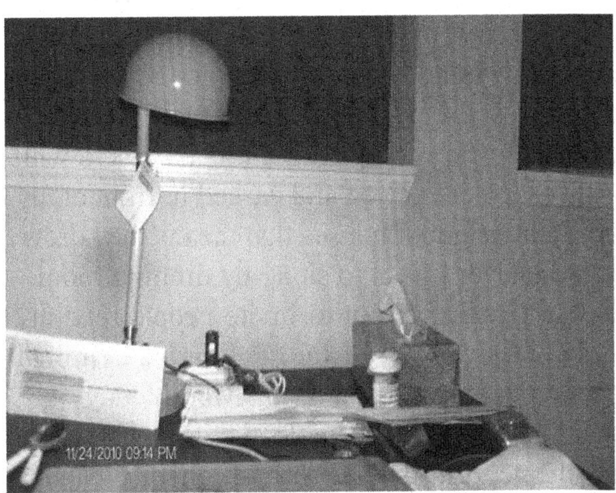

November 24, 2010 9:14 P.M.

They attacked to Phiem's face when she was sitting at her computer, she took this picture was in this color she wanted to share; expertise will say it was the form of Nanotechnology.

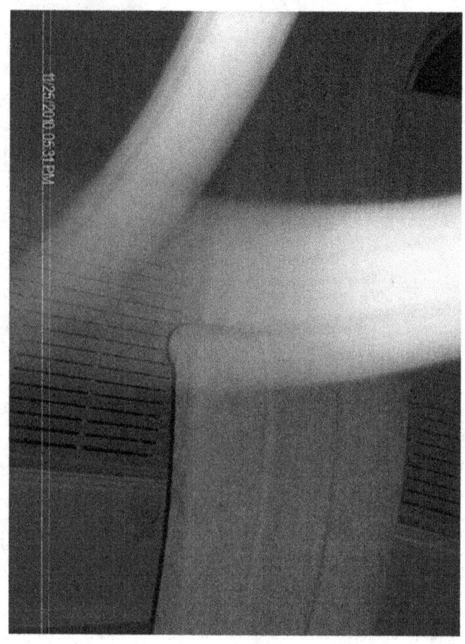

November 25, 2010 5:31 P.M. (1)

Today is the Thank-giving holiday in US, I had dinner at my dinner room as usually I am, they shot to my ear so hard, I took these pictures then I went outside to take picture if I could catch the force they were using and by whom, I saw the person at the neighbor window immediately left that site, I wonder if they are the one who was attacking me, the guess with cars parked in front. For continuously years I saw cars were driven and parked in front of my house or the opposite neighbor houses or my adjacent neighbor houses that means they drove and parked in surrounding my neighbor houses whenever I went to sit at my dinning room.
I went upstairs to take my website visit cards that I will give out to invite people read my books because people have to read my books and have to read the victims of Criminal Psychotropic Weapons to know what was happen in this nation and in this world today.
I knew the ground base was using cars, neighbor houses, portable devices they were attacking me. I read the victim petitions and the reports they recruit neighbors, friends relatives and even parents to become Perpetrators, attackers and controllers.
This is the horrible problem people and I would not imagine it happen into this mankind.

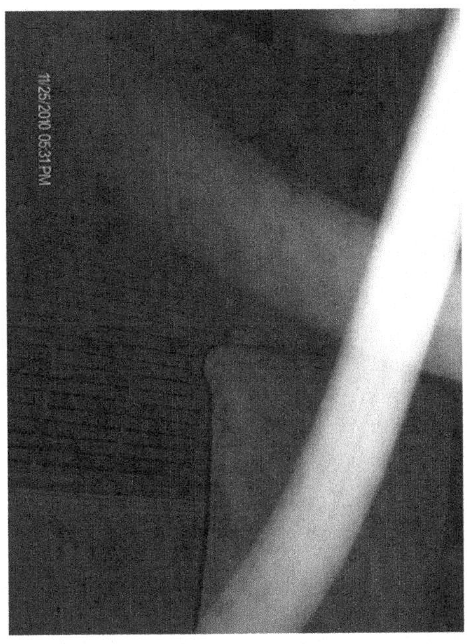

November 25, 2010 5:31 P.M. (2)

They attacked to Phiem's ear when she had dinner at her dinning room.

November 26, 2010 7:37 A.M.

They attacked Phiem's when brushed teeth they're attacking her in her bathroom then went outside to go downstairs at the kitchen and the whole house was set up like that.

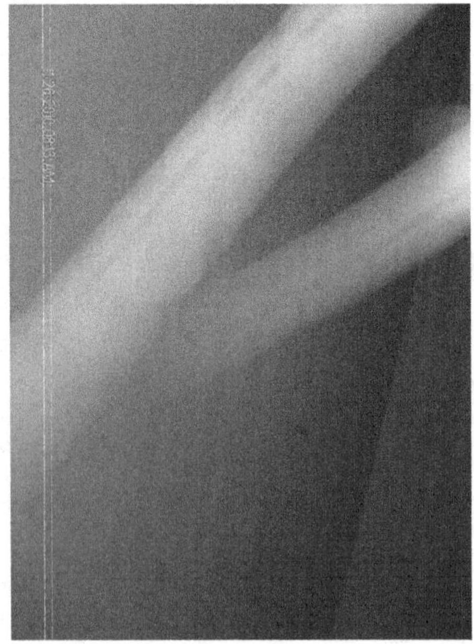

November 26, 2010 8:13 A.M. (1)

They attacked to Phiem's ear and body when she exercises, people could not live like that. They are the tortures, abusers, murderers and rapist.

November 26, 2010 8:13 A.M. (2)

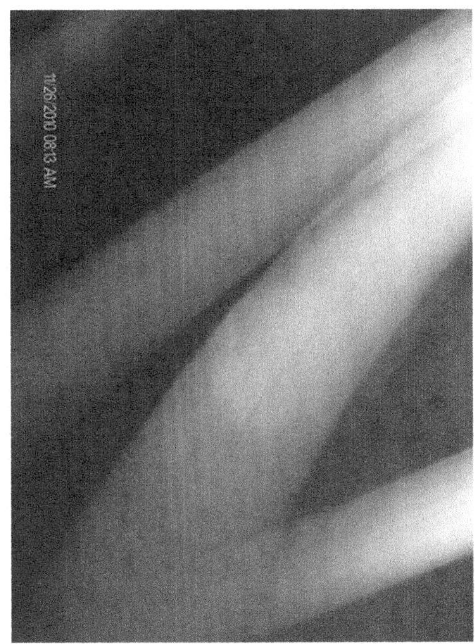

November 13, 2010 8:13 A.M. (3)

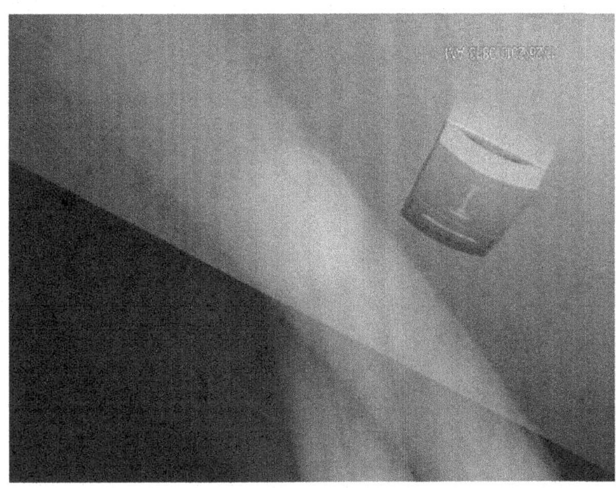

November 26, 2010 8:13 A.M. (4)

November 26, 2010 8:13 A.M. (5)

November 26, 2010 8:14 A.M. (6)

These pictures above were taken they were attacking during the time Phiem exercise.

November 26, 2010 9:02 A.M. (1)

They were attacking to Phiem when she was sitting at her computer.

November 26, 2010 9:07 A.M. (2)

They attacked to Phiem when she was sitting at her computer. I repeat these sentences so often in my DVD and in my book but it was useful when it did not have a tag note I could not remember the detail of the pictures to explain however readers were familiar with my house so you can guest it and me too.

November 26, 2010 11: PM (1)

They attacked to Phiem's abdomen when she was sitting at her computer.

November 26, 2010 11:52 PM (2)

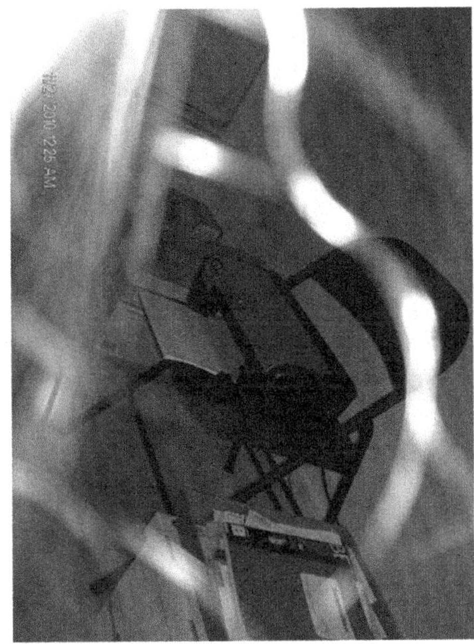

November 27, 2010 12:25 (1)

They attacked to Phiem's ear when she was sitting at her computer.

November 27, 2010 12:26 AM (2)

November 27, 2010 12:30 AM (1)

November 27, 2010 12:30 AM (2)

November 27, 2010 10:32 PM

They attacked to Phiem's ear when she was sitting at her computer.

November 27, 2010 2:45 AM (1)

Phiem took these pictures when she felt they attacked to her ear, she let camera faced to her ear in these pictures how she micro magnetic wave affected to her ear that everyday they beamed to her ear constantly since 2004.

November 27, 2010 2:45 AM (2)

November 27, 2010 2:46 AM (1)

They attacked to Phiem's ear when she was in her bed.

November 28, 2010 10:27 AM (1)

They attacked to Phiem's ear when she was sitting at her computer.

November 27, 2010 2:48 AM (2)

They constantly beamed the Nanotechnology Micromagnetic beam to Phiem's ear when she was sitting at her computer as you see in this these pictures and time.

November 28, 2010 10:29 AM (3)

They bombarded to Phiem'ear canal by Micromagnetic ray gun to her ear constantly as you recognize their processing.

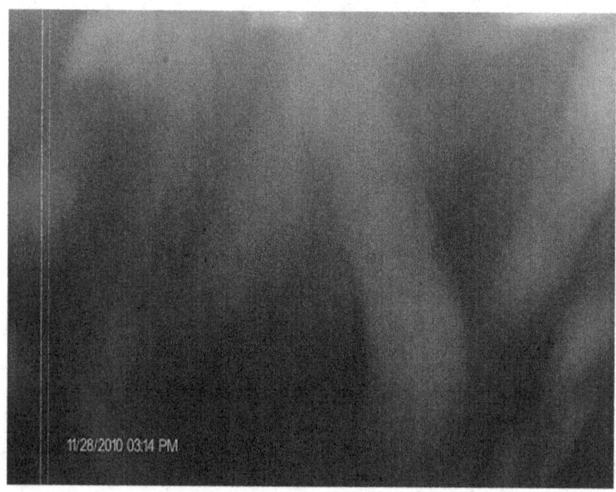

November 28, 2010 3:14 PM (1)

They bombarded to Phiem' head when she was sitting at her computer, she wanted to prove how they murder her day and night constantly since 2004 until today and it is continuing.

November 28, 2010 3:14 PM (2)

November 28, 2010 3:15 PM (3)

They bombarded to Phiem's center of two brain sphere (central nervous system).

November 28, 2010 3:15 PM (4)

This picture was taken from Phiem's back head.

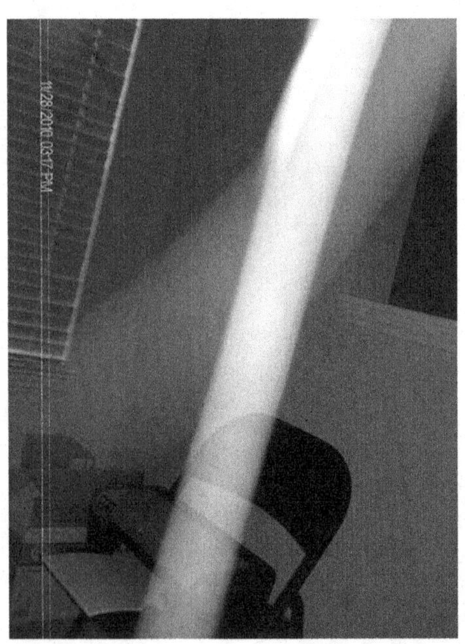

November 28, 2010 3:17 PM (1)

They used Nanotechnology to bombarded Micromagnetic to Phiem's ear when she was sitting at her computer. These following pictures stated the situation how they attacked to torture and murder and harm her, it was shown in these evidences and time to prove it.

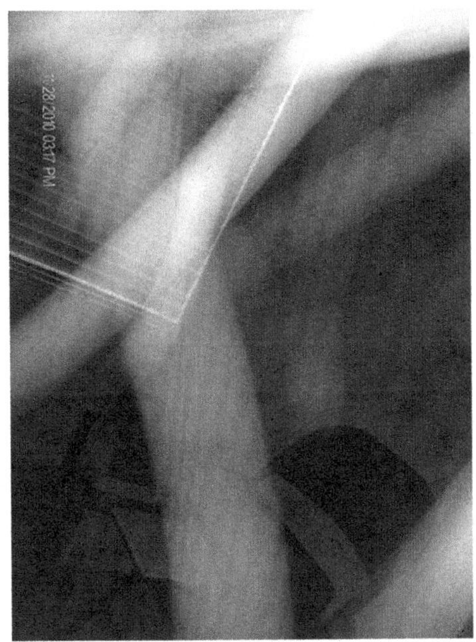

November 28, 2010 3:18 PM (2)

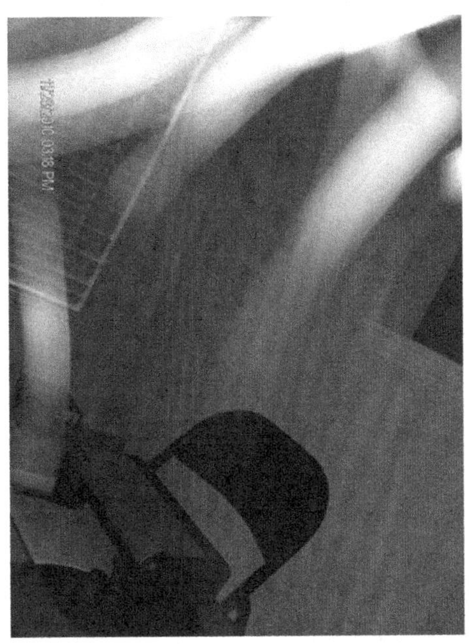

November 28, 2010 3:18 PM (3)

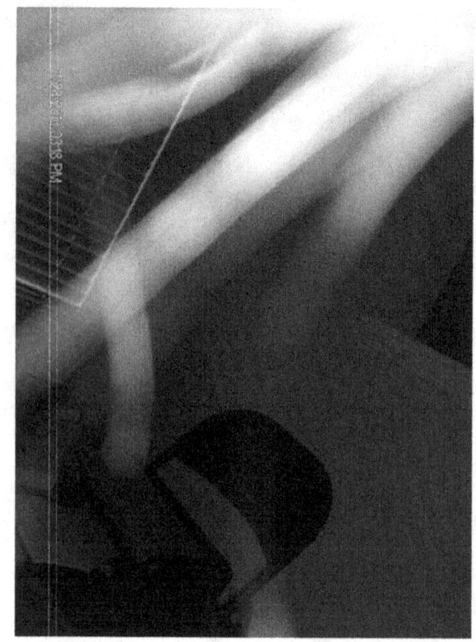

November 28, 2010 3:18 PM (4)

November 28, 2010 3:21 PM (1)

They attacked to Phiem’s neck when she was sitting at her computer.

November 28, 2010 3:21 PM (2)

November 28, 2010 3:22 PM (3)

November 28, 2010 3:22 PM

They attacked to Phiem's ear when she was sitting at her computer, in this picture it was shown only the pink color, it should be another Nano image or pink laser.

November 28, 2010 3:40 PM (1)

They attacked to Phiem's ear when she was sitting at her computer.

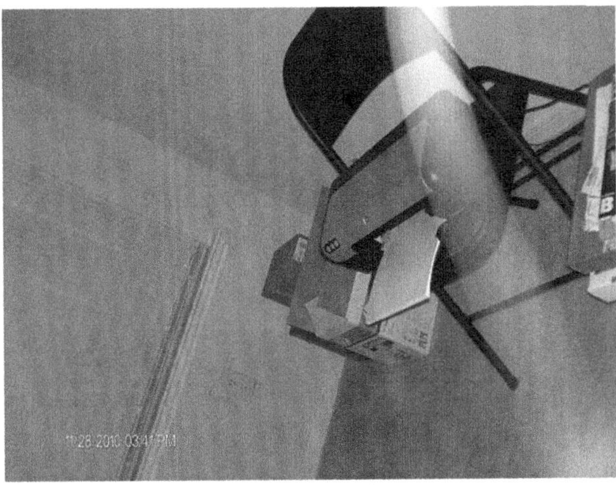

November 28, 2010 3:41 PM (2)

November 28, 2010 6:55 PM (1)

They attacked to Phiem's back she took these picture to prove the force and the color of Micromagnetic on her hairs at her back at that time.

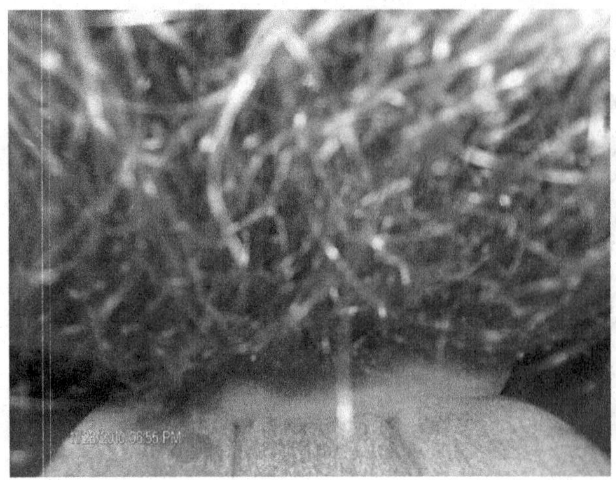

November 28, 2010 6:55 PM (2)

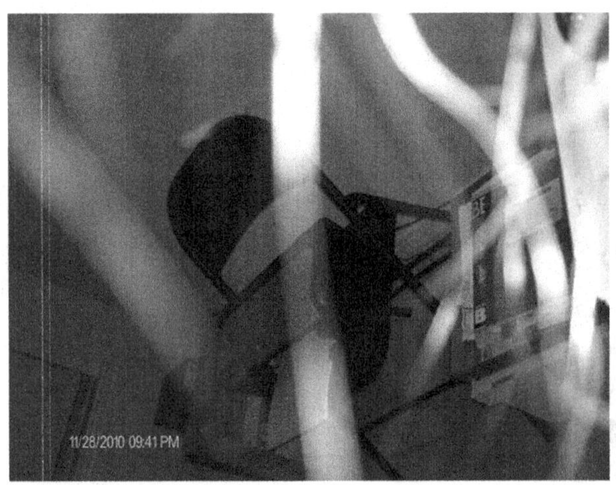

November 28, 2010 9:41 PM (1)

They attacked to Phiem's ear when she was sitting at her computer.

November 28, 2010 9:41 PM (2)

November 28, 2010 9:42 PM (1)

November 28, 2010 9:46 PM (2)

They beamed to Phiem's ear when she was sitting at her computer.

November 28, 2010 9:46 PM (3)

They bombarded to Phiem's ear when she was sitting at her computer.

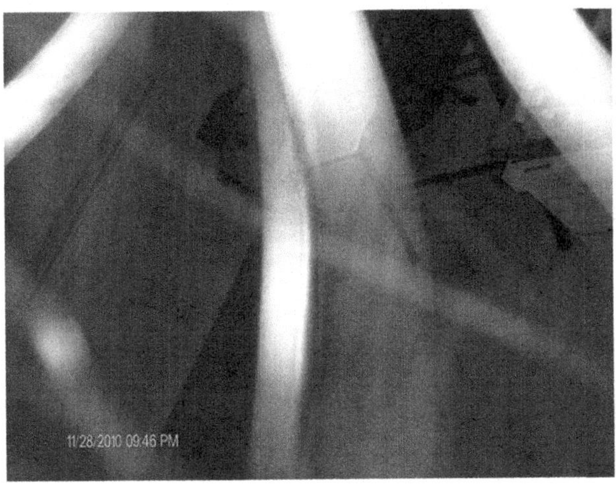

November 28, 2010 9:46 PM (4)

They attacked to Phiem's ear when she was sitting at her computer.

November 28, 2010 9:48 PM (5)

They attacked to Phiem's ear when she was sitting at her computer, they are patient meticulous murderers but they are faceless and fingerless, secretly murder process.

November 27, 2010 2:48 AM (2)

November 27, 2010 7:27 PM (1)

They attacked to Phiem abdomen when she was sitting at her kitchen table for dinner.

November 27, 2010 7:27 PM (2)

November 27, 2010 7:34 PM

They attacked to Phiem's ear when she was sitting at her kitchen table for having dinner.

December 17, 2010 9:08 PM

They attacked to Phiem's neck when she was in her bed she got flu symptom since Thursday 16, 2010, severe flu she got it.

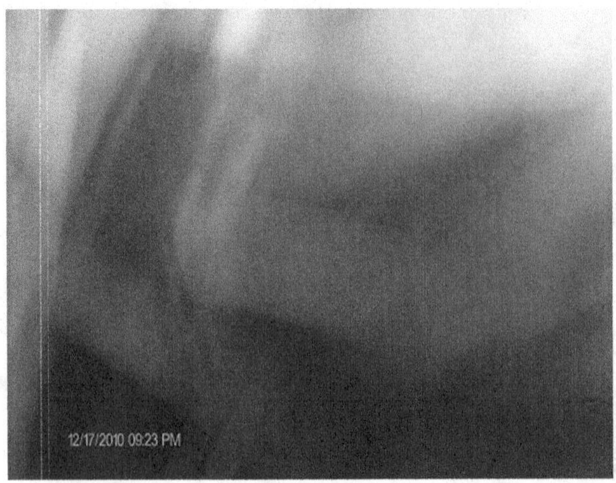

December 17, 2010 9:23 PM (1)

They attacked to Phiem's back head when she was in bed caused flu symptom.

December 17, 2010 9:23 PM (2)

They attacked to Phiem's back head when she was in her bed caused flu symptom.

December 17, 2010 9:26 PM (3)

They attacked to Phiem's back head under her hairs when she was in her bed caused flu symptom.

December 17, 2010 9:50 PM (1)

They attacked to Phiem's ear canal when she was in her bed she got flu symptom.

December 17, 2010 9:51 PM (2)

They attacked to Phiem's ear canal when she was in her bed caused severe flu symptom.

December 17, 2010 11:53 PM (1)

Phiem saw the manmade object was flying on the air circle tours it was passing her window several times before but she thought it was from the plane but this night she noticed it the second tours so she went to the window to see the plane but she did not see any plane there but the milky white oval at the size from 16 inches to 22 inches circle above the roof of her neighbor houses and passing her window, she took camera to take pictures but it was hard to see it in this picture with the flash on. She could see the two brown nanowires through her window; these small white strings are the light reflection curtain strings.

December 17, 2010 11:59 PM (2)

The manmade object was flying circle tour and passing Phiem window she captured it on her camera, this picture was flash off.

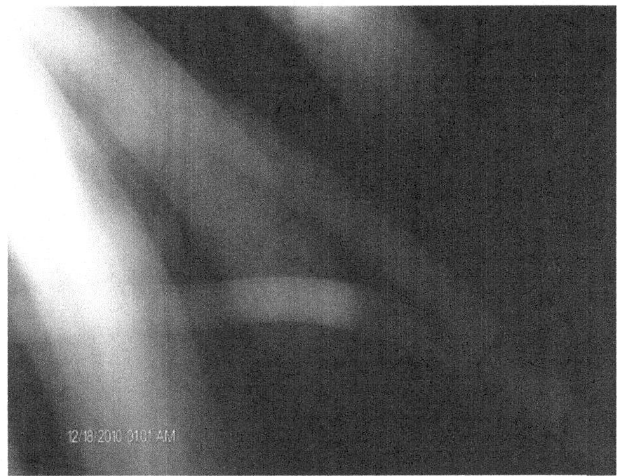

December 18, 2010 1:01 AM (1)

They attacked to Phiem's ear canal when she was in her bed in heavy flu she wonder if this flu symptom was similar to Russian flu symptom she just saw the title on the internet news.

December 18, 2010 1:01 AM (1)

They attacked to Phiem's ear canal when she was in her bed in heavy flu she wonder if this flu symptom was similar to Russian flu symptom she just saw the title on the internet news. On Friday she saw her next neighbor had two cars one red is Biotech and another is white car with cover pickup nap, she opened her window to see they did work on the electric boxes she heard the white man talk to the black man "this is the death ray".

December 18, 2010 1:10 AM (1)

They attacked to Phiem's stomach side when she was in her bed cause flu symptom.

December 18, 2010 3:18 AM

They attacked to Phiem's ear frame she took this picture, she did not know what they tried to do to her body for the whole night, they woke her up several times during the night, they made her body pain so she had to do massage when she woke up this morning but she did not know it was from her flu symptom or cause from their actions.

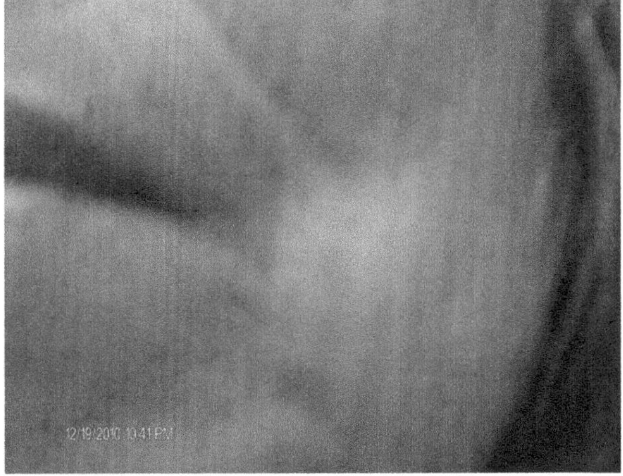

December 19, 2010 10:41 PM

They attacked to Phiem's mouth when she was in her dinning-room the patch of dark color at her mouth was shown in this picture, now she knew they created age instantly spots it was not over night as she saw on her face when she woke up, she could say they are spies and they were using spy technique to camouflage and now they used it to degrade natural human beauty and handsome to punish the targets they aim at.

In this picture readers could see clearly they made her saggy cheeks as she described it before but she did not take pictures them to show.
This evening they shot to her sole before they attacked her mouth but she could not take picture it clearly to show the tiny chip she could feel at her sole but she could not take it out.
This evening Phiem saw the plane was passing by her window then following the attacking but she did not know for sure it was from air base or it was from ground base attacking.

December 26, 2010 5:11 AM

They attacked to Phiem's left ear when she was in her bed.

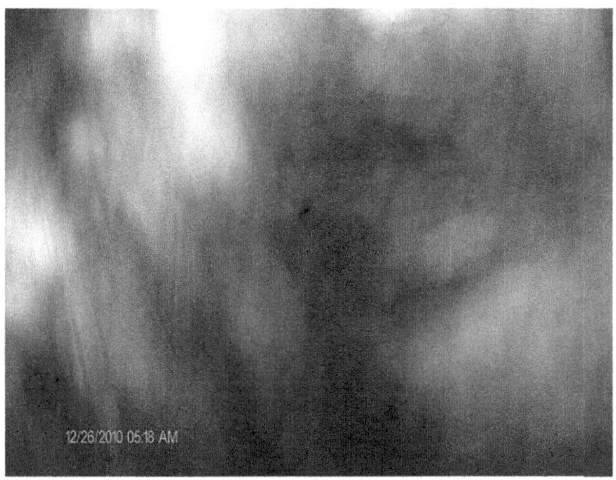

December 26, 2010 5:18 AM (1)

They attacked to Phiem's back head when she was in her bed, these pictures were taken under her hairs.

December 26, 2010 5:18 AM (2)

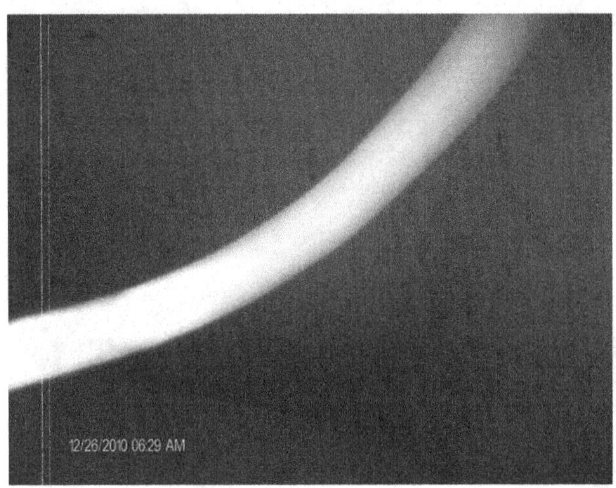

December 26, 2010 6:29 AM (1)

They attacked to Phiem's right ear when she was in her bed.

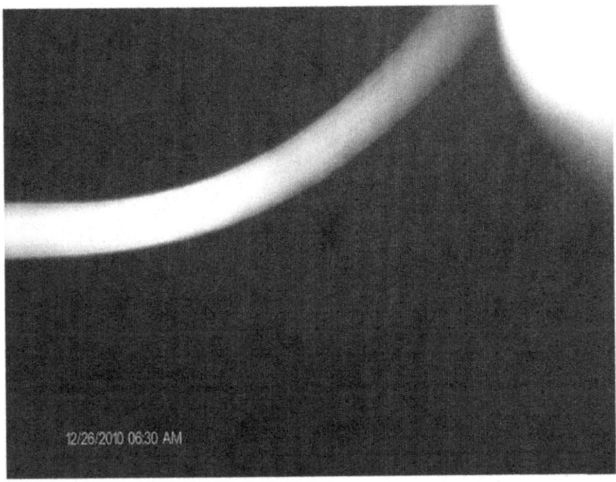

December 26, 2010 6:30 AM (2)

They attacked to Phiem's right ear when she was in her bed.

December 26, 2010 6:33 AM

They attacked to Phiem's fore-front head when she was in her bed.

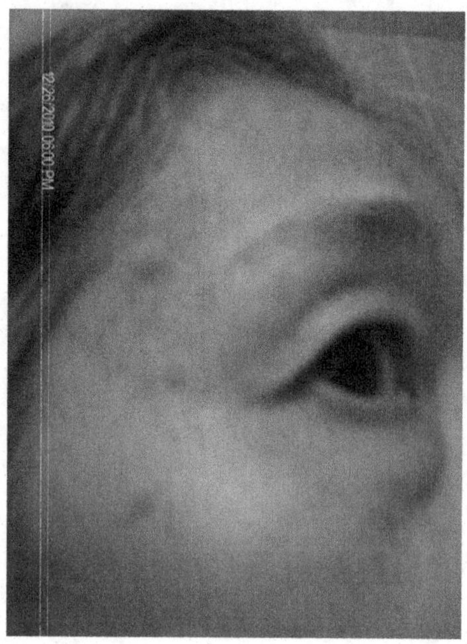

December 26, 2010 6:00PM

They implanted microchip into Phiem's right tempo when she saw it she took these picture she did not know when they did it.

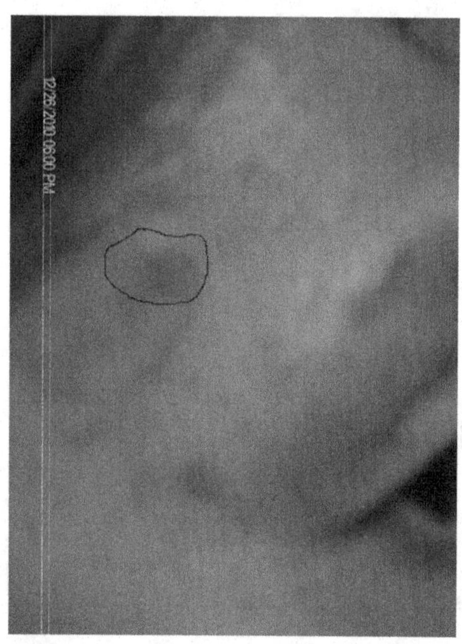

December 26, 2010 6:00PM

They implanted microchip into Phiem's right tempo when she saw it she took these pictures she did not know when they did it.

December 28, 2010 11:49 PM

They attacked to Phiem's ear face when she was in her bed.

December 30, 2010 12:43 AM

They attacked to Phiem's ear when she was in her bed.

December 30, 2010 12:47 AM (2)

They attacked to Phiem's ear when she was in her bed.

December 30, 2010 8:01 AM (1)

They attacked to Phiem's ear when she was at her kitchen.

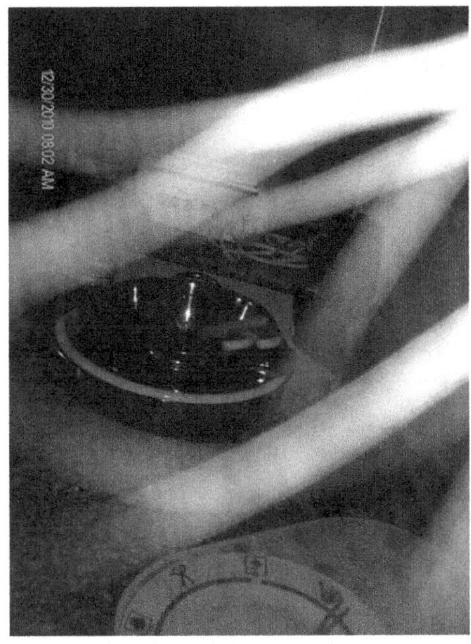

December 30, 2010 8:02 AM (2)

They attacked to Phiem's ear when she was at her kitchen.

December 30, 2010 8:03 AM (3)

They attacked to Phiem's ear when she was at her kitchen.

December 31, 2010 8:53 AM

They attacked to Phiem's ear when she was sitting at her computer.

January 1, 2011 11:59 PM (1)

They attacked to Phiem's ear when she was sitting at her computer.

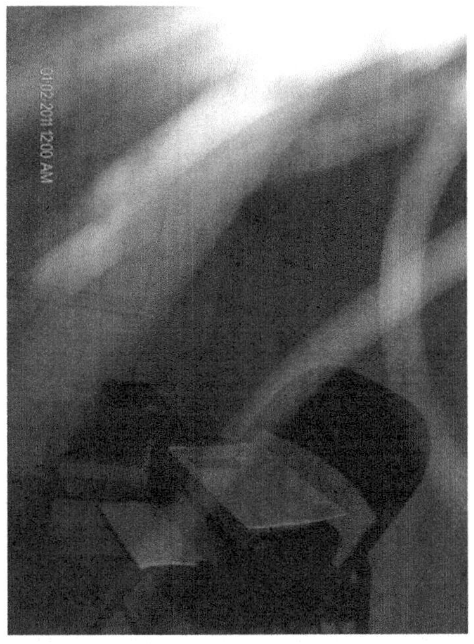

January 2, 2011 12.00 AM (2)

They attacked to Phiem's ear when she was sitting at her computer.

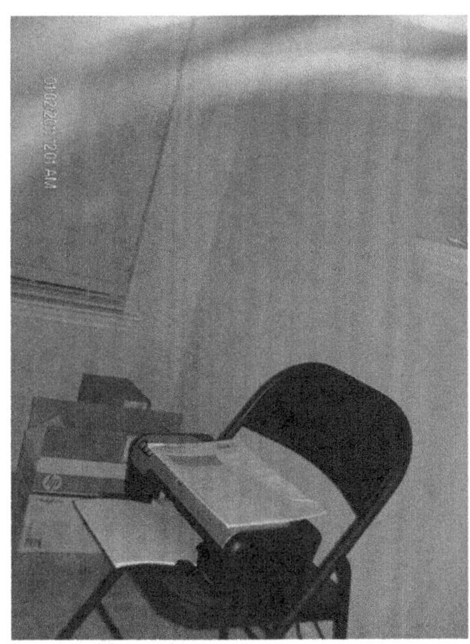

January 2, 2011 12:01 AM (3)

They attacked to Phiem's ear when she was sitting at her computer.

January 2, 2011 3:43 PM (1)

They used MicroNanowires attacked to Phiem's left fore-front head she took this picture camera faced to outside from her head, the two small bright lines with pencil deleted marks in this picture were the reflection from the sun light.

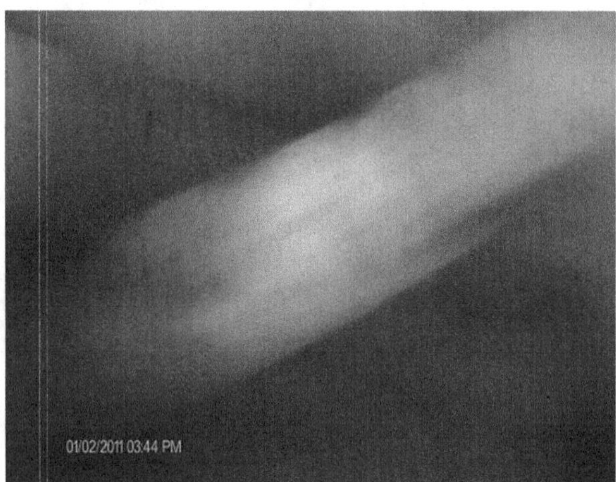

January 2, 2011 3:44 PM (2)

They used Micronanowire to attack to Phiem's fore-front head when she was sitting at her computer, this picture was taken camera faced to her head.

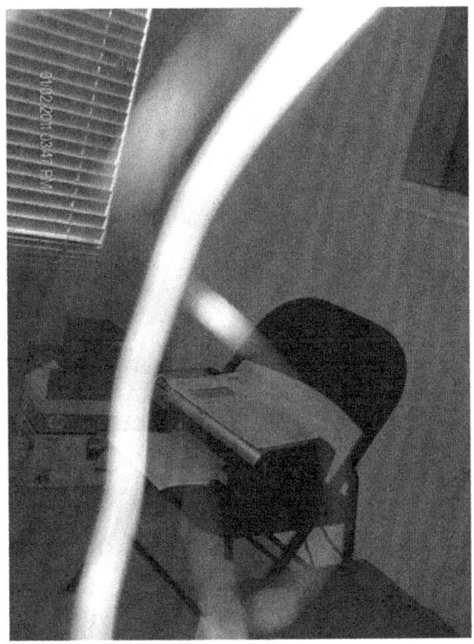

January 2, 2011 3:47 PM (1)

They attacked to Phiem's ear when she was sitting at her computer.

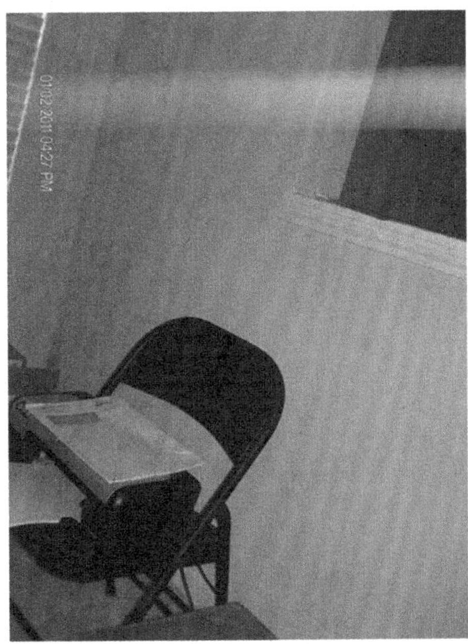

January 2, 2011 4:27 PM (2)

They attacked to Phiem's ear when she was sitting at her computer.

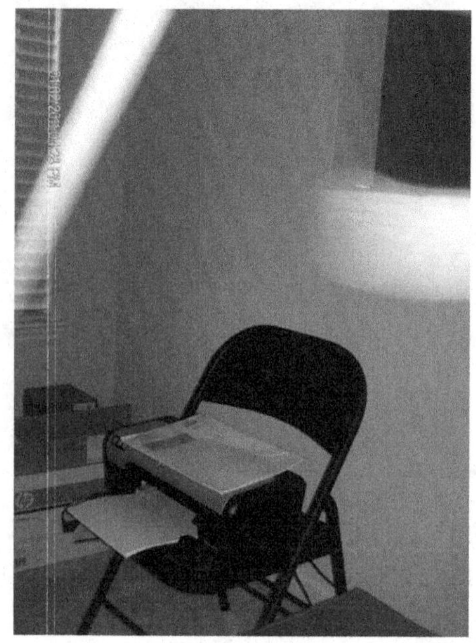

January 2, 2011 4:28 PM (3)

They attacked to Phiem's ear when she was sitting at her computer.

January 3, 2011 6:11 AM

They attacked to Phiem's ear, face when she was in her bed.

January 4, 2011 11:17 AM (1)

They attacked to Phiem's ear when she was in her kitchen.

January 4, 2011 11:18 AM (2)

They attacked to Phiem's ear when she was in her kitchen.

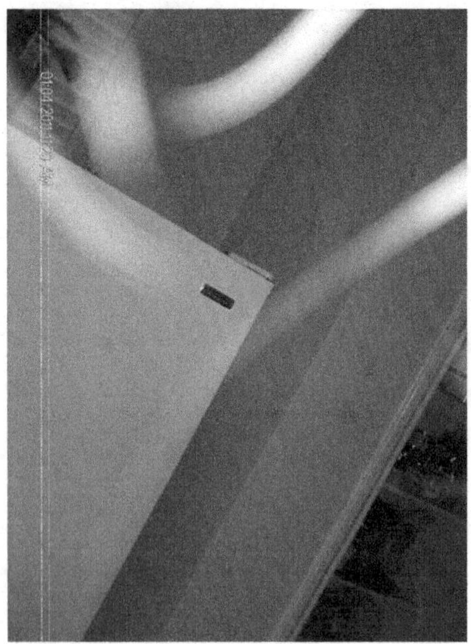

January 4, 2011 11:20 AM (3)

They attacked to Phiem's ear when she was in her kitchen.

January 4, 2011 11:22 AM (4)

They attacked to Phiem's ear when she was in her kitchen she took this picture camera faced to her ear.

January 4, 2011 11:22 AM

They attacked to Phiem's face when she was in her kitchen.

January 4, 2011 12:09 PM

They attacked to Phiem right ear and head when she was sitting at her computer.

January 4, 2011 12:24 PM

They attacked to Phiem's left ear when she was sitting at her computer.

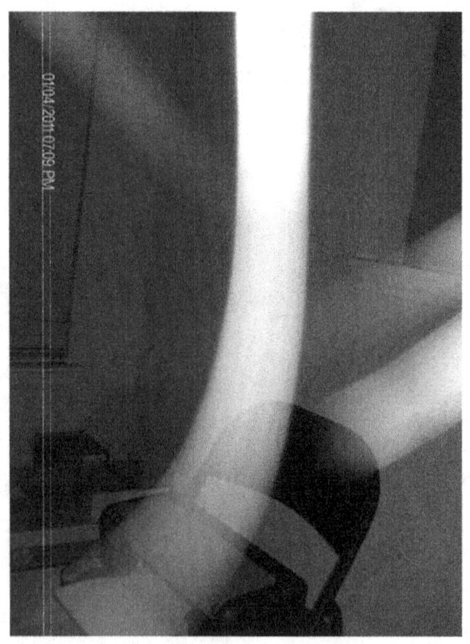

January 4, 2011 7:09 PM (1)

They attacked to Phiem's left ear when she was sitting at her computer.

January 4, 2011 7:09 PM (2)

They attacked to Phiem's left ear when she was sitting at her computer.

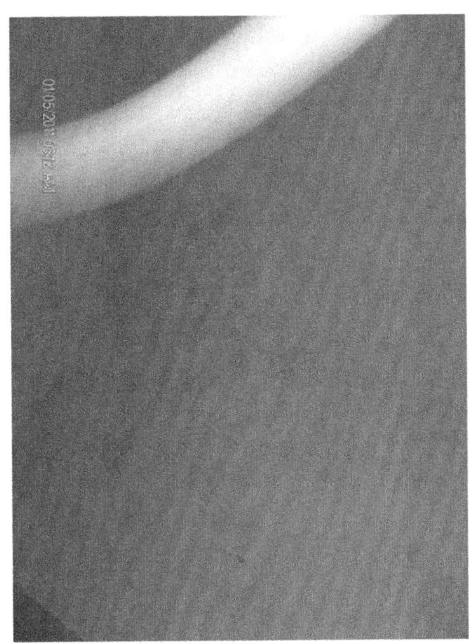

January 5, 2011 6:12 AM

They attacked to Phiem's left ear when she was in her bed.

January 5, 2011 6:17 AM

They attacked to Phiem's left ear when she was in her bed this picture was taken camera faced to her ear.

January 5, 2011 6:18 AM

They attacked to Phiem's left ear when she was in her bed this picture was taken camera faced to her ear.

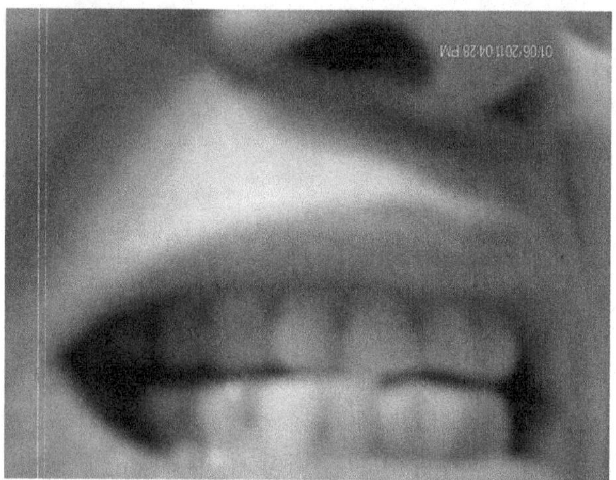

January 6, 2011 4:28 PM

Phiem did not know why her gum like that she thought it could be her tooth was pull out but she just read the document stated that was cause from microwave and directed energy bombarded to her head, face and body.

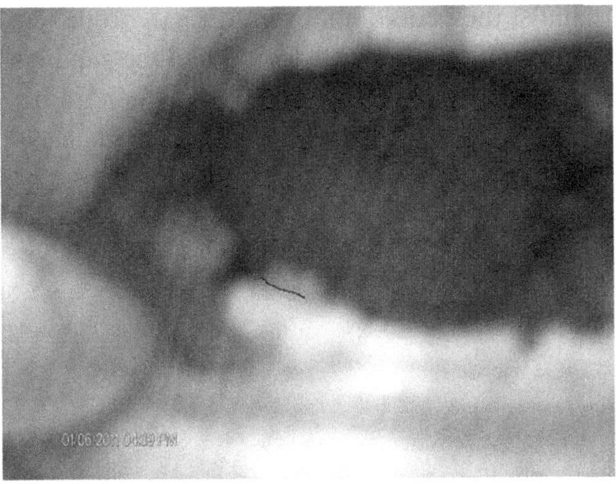

January 6, 2011 4:39 PM

They sew off Phiem tooth as it was shown in this picture in order she could not chew her food, they did it during the time she was sleeping because she never see they did it to her when she was awakening.

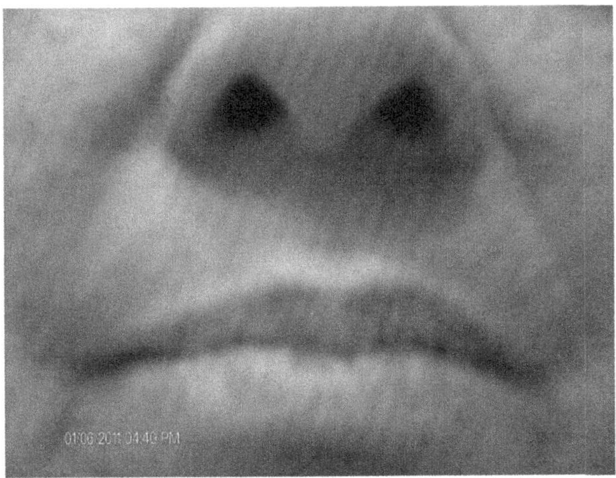

January 6, 2011 4:40 PM

Phiem did not know what they did to her mouth and to her upper lip during the time she was sleeping during the night, she woke up she felt strange and uncomfortable to her mouth and to her lip she took this picture to show. My nose at the left side they tried to change it shape that I only felt the itchy boring me all the time at that place then I saw my left side nose appeared thinner and it was changed to the different shape. They use Nanotechnology wire to implant the cells to my cheek and it was grown to destroy my original cells to make my face aging and saggy and they used their technique to sabotage my face, my unique, they were laughing when they did it to my face, my beauty.
Yesterday I felt so painful to both side of my jaw I did not know what they did to my jaw, they want to change my face to another face or they beamed to my head by both side of my

neck because I used ear plugs to close my ear canals, they could not beam directly to my ear canals. I could not take picture my ear canals by myself to show but I could feel the sandy at my ear canals and I could see and feel several microchips were implanted at my ear frames for a long period of time.

January 6, 2011 8:31 PM (1)

They attacked to Phiem'ear when she was sitting at her computer.

January 7, 2011 8:32 PM (2)

They attacked to Phiem'ear when she was sitting at her computer.

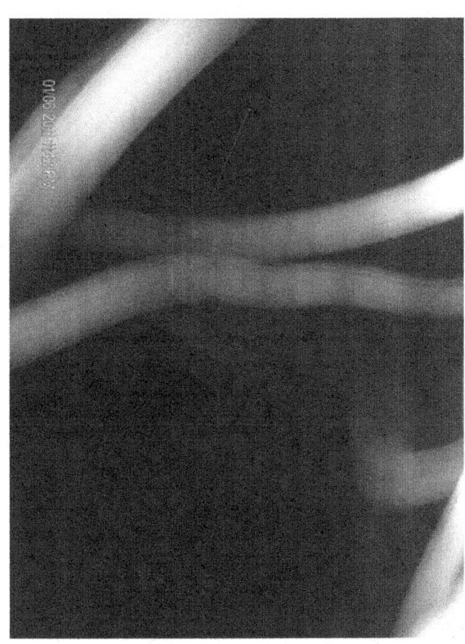

January 6, 2011 11:42 PM

They attacked to Phiem's left ear when she shut down and left her computer desk.

January 7, 2011 12:21 AM

They attacked to Phiem's neck at the place under her ear when she was in her bed.

January 7, 2011 6:53 AM (1)

They attacked to Phiem's left ear when she was in her bed.

January 7, 2011 6:54 AM (2)

They were constantly attacked to Phiem'left ear when she was in her bed, in this picture was captured the red color of microwave.

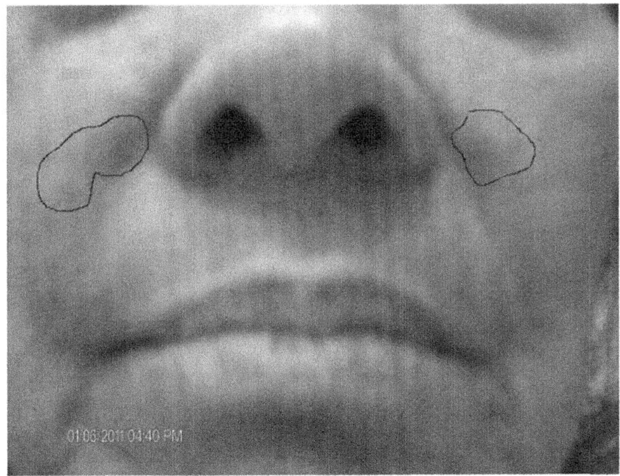

January 6, 2011 4:40 PM (1)

They used Nanotechnology wire to implanted the cells into Phiem's cheeks in order to grow their deform cells then destroy Phiem cheeks original cells to degrade to sabotage her beauty, her unique.

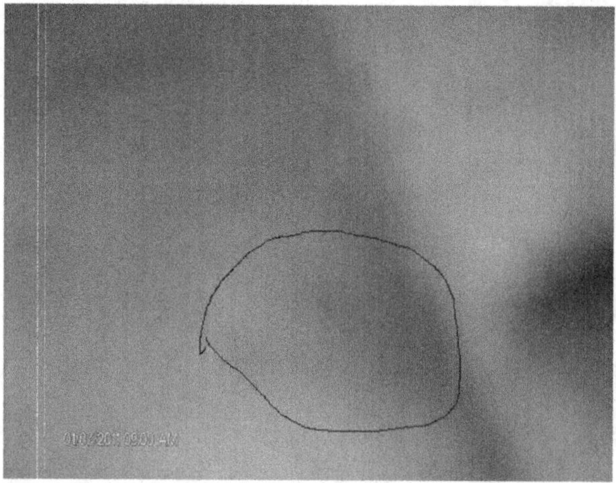

January 7, 2011 9:00 AM (2)

Phiem took this picture her left cheek this morning at the place they implanted microchips or cells into her left cheek.

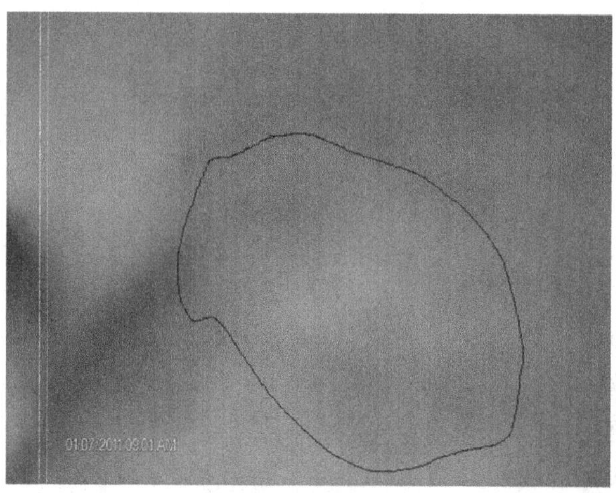

January 7, 2011 9:01 AM (3)

Phiem took this picture the place they implanted microchips or cells into her right cheek, it will be working in that place to form my cheek as they want it to be, it was swollen then it looked saggy, her face looked too old, they sabotaged her beauty.

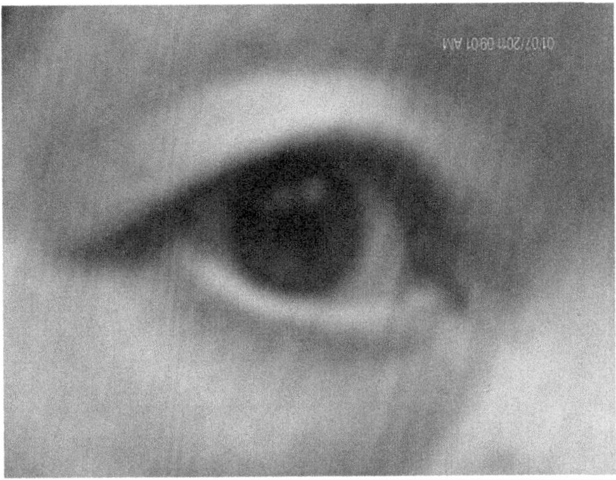

January 7, 2011 9:01 AM

Phiem saw her eye lids were swoopy like that she took this picture to show, her eye lids were double eye lids it were not like that.

January 7, 2011 11:39 AM (1)

They set up every ware in Phiem's house when she went downstairs to her kitchen she captured the Nanomicrotechnology to attack from everywhere directions in her house to attack her that she could not avoid the force was set and activated.

January 7, 2011 11:40 AM (2)

January 7, 2011 11:40 AM (3)

They attacked to Phiem's ear when she went downstairs to her kitchen they attacked her from every where she went.

January 7, 2011 7:01 PM

They attacked to Phiem's ear when she was in her kitchen.

January 7, 2011 7:04 PM (2)

They constantly attacked to Phiem's ear when she was in her kitchen.

January 8, 2011 3:54 AM (1)

They attacked to Phiem's left ear when she woke up then went back from bathroom; she captured the microwave color in surrounding her bedroom.

January 8, 2011 3:55 AM (2)

They attacked Phiem's left ear when she was in her bed room, they might woke her up and they might do something to her body during she was sleeping, she captured these pictures with microwave color was using to bombarded to her head through her ear canal.

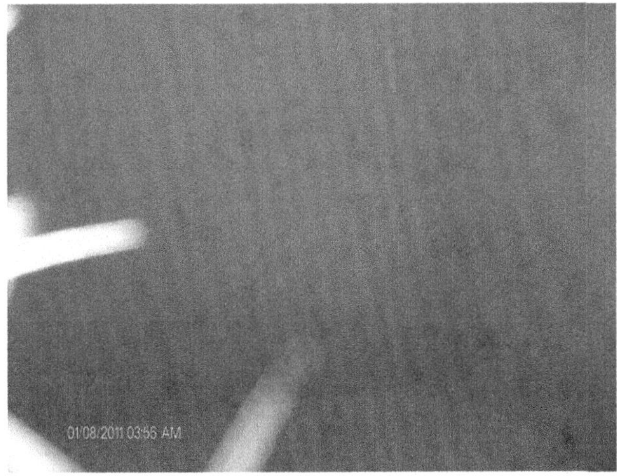

January 8, 2011 3:56 AM (1)

They attacked to Phiem's right ear when she was in her bed as she described above that they beamed to her left ear.

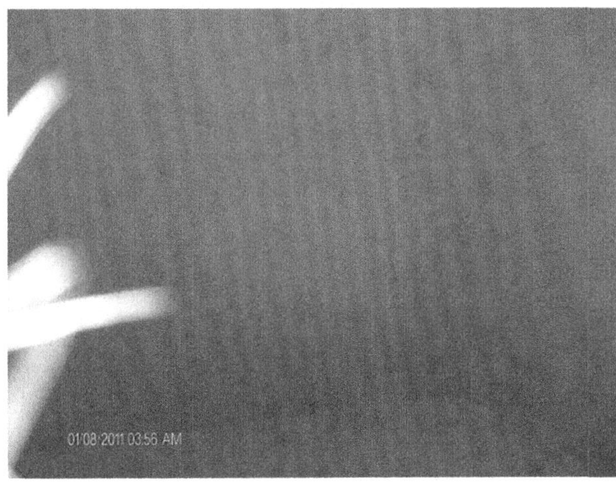

January 8, 2011 3:56 AM (2)

They beamed Nanomicrotechnology to Phiem's right ear when she was in her bed.

January 8, 2011 12:30 PM (1)

They attacked to Phiem's left ear when she was sitting at her computer.

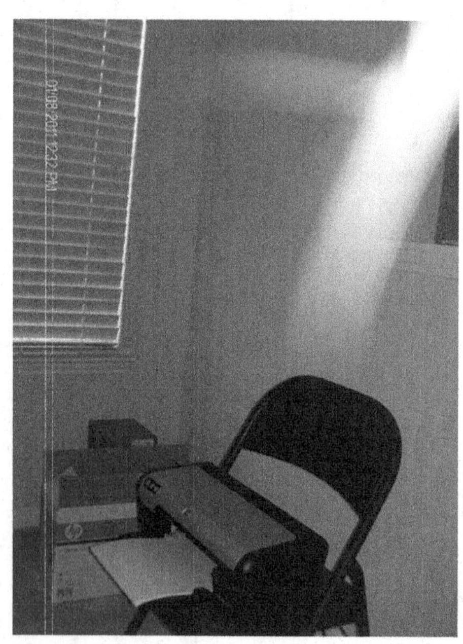

January 8, 2011 12:32 PM (2)

January 8, 2011 12:32 PM (3)

They constantly bombarded Nanotechnology Micromagnetic to Phiem's left ear when she was sitting at her computer desk.

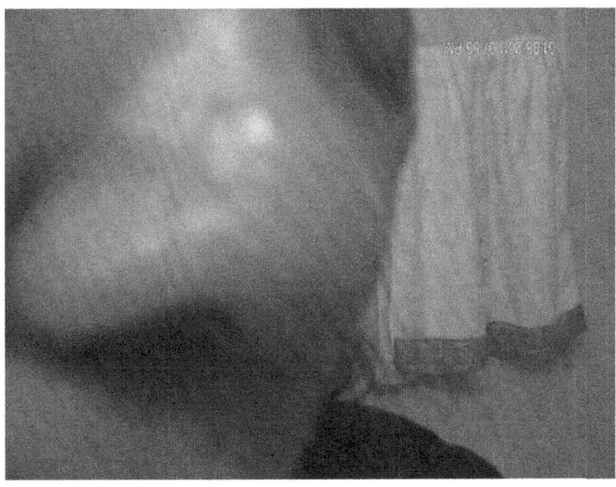

January 8, 2011 7:56 PM (1)

Phiem original nose (canh mui), this is her right side nose.

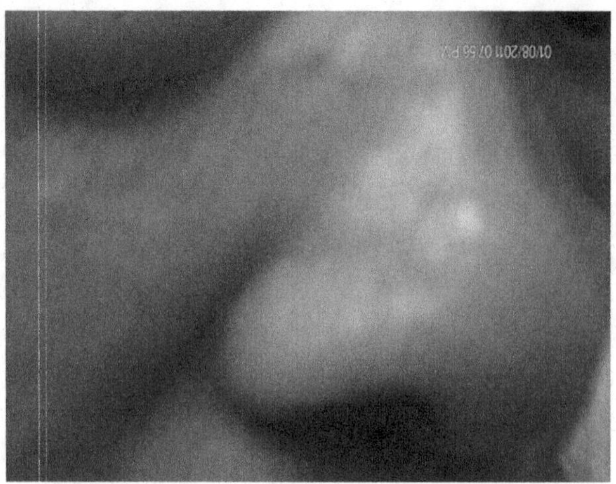

January 8, 2011 7:56 PM (2)

Phiem original nose (canh mui), this is her right side nose.

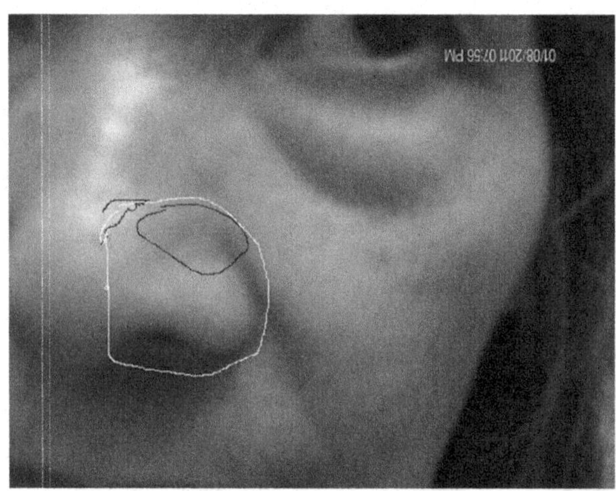

January 8, 2011 7:56 PM (3)

They changed shape Phiem's nose, this is her left side nose.

January 11, 2011 3:24 PM (1)

They attacked to Phiem's left ear when she was sitting at her computer; the three small bright lines are sun light reflection not the Nano Micromagnetic rays.

January 11, 2011 3:24 PM (2)

They attacked to Phiem's left ear when she was sitting at her computer, the three small bright lines are sun light reflection not the Nano Micromagnetic rays.

January 11, 2011 3:26 PM (3)

They attacked to Phiem neck under her ear to beam Nano Micromagnetic wires, rays to her ear canal because she locked her ear canal; she was sitting at her computer.

January 11, 2011 3:27 PM (4)

They attacked to Phiem neck under her ear to beam Nano Micromagnetic wires, rays to her ear canal because she locked her ear canal; she was sitting at her computer.

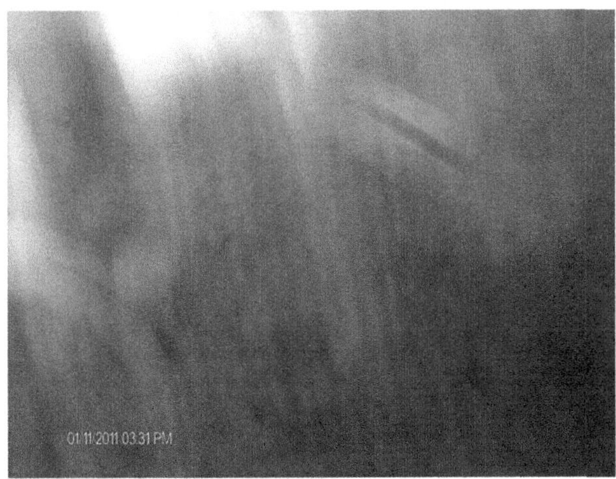

January 11, 2011 3:31 PM (1)

They attacked to Phiem's back head at her back ear.

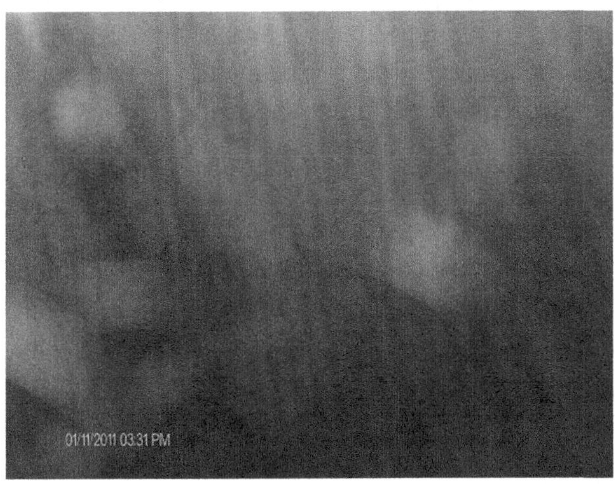

January 11, 2011 3:31 PM (2)

They attacked to Phiem's back head at her back ear.

January 11, 2011 3:31 PM (2)

They attacked to Phiem's back head at her back ear, what they tried to do to her head? They wanted to control her mind, to sex slave, to sex abuse, to humiliate her, to change her behavior, to change her thought, to do what they wanted her to do, they 24/7 constantly doing these things on her. They are not tired, their aims are steal people lands, money and love sex. Everything she said is true they constantly attacked to Phiem female to sensation her female and made her think as they wanted her think but she aware of that so she averse he thought if human did not know about that how human naturally react differently. Several actions they assault to her female but she did not know how to explain that, they knew how and what they did to her or others can describe it.

No doubt about the attacking they posed to Phiem back head at her back ear it made her could not use her brain to think to work with brain, it made dizziness like they polluted her entire house with chemical and their microwave radiation beamed to her head and to her body. Mind control method and abuse and high-tech rape.

January 12, 2011 3:18 AM

They attacked to Phiem's neck and ear when she was in her bed. She woke up then went to bathroom then back to her bed then attacked her as the force was captured in this picture. They might did something to her body and her subconscious then they woke her up in the condition she needed to go to bathroom in urgent then they attacked her body her ears when she went back to her bed, they did it several times before so she rose the question mark recently.

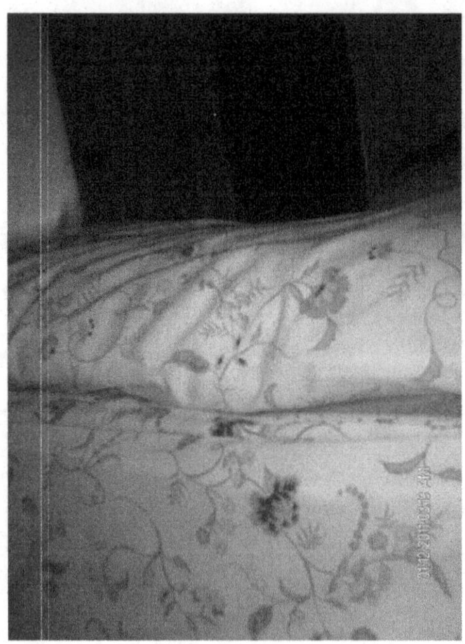

January 12, 2011 3:20 AM

Phiem stood up beside her bed to avoid the Nanomicromagnetic radian beams to her neck and ear then they beamed to her female she took this picture to show, she did not know what it was.

January 12, 2011 3:31 AM

They attacked to Phiem's right ear when she was in her bed and this was a series of attacking after she woke up or be woken up then beamed Nanomicromagnetic rays (wires) to her body, her head through her ears.

Microwave high frequency burned the flesh inside body, they use Microwave at the low frequency enough to kill cells, tissue my (Phiem) body, it turned aging to her hang at her female, her buttocks, they used Nanomicromagnetic technique to attacked to her body which part they want to change shape and which part they want to damage, they did it to her female, her face, her whole body.

Few nights ago Phiem did not know what they did to her back when she woke up she felt hurt and it was not comfortable.

January 14, 2011

Last night Phiem was in bed she felt so painful to her stomach she had to take the tin can and the heavy sponge to cover her stomach although she had cover her body with blanket and her fake leather jacket, she knew immediately they wanted to murder her, they increase the power to attack her stomach her organs, she knew it because in 2006 they attacked to her abdomen, her ovaries she placed her hand to cover the place was hit then the day after they increased power to attack her stomach she placed her hand to cover as she did the day before, it was hurt her hand so much so she got out of bed to take her jacket to cover her body since every night she in bed.

Phiem just watched video Mind Control Possible and HARP project human made the choice between God and Evil and if it was in the wrong hands the pities world problem could not be imaginable and could not be solved.

Criminal Psychotronic Weapons part IV

January 17, 2011

Phiem saw the 2 green black spots at her right buttock she took these pictures but she did not know when and how they did it to her body.
They made it vibration she could feel it when it was activated, they destroyed her entire body they squeezed, twisted her vain legs.

January 21, 2011

Phiem brushed her teeth she bent her body they beamed the Nanomicromagnetic ray to her kidney she could not go away to avoid it so they were continuing to attack to her left kidney then they made vibration her kidney to her left lung, they murder her like that constantly day and night, after she finished her brushing teeth she went out to take camera to take picture to show.

January 22, 2011

Last night Phiem sat at her computer they attacked to her side stomach and her right shoulder they made her arm could not move she had to take some thing like metal to place at her shoulder to absorber some radiation.
This morning Phiem was in her kitchen cooking they attacked to her female her lower abdomen sides then her stomach, they made her stomach felt sick. Now people could tell they murder people all the time, how could people live the life like that, this is natural law the earth will be recycle itself to bring back the normal nature to balance this universe if you do believe science. I said do not blame nature but blame yourself.

January 23, 2011

Last night when Phiem just lied down into bed they made the laser line ran across her upper lip then she immediately fall into sleep right away she could not resisted but she do not know if she was so tired or from their controlling.
Day and night they constantly attacking her from head to toes from inside to outside then during the time she's sleeping they invaded her subconscious to abuse to humiliate to control and to change into what they wanted.
Phiem is so angry she said she could not live the life like that and human can not live the life like that so evils will be destroyed, all the evils.
Phiem was so angry this morning when she talk to her family member that they murder her, she had to pay the Doctor bills US$3000.00 the Hospital bills will be more than US$16000.00, she does not have Insurance. How can she buy Insurance without income since 1980 with depending tighten budget, she tried to save money to buy Insurance but she could not do it, they tried to prevent her on everything.

January 24, 2011

They damage Phiem's woman organs, her ovaries, her veins at her hang to control her leg veins, she wrote about it but she did not take picture of it, this morning she felt pain when she woke up she felt her entire stomach, her lower abdomen were painful, they tortured, abused, they shot to damage, they implanted, she took these pictures to show.

Phiem did not know what they will abuse her next, last night she dreamed in the pattern mind solution, she woke up in the conscious to following the finding solution continuing from the dream, she did not want to continue it, let see what they tried to abuse next. In her fragment subconscious or their subconscious set up each night they wanted her to think as they wanted it to be.

January 25, 2011

This morning Phiem felt so terrible hurt at her left thigh so she took picture at her left thigh to show how they damage her thigh by Microwave heat to damage her cell thigh. They did not do it last night only but long period time they heat her hang, her buttocks her female like that, the pictures will show the evidences.
Unfortunately, I could not upload my file to computer because the virus in my memory card or they changed my memory card. I could say they wanted to block it.

January 29, 2011

As everyday I go to bed to shield my body with metal sheet, sponges, blanket and jacket as I show these pictures.
I enter this diary at 5:35 AM, I went to bed at midnight then they attacked my head, my ear, my stomach and two side stomachs, my lower abdomen, my female and my spinal cord, I felt hurt then I did massage my back because I felt hurt at my back.

January 31, 2011

Last night I went to bed early because I was too tired for cooking then I woke up at 12:45 AM I went to bathroom then back my bed I was in attacking form them so I got out of my bed to go outside my bedroom. They shot to my head I could not work with my brain, they used Micromagnetic to attacked to my thighs to burn my cells at my thighs, my hang, my ovaries places.
They damaged my buttocks and my hang, people could not see because it was private and it was in my back I could not take pictures of it.
Pictures I took I could not upload it because the memory card problem, I just order the new one whenever I have it I will show it in this diary.
Few days ago, my computer was affected with virus files. How can this crime be stopped I asked it on the face book, this is not suffering only the victims but it could be the authorities too because you could not escape that, your privacy, your body, your life and your pass words

and also your plans could be read, you created fire wall but when it will be affected virus like the case on computer, you will be defeated.

February 1, 2011

This morning when I was brushing my teeth they attacked to my lower abdomen like they cut and injury inside my abdomen through to my female. I did not know what they did to me. They shot to my leg, my toe. This evening when I was eating at dinning room they shot to my back head, my top left side head then two side of my lungs so hard, so hurt, I took the two metal things to cover it.

I saw the thing went wrong today I log in White House website to post my opened letter but I could not write in the wall so I just post it at my side I hope that our government notice it and do something to stop it.
I copied the letter here.

This opened letter I am sending to our Government United States of America

Phiem Nguyen

February 1, 2011

Dear Mr. Barack Obama and the Government of United State of America:
Dear Senators and Congress of Legislation of United State of America:

Grassroots movement was the voices of citizens in community to voice the necessary community need to the government.
I am a citizen want to express the situation I am the victim of Criminal Psychotropic Weapons and all the victims in America and around the globe.
Please search on Internet about this subject government will collect all the information and the victim petitions were placing there or link to my face book to do research.
How technology was developed and how it was using on human and how it tortured innocent victims.
The dangerous technology, the invisible technology, the powerful and detriment technology intended to destroy the entire population and this earth with the ambitious governments.
The powerless victims are loyal patriotic citizens were placing under harassment, torture, rape, abuse, humiliate, murder and deprive, isolation and financial ruin, powerless in legal it looked alike taped your mouth shut, no body knows what was going on in the deep societies.
Victims have lived in grievous lives with mental abuse, physical damaged and well-being human was deprived in the meticulous scenarios set up trap.
I and a lot of victims sent letters to the government but this issue seemed silent as it was ordering to execute on victims, this violation civil liberty is secretly and silently, we have learned this in history since this human history was written.
This Criminal Psychotropic Weapons is dangerous more than nuclear and drug problem, the entire planet will be paralyzed if government kept ordering it silent.

You have to wake up or you have to order an investigation to know the truth and to learn how dangerous this trend of weapons you will be next, you will not escape that, and you will be surrendered.
Please do something in urgent to this weapon issue to ban it, to stop it, if it is not too late to action.
Government has to look back and see you fell to protect citizens, the innocent victims do not know where to report the crime, do not know where to seek the legal to protect.
Government has to end this exercise research, bring honorable human life back to victims and compensate for all the victims.

February 2, 2011

Phiem went to bed at 1:00 AM but she could not sleep because they harassed her so she went to bathroom then to her computer now 3:03 AM. She said she would be free when all of the evils were died. She was so angry.
This is not fiction but the fact base on the history, she did not know who manipulated the cause but the result communism uprising and control. Rewrite history with the new kind of weapons, at this time the world will be accepted the ancient time fact.

Yesterday when Phiem's brushing her teeth they shot then they did something to her eyes and they did it before Phiem felt soar to her eyes then yesterday she read on Internet she felt soar to her eyes too, it was bothering her reading, they implanted Micro object to outside her left eyes then to her right eye now, it's still there when she wrote these sentences.

February 03, 2011

They are constantly murder Phiem, they used Micromagnetic to damage her organs everyday when she sat at her computer, when she was brushing her teeth and when she was in her kitchen and the night she was in her bed, they are not just attacking her female, they are not just rape, they also damage, and changed shape her female, of-course damage her body from her head to her toes, from subconscious to conscious.

Phiem does not know what they took inside her head they pressed her head as she saw it was changed shape.

February 4, 2011

This morning when Phiem woke up she felt pain at her born Macro she know it was from attacking there during the time she was sleeping, she was not covering at that place last night, hat was so terrible how people can live the life like that; the evils should be destroyed.

February 6, 2011

Phiem does not know what they did to her lower lip last night during the time she was sleeping when she woke up this morning she saw the swollen and felt hurt at her lip, she saw the bleeding at the wound on her lip, she took pictures but her memory card could not be read by her computer so she could not show it here. They damaged her lower lip in 2006 she described it in her book God Universe and Me.
Few days ago and yesterday they shot to her heels, she took picture the trace of big red dot at her right heel, it felt hurt too then 2 days later she felt at that place of the dot became harder skin then it was split broken skin, it was hurt.
They destroyed Phiem's beauty, her lip, her mouth, her eyes, her cheeks, her chin, her eye brows, her fore head, they pressed her head dented in to change shape, they damage her woman body, her breast, her female, her buttocks, her thighs, her legs, enter her body, her organs, her brain and her subconscious.
She has to have things to cover her body to avoid their attacking forces but she could not do it all the time and entire her body, during her sleeping time she's paralyzing.
Their governments have to pay for what they did, I sued them, they have to pay for and they have to bring the honorable lives back to me and the victims then they have to stop these criminal actions to human if not they have to face the law of the universe or people will action to rescue this mankind.
Evils should be destroyed.

February 7, 2011

This morning Phiem's continuing applied ices to her lips, yesterday she applied ices to her lips then the gray color was gone. The lover lip was in injury by convulsion force attacking to her lip during the time she was sleeping and the trace of implant the tiny microchips into her lip, she tried to pull it out but it still inside her lip, she saw the white tiny microchips there.

February 11, 2011

Yesterday they shot to my head, my upper lip then today when I take shower they shot to my right lower leg, they constantly attack to my head, my ears, stomach, chest, legs, hips, lower abdomen an my female.
This evening they shot to my both forefront head and at the tempos it made me feel head ache and dizzy that made me could not do stock work, they tortured like that, they prevent on doing everything, eating, doing dishes, cooking, sleeping, brushing teeth, reading and I could not rest when I was tired. They abuse, murder, torture like that, they are cowards dinosaurs I named it and what I wish for those dinosaurs.

February 15, 2011

I could not sleep because they attacked to my female, they did something to my female so I came out my bedroom 4:00 AM, I went to bed at 2:00 AM, I was afraid of sleeping because

I did not know what they did to my female when I was sleeping. They are group of people but I am alone and I am human how could I resist sleeping to guard for my body that was the reason they rape, murder, humiliate, harm, deform, degrade and sabotage to my body, my beauty, my organs, my heath. I wish for these ill evils will be destroyed.
They beam, they shot, they activate chips to control my whole body 24/7, I took pictures but I could not upload those pictures to my computer recently.

February 16, 2011

They shot to Phiem's neck it made soar throat when she does dishes, they did all time 24/7 attacking to Phiem form head to toes from inside organs to her skin, from conscious to subconscious. I want them to be destroyed.
Today I mailed letter to collector debt that I paid my Hospital and Doctor bills by my credit cards because I did not have health insurance, I supposed to let them know that was case of murder they did on my organs.

They implanted chip into my female then they activated to sensation all day today, they made itchy to my female to trigger the sensation, the chips are inside my female were working to deform my female with their attempted to sabotage my body to humiliate me.

February 17, 2011

I just found out all pictures on the memory card that could not read by my computer were gone, they stole my memory card or they control my digital camera so they did not get in my house to steal the pictures, all pictures my privacy pictures were taken by myself to proved what they did to my body.
Last night I could not rest after I was finished working on my website, I sat outside my bedroom until 5:00 AM. I had lunch time around 3:00PM then could not clean my dishes because the radio wave they sent it through phone line busted into my kitchen smelt like heroin or drug or something, in my bathroom smelt like human waste.

February 19, 2011

Today I cleaned my bathroom after I finished it I heard the strange sound was siren, it like hurricane wind in my bathroom at the toilet, I went outside to check but nothing outside the bathroom, it was heard inside the bathroom only.
This evening I had dinner at my dinning room I saw the plan past by my window at least 3 tours then the shooting began to my under arm, my back the right lung and my left ovary.
They constantly shot to my stomach, organs and stomach side organs, the pictures below show my stomach was cover with sponges and plastic sheet to shield my stomach but they increase the power to shoot through these things, I watched the victim video on YouTube, he had the hard thick stainless steel sheet to shield his stomach. I said, they have to stop these evil things or they should be destroyed.
This evening Phiem sat at her computer they shot and activated to her female to sensation and did harm her female, they tried to humiliate her and transformed her female and her

female organ. What they are doing on Phiem's body? They shot to her stomach or they activated or they control mind, she felt so terrible pain at her inside stomach when she was sitting at her computer. Phiem was afraid of going to bed each night, she was awaken whole night this night too, now it is 6:08 AM

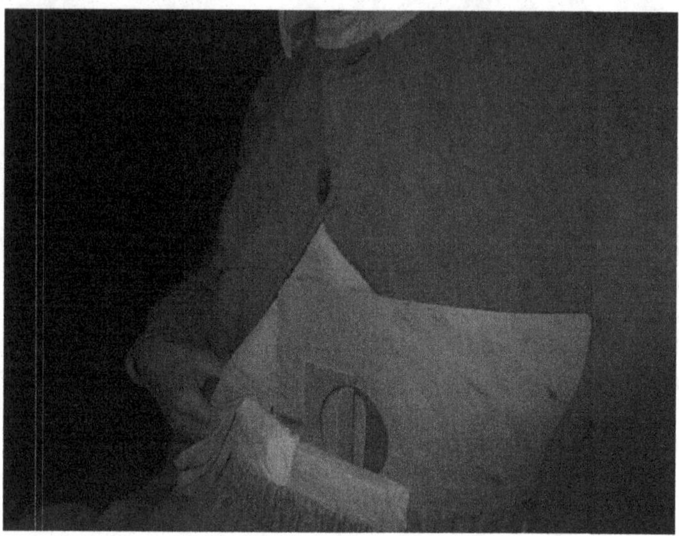

February 18, 2011 11:00 PM

Phiem covered her stomach with these things, sponges and plastic mouse pat, Phiem used another camera because it can read the memory card she just ordered, it is bigger and heavier than HP camera so she reduce the pictures to show the evidences in this part of her book. They murdered.

February 21, 2011

Yesterday Phiem woke up at around 10:00AM she went to bed at 7:00 AM she was in awaken all night because she's afraid of in their changing pastel something to her subconscious and they might doing something to her female sex, they activated their chips at her female to make sensation when she was sitting at her computer, that why she was afraid of going to bed.

Last night she went to bed as usual at night, she woke up at 4:00 AM to go to bath under their controlling to wake her up by sensation their chips at her female, she felt head each, her face was pain then she back to sleep, during that time she was sleeping what they did to her body when she woke up she felt her entire body hurt by chips controlling on entire her body and her face also.

She had to do exercise after she did it she felt ease.

The important thing she noticed that each time they conduct the pattern to her subconscious like changed emotion, thinking and etc. head each traditional using in 1980s, recently they shot to the fore front head at tempos.

February 23, 2011

Every night they invade Phiem's subconscious they injected their created dreams as people called that "outcome dreams"
Yesterday evening when Phiem was sitting at her dinning room she saw the plane was past by her window 4 tours, first she noticed the shot at her back then she saw the first tour then the second tour came with the attacking to her ear, the second tour shot to her head, the third tour shot to her right side ovary, her head, the fourth tours came she left the table, she wondered how many people here under this surveillance and murder and who paid for that and how much money they spent to harass those citizens and now I knew they will shut down government on April 03, 2011, Phiem took these pictures but could not present it here, the problem the memory card was changed by them her computer could not read it.
During the time Phiem typed this entry diary they shot to her left ear she took these pictures too as she described above.
Phiem noticed it they used the plane and they used mobile or portable the radiation isotropic bullet gun from Medical field to do that harm and murder Phiem just knew it from the face book friend revealed it.

Attention! Good News

They returned my memory card back or they activated my computer can read my (Phiem) memory card I did not know but I tried it again at this moment I found out that I can copied those pictures which I present here to show how the plane was attacking my body last evening however they stole several pictures included my private pictures too that I took since I knew my computer could not read my memory card.

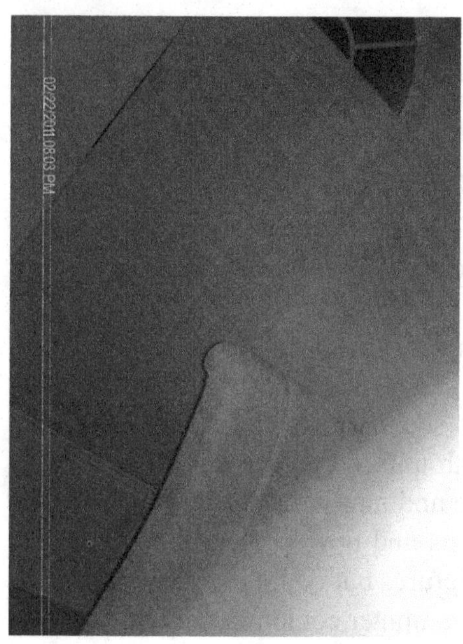

February 22, 2011 8:03 PM (1)

The plane was carried out their attacking to Phiem' head and ear when she was in her dinning room this evening.

February 22, 2011 8:03 PM (2)

The plan carried out attacking to Phiem' head and ear when she was in her dinning room.

February 22, 2011 8:20 PM (3)

These pictures Phiem took it when the plane was attacking her right ovary she did not know what it was she had to show it.

February 22, 2011 8:20 PM (4)

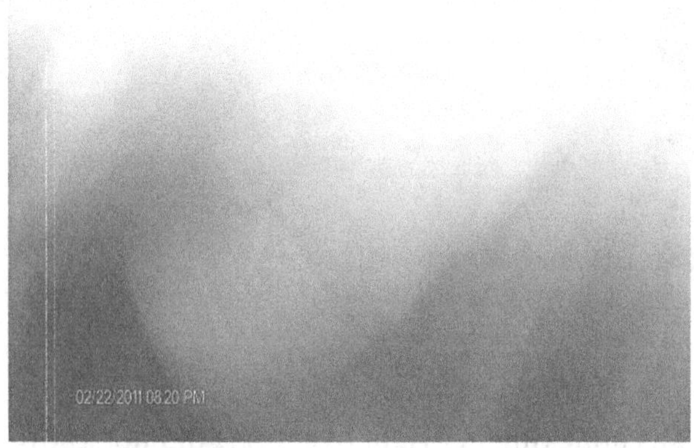

February 22, 2011 8:20 PM (5)

They attacked to Phiem's head

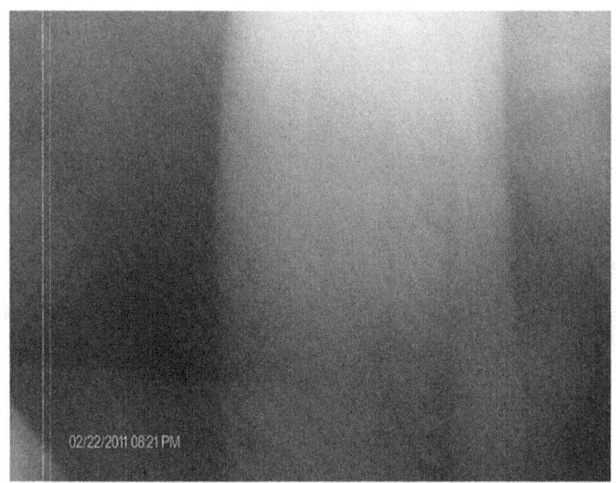

February 22, 2011 8:21 PM (6)

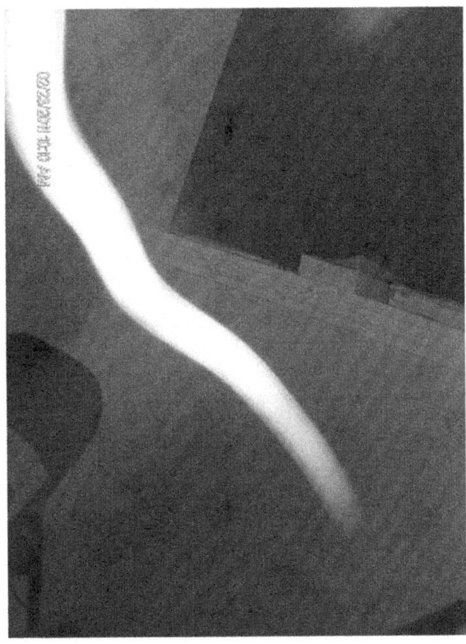

February 23, 2011 10:10 AM (1)

This picture was taken during the time Phiem was typing this diary they beamed to her left ear.

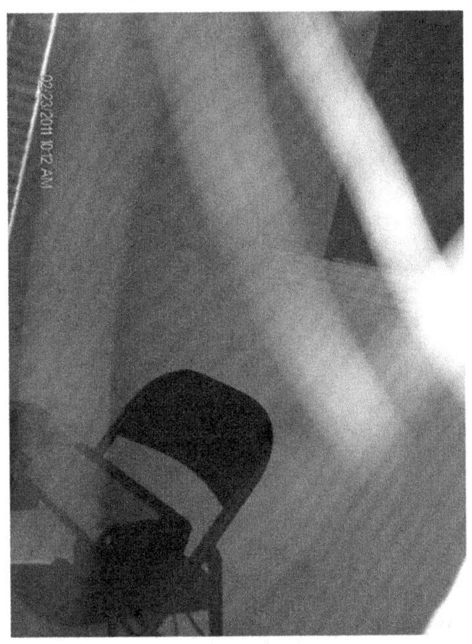

February 23, 2011 10:10 AM (2)

This picture was taken during the time Phiem was typing this diary they assaulted to her left ear.

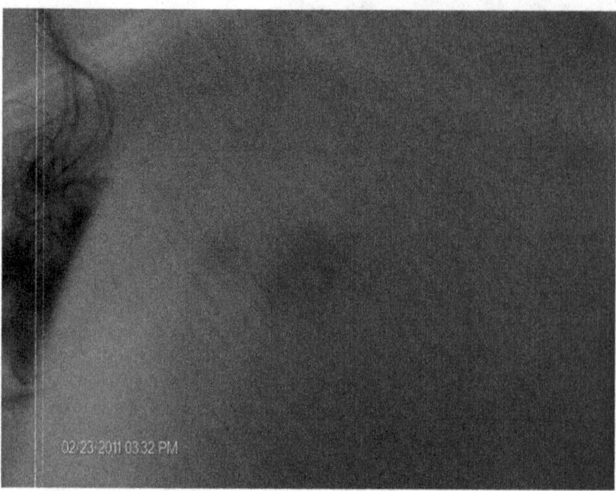

Image # 1

The date Phiem took this picture was not the date this happened to her knee but it was few days ago when she woke up she saw it but she could not upload her pictures to her computer, yesterday she found out her memory card was returned or they connected or someone might activated or set up so I copied this picture to show.

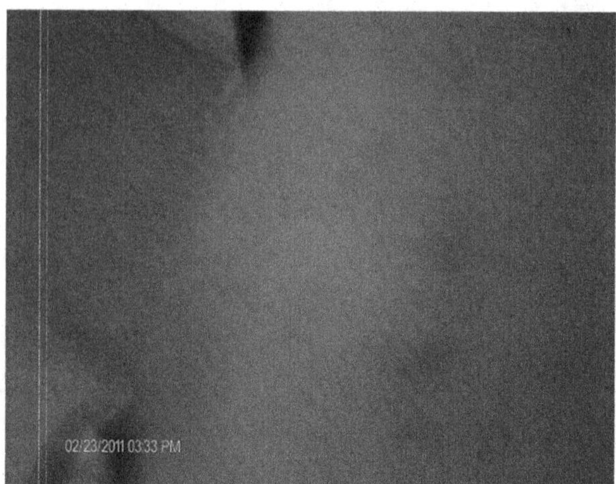

Image # 2

Phiem saw the scratching at her knee but no blood on that place and no soar for that injury she did not know what they did to her body during the time she was sleeping, she took this picture to prove it.

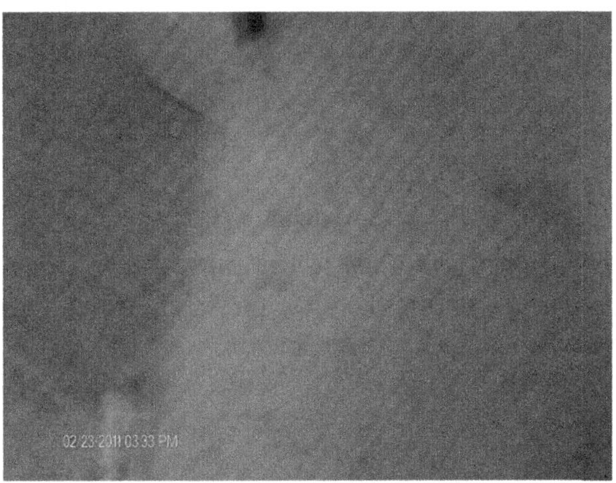

Image # 3

The whole picture of Phiem's knee.

February 23, 2011 8:53 PM (1)

Phiem had dinner at her dinning room first she felt the shot to her head then she saw the plan past by her window then the attacking began they assaulted to her ear, these pictures were taken during that time, she took her cell phone to capture the force they were using that would notice from the cell phone tower and what we can see in these pictures.

February 23, 2011 8:54 PM (2)

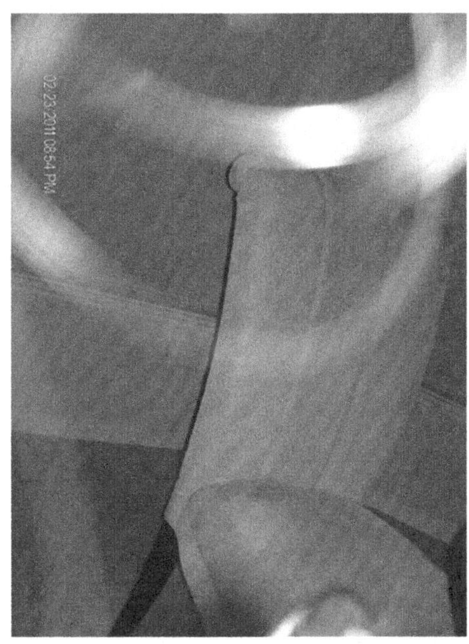

February 23, 2011 8:54 PM (3)

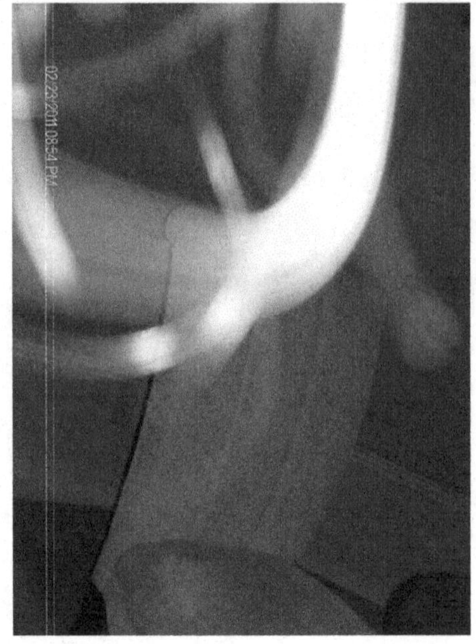

February 23, 2011 (4)

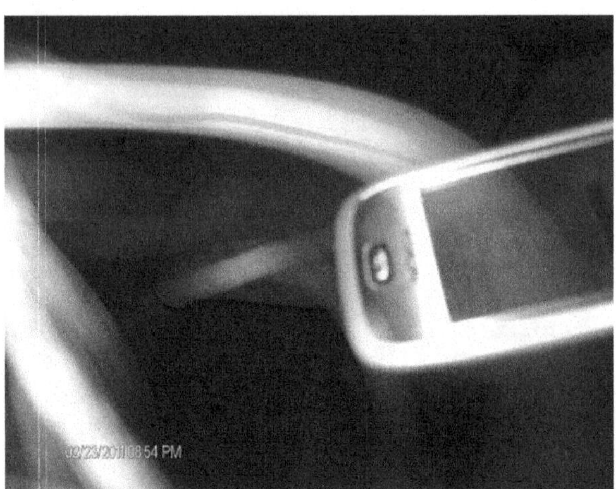

February 23, 2011 (5)

February 23, 2011 8:55 PM (6)

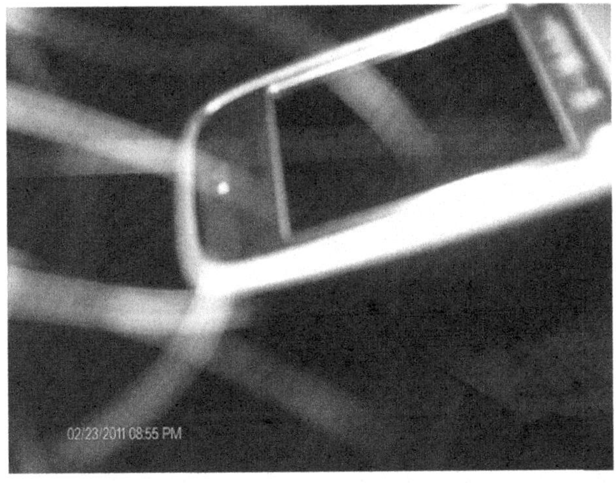

February 23, 2011 8:55 PM (7)

February 23, 2011 8:55 PM (8)

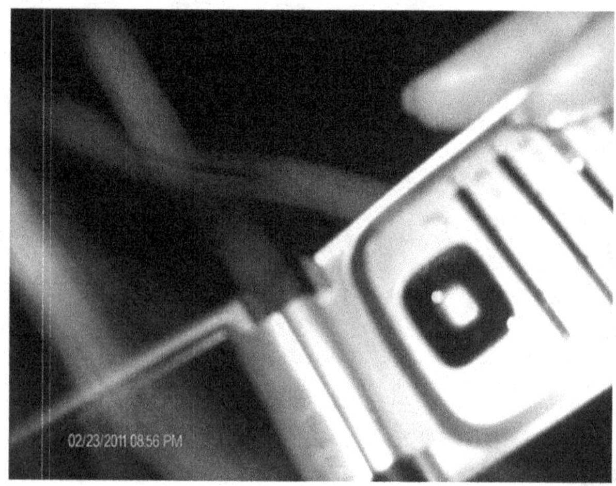

February 24, 2011 8:56 PM (9)

February 23, 2011 9:02 PM

They shot to Phiem's head when she was in her kitchen.

February 24, 2011 7:50 AM

They shot to Phiem's head when she was in her kitchen.

February 24, 2011 8:11 AM

They beamed to Phiem's left ear when she was in her kitchen preparing for her cooking.

February 24, 2011 8:28 AM

They were attacking to Phiem's stomach side organ when she was in her kitchen cooking.

February 25, 2011 3:05 AM (1)

They assaulted to Phiem's left ear when she was in her bed, after they woke her up to go to bathroom the she went back her bed.

February 25, 2011 3:06 AM (2)

They assaulted to Phiem's left ear when she was in her bed, after they woke her up to go to bathroom the she went back her bed.

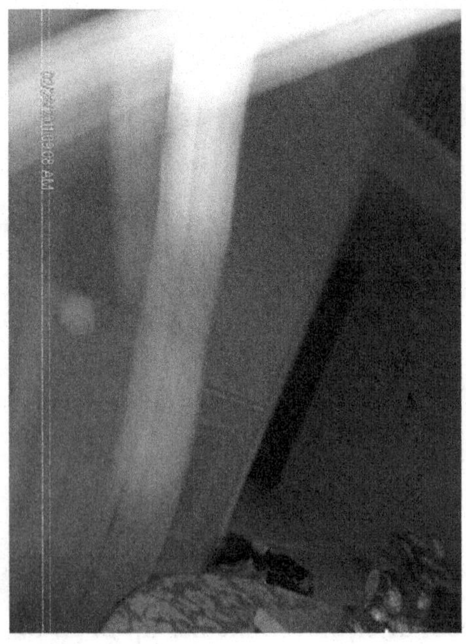

February 26, 2011 9:08 (1)

Phiem's having rice soup she cooked this morning because she had fruit allergy yesterday she was in bed from yesterday afternoon until this morning. They beamed to her left ear when she was at her dinning table to eat, they beamed constantly from 9: 08 AM to 9:12 AM these pictures will prove it.

February 26, 2011 9:12 AM (2)

February 26, 2011 9:12 AM (3)

These pictures above were proved the time on these pictures.

February 27, 2011

What kind of weapon they tortured Phiem to woke her up to deprive her sleeping to murder her by this method. They are using laser micro magnetic gun to shot to her left toe, left sole, left thigh, her female, stomach, lower abdomen, chest, head and shoulder, she sat at the chair outside her bedroom then she turned on her computer to note this diary, it was hard to catch the images of the gun so it was like these pictures below.

02/27/2011 02:35 AM

February 27, 2011 2:35 AM (1)

February 27, 2011 3:07 AM (2)

February 27, 2011 6:16 AM (1)

Phiem was awaken until this time it was shown on this pictured she took when they were attacking her.

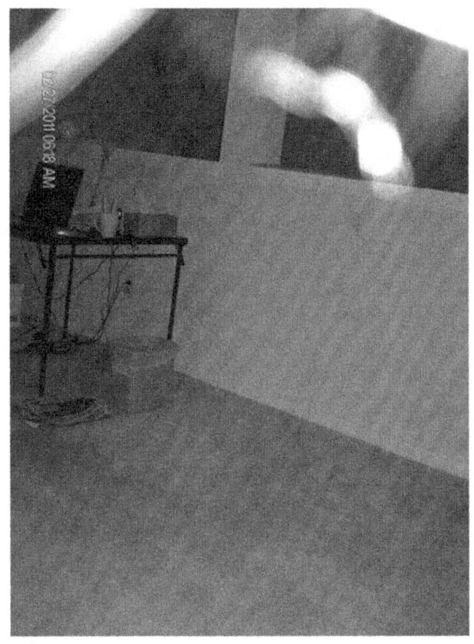

February 27, 2011 6:18 AM (2)

February 27, 2011 6:20 (3)

They were constantly attacking to Phiem these pictures proved the time on it.

February 27, 2011 11:41AM (1)

Phiem went to bed at 7:00 AM they woke her up about 8: 45 AM she went to bathroom as they activated on her body then she went back sleeping later then they woke her up at about 10:45 AM, she brushed teeth then went down her kitchen to fry the left over rice and vegetable with dumpling meat yesterday for lunch.

They shot to her stomach and her side stomach organs to murder her.

February 27, 2011 11:41AM (2)

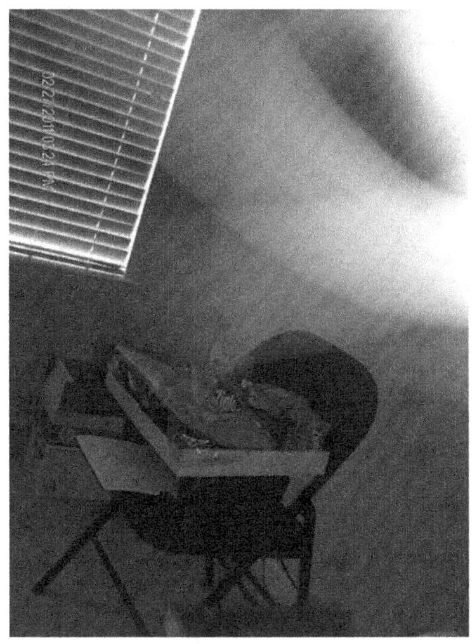

February 27, 2011 3:25 PM (1)

They attacked to Phiem's ear when she was sitting at her computer to prepare her work for her website.

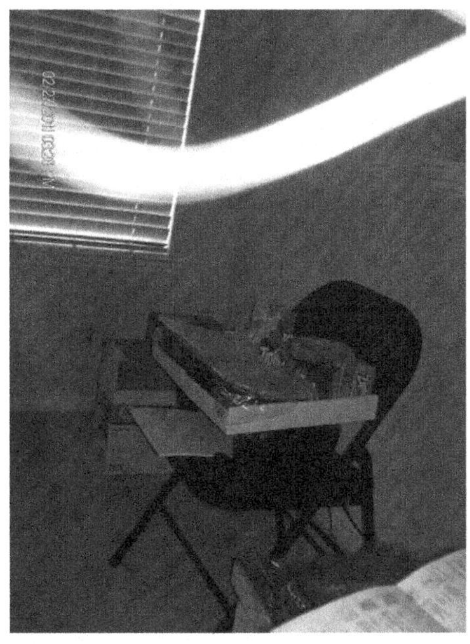

February 27, 2011 3:26 PM (2)

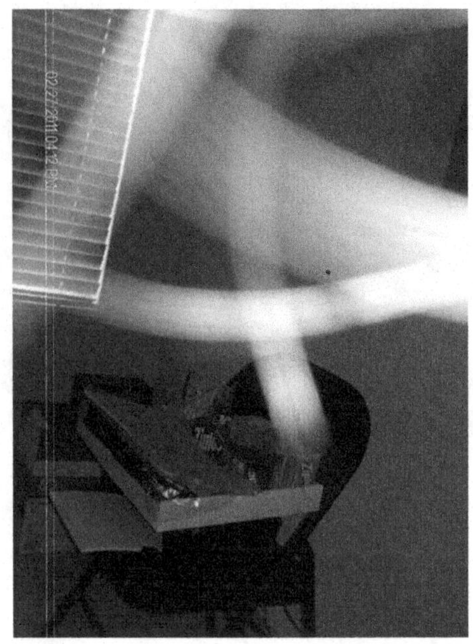

February 27, 2011 4:12 PM (3)

February 27, 2011 4:12 PM (4)

They constantly tortured Phiem during the time she did her work like that, it was shown the time on these pictures she just copied some of them to prove.

February 27, 2011 5:00 PM (5)

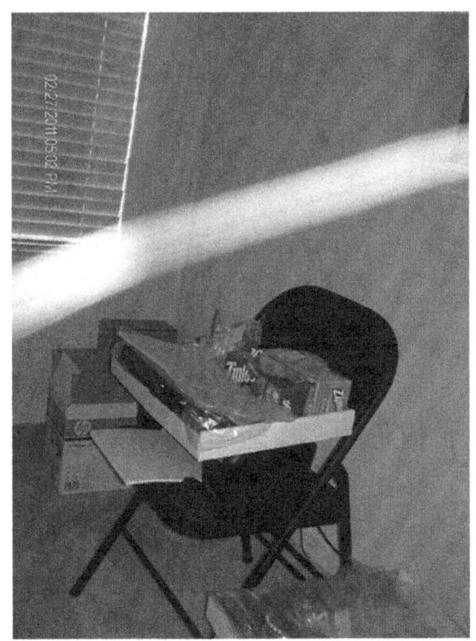

February 27, 2011 5:02 PM (6)

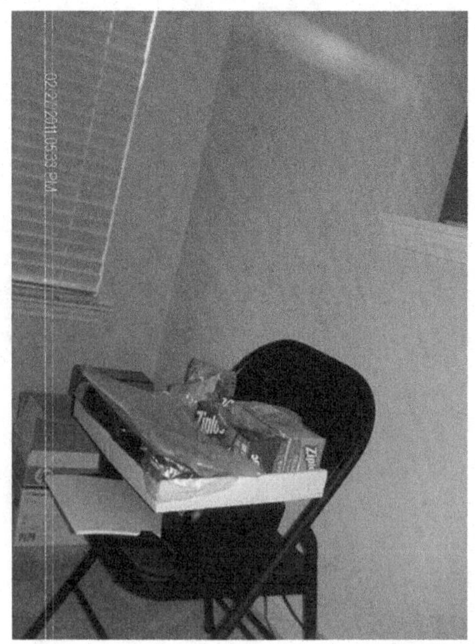

February 27, 2011 5:33 PM (7)

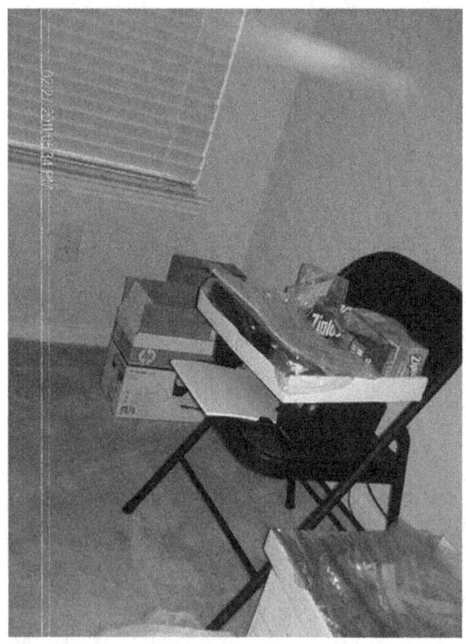

February 28, 2011 5:34 PM (9)

From the beginning to the end of their gun power were shown on these pictures patiently manner and ambitious behavior at the target, the victim with nothing to defend for herself, it was so terrible enemies.

February 28, 2011 8:13 PM (1)

This is the series of pictures Phiem took to prove that they murdered her by shooting Micromagnetic Directed Energy Weapons assaulted to her head when she just sat down at the dinning room, that made her so terrible head ach, dizziness and unbalance, she had to control herself not to fall down. They attacked to Phiem's head at the top first then back of the head then her front head and her eye-brow. They can kill people easily by murdering people like that.

They might using the car portable devices, she saw the plan was past by her window 1 tour however she saw the plan was on the air for so long she could notice it after she finished her meal, cleaned then went upstairs.

Phiem read the news the ugly medical researched in the past was ordered an investigation, why this crime was executed in present was zipped in silent then when all the victims died at that time will make the show.

February 28, 2011 8:13 PM (2)

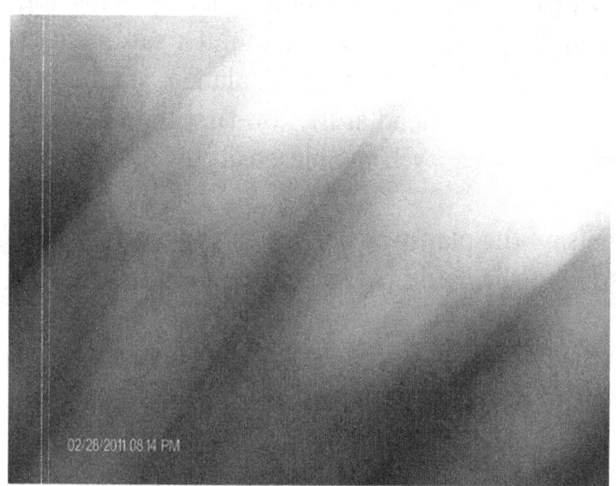

February 28, 2011 8:14 PM (2a)

February 28, 2011 8:14 PM (3)

February 28, 2011 8:16 PM (4)

February 28, 2011 8:21 (5)

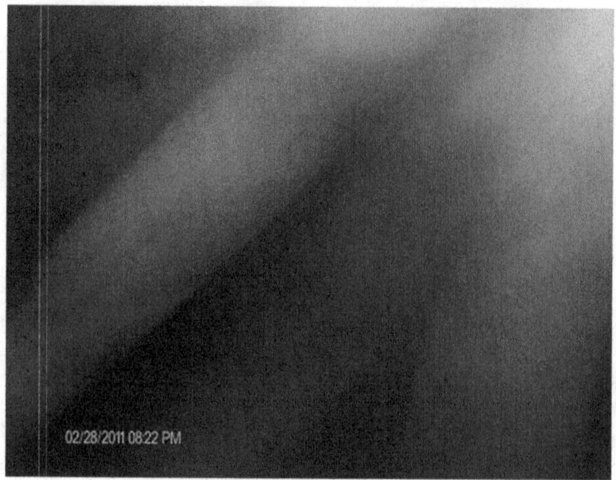

February 28, 2011 8:22 PM (5a)

February 28, 2011 8:22 PM (6)

February 28, 2011 8:25 PM (7)

February 28, 2011 8:25 PM (8)

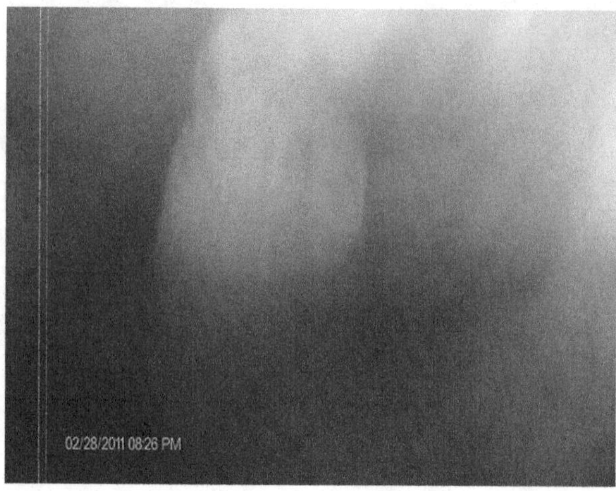

February 28, 2011 8:26 PM (9)

March 01, 2011

Today Phiem went to bank Phiem realized that authorities were in charge to protect citizens, she saw woman police at the bank, lady walked with
K-9 she guessed and the policeman motor on the street, authorities answered us do nothing to hurt yourself we know how to handle that.

March 02, 2011

Yesterday I went to bank I saw the Electric service truck and some other cars but I did not pay attention, in my mind I was afraid of last time they snooze to my female then on the way back home after I past that intersection for about 10 minutes later I knew that something was happened like they activated chips to my ure organ inside my house that I just learned from reading that created ure sex but I really did not know for sure who did that. They are sick evils I could say, in the evening they attacked to my head then during the night they attacked to my female but it might be interfered by some preventing force so I had not be woken up after one hour sleeping for going to bathroom.
Today the whole day they attacked to my head, asked them, they murdered me.

Below Phiem presented the series of pictures.

March 01, 2011 8:29 PM (1)

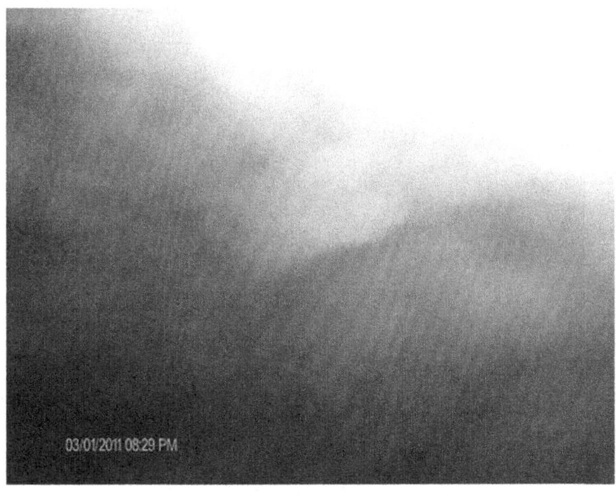

March 01, 2011 8:29 PM (2)

March 01, 2011 10:23 PM (3)

March 01, 2011 10:24 PM (4)

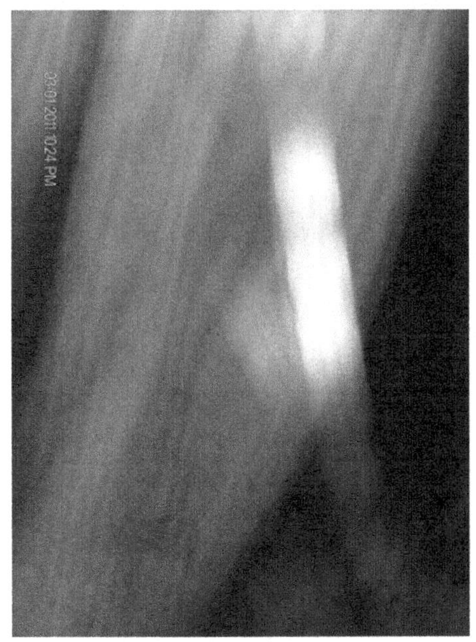

March 01, 2011 10:24 PM (5)

March 01, 2011 10:24 PM (6)

March 01, 2011 10:26 PM (7)

March 01, 2011 10:26 PM (9)

March 01, 2011 10:29 PM (9)

Phiem did not know when they implanted chip to her outside ear, this one at the left side and the other one at her right back ear then they activated severe pain, she could not take picture her back by herself, these series of pictures to prove the evidence. They were usually implanted chips to her ear canal but recently Phiem used ear plug to block her ear canals so they implanted chips outside her ears.

March 03, 2011 9:53 AM (1)

March 03, 2011 9:54 AM (2)

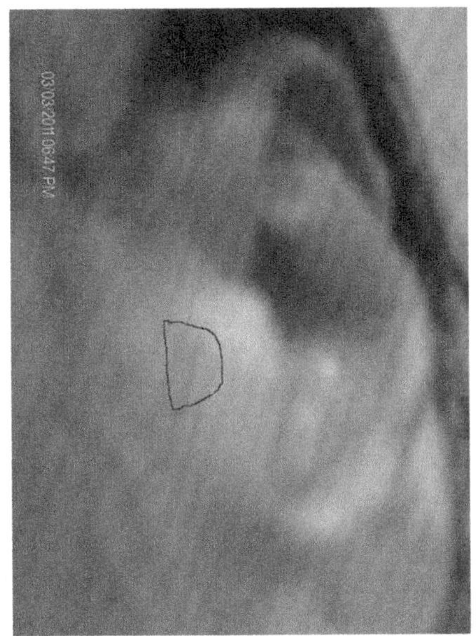

March 03, 2011 6:48 PM (3)

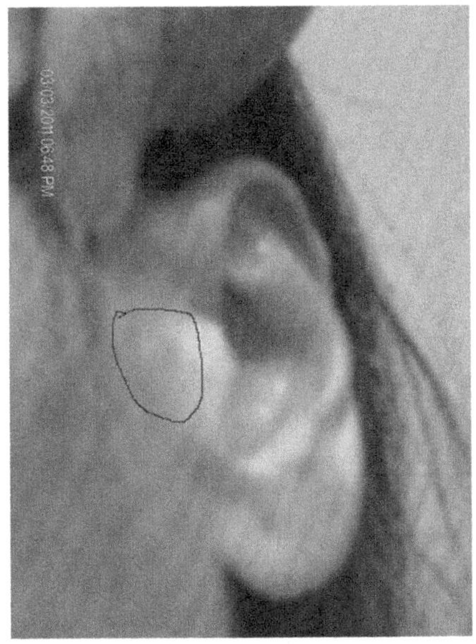

March 03, 2011 6:48 PM (4)

March 03, 2011 6:43 PM (5)

Phiem wanted to prove how she took these pictures of her ear by herself.

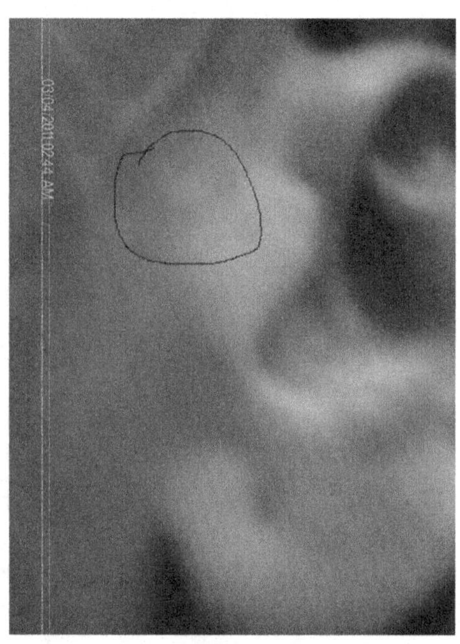

March 4, 2011 2:44 AM (6)

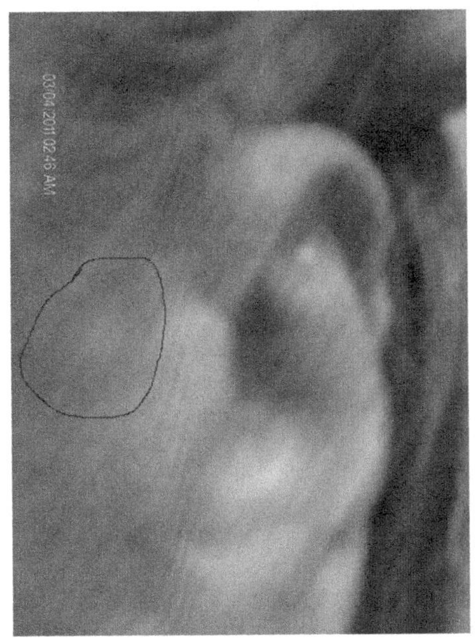

March 4, 2011 2:46 AM (7)

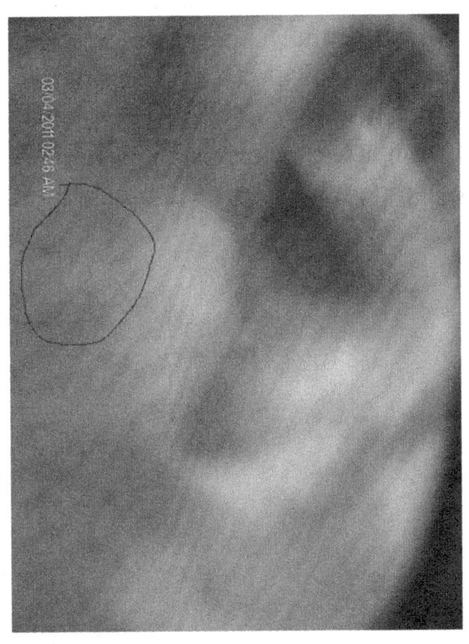

March 4, 2011 2:46 AM (8)

March 4, 2011 2:45 AM (10)

Phiem proved these pictures above she took her ear by herself at that time because they attacked to her female she could not sleep in resentful situation so she took these pictures her outside ear implanted again to prove.

Last night before Phiem goes to bed she emailed her files to
Presidential Commission for the study of Bioethical Issues, Phiem just watched the video all supporters and victims were presenting in persons to testify and hand out the evident information to the Presidential Commission for the study of Bioethical Issues, she saw Dr. John Hall who is the hero of Targeted Individuals and History Investigator and Professional, Professor there too. Phiem hope this crime will be solved soon it will be not waiting until all the victims were died and she's happy citizen voices were heard and government took action immediately. Phiem thank to God and all supporters and her savior.

March 4, 2011 7:57 PM (1)

Phiem was sitting at the dinning room she felt the first shot to her right head then she saw the plan past by her window then she felt the shot to her right stomach organs then her left ear at the place they just implanted chip she presented pictures above, this is the series of pictures.

March 4, 2011 7:58 PM (2)

March 4, 2011 7:58 PM (3)

March 4, 2011 7:59 PM (4)

March 4, 2011 8:08 PM (5)

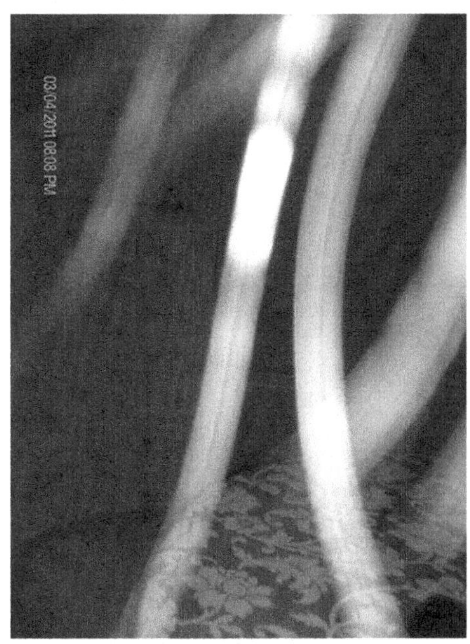

March 4, 2011 8:08 PM (6)

March 4, 2011 8:08 PM (7)

March 4, 2011 8:09 PM (8)

March 4, 2011 8:09 PM (9)

March 4, 2011 8:11 PM (10)

March 4, 2011 8:12 PM (11)

They attacked to Phiem from the plan flew by her window she took this picture to show the light technique was using from the plan regularly.

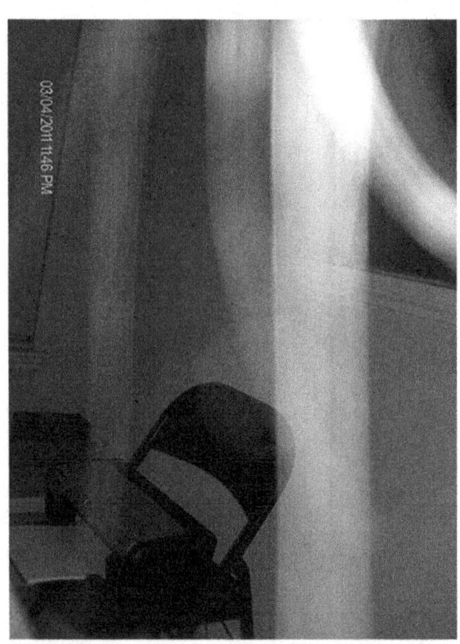

March 4, 2011 11:46 PM (1)

They assaulted to Phiem's ear when she was sitting at her computer.

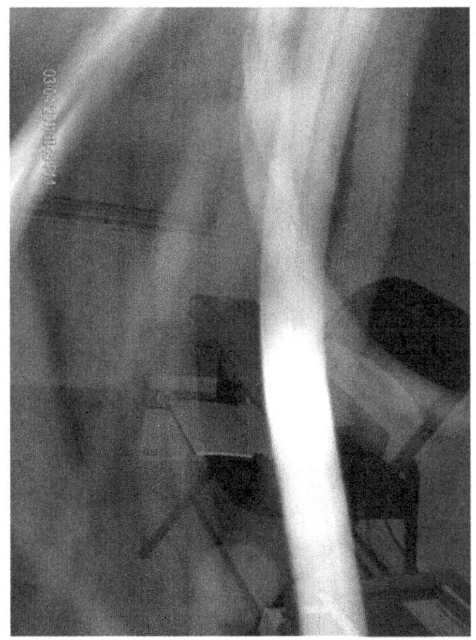

March 4, 2011 11:46 PM (2)

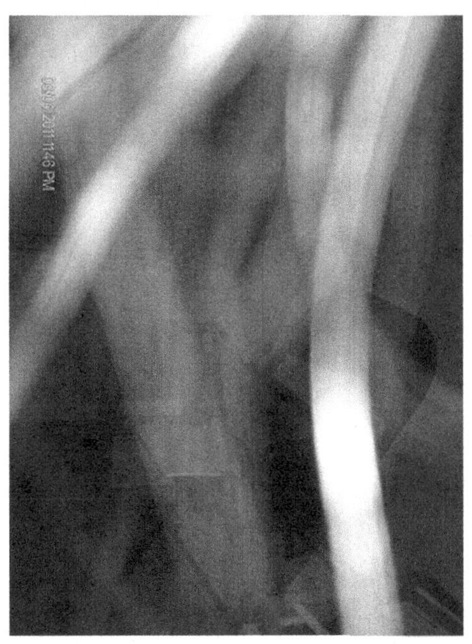

March 4, 2011 11:46 PM (3)

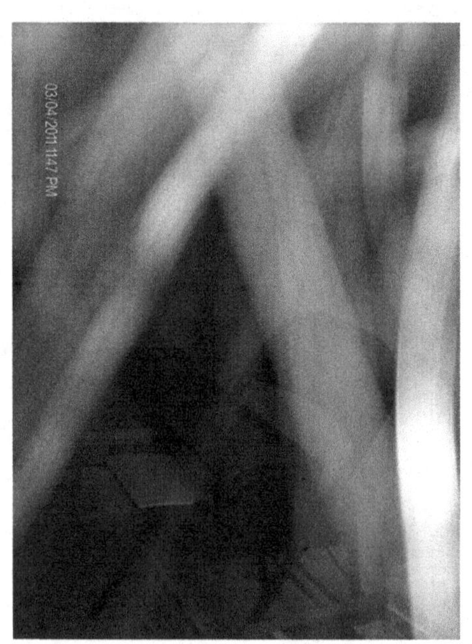

March 4, 2011 11:47 PM (4)

March 5, 2011 5:53 AM

They assaulted to Phiem's ear when she was back in her bed after she went to bathroom.

Phiem woke up or they woke her up to go to bathroom, she did not know what they did to her female organ and her uterus she felt hurt entire her lower abdomen when she woke up to go to bathroom, during the time she was sleeping they patched their fragment to her subconscious or they pick out from her subconscious or they did make sensation insider her uterus or they raped her during the time she was sleeping or it was the dream they wanted her to remember when she woke up only that sensation part nothing more. After she go to bathroom she went back her bed she thought in the morning she does not need to wave her rod to check if someone was hidden in her room they wore the invisible clothe so she just lock her room and the locking stand rod to against her door to open from intruder outside her room, her house turned on security system, door locks then the rod lock stands then her room door lock and the rod lock stand she mention it was dangerous. When she woke up again this morning she did not see the rod lock stand, it was mysterious, they came into her house then get in when she went to bathroom or they get into her house from the roof or underground in order to rape mannequin, because if her conscious did not know it or it was from their fragments to order people, it considered crime and rape mannequin, they will be proud of they raped mannequin. They are so terrible sick since 1944 until now and they want it to be continuing, is that right?

March 6, 2011 1:29 PM

They assaulted to Phiem's head when she was sitting at her dinning room at lunch time.

March 6, 2011 1:56 PM

They assaulted to Phiem's right ear when she was sitting at her dinning-room having lunch.

March 7, 2011 12:47 AM

Phiem sat at her bed they beamed to Phiem's ear, she have light on each night because evils love the dark.

March 7, 2011 1:07 AM

Phiem went outside her bedroom to sit at her game-room they shot to her female.

March 7, 2011 1:12 AM

Phiem went outside her bed room to sit at her game room they beamed to her ear.

March 7, 2011 1:15 AM

They shot to Phiem's ear

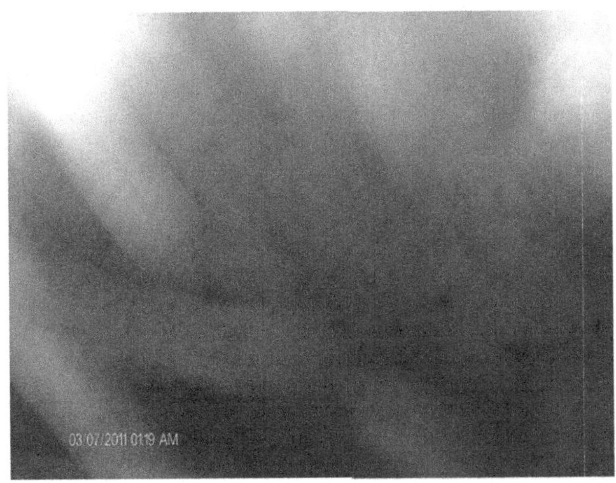

March 7, 2011 1:19 AM

They shot to Phiem's head

March 7, 2011 1:38 AM (1)

They shot to Phiem's ear

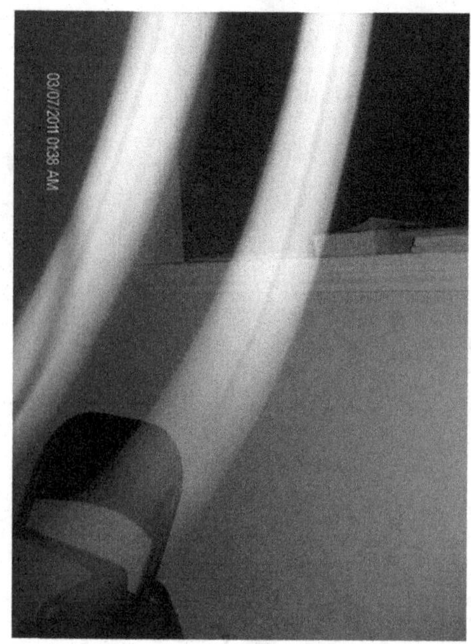

March 7, 2011 1:39 AM (2)

March 7, 2011 1:40 AM

They shot to Phiem's head

March 7, 2011 3:05 AM (1)

They shot to Phiem's ear, this is new kind of force they used Phiem was familiar with this when they use to attacked to her female.

March 7, 2011 3:06 AM (2)

March 7, 2011 9:40 PM

They attacked to Phiem’s ear when she was sitting at her computer.

March 7, 2011 9:41 PM

They attacked to Phiem’s head when she was sitting at her computer.

March 7, 2011 9:43 PM (1)

March 7, 2011 9:44 PM (2)

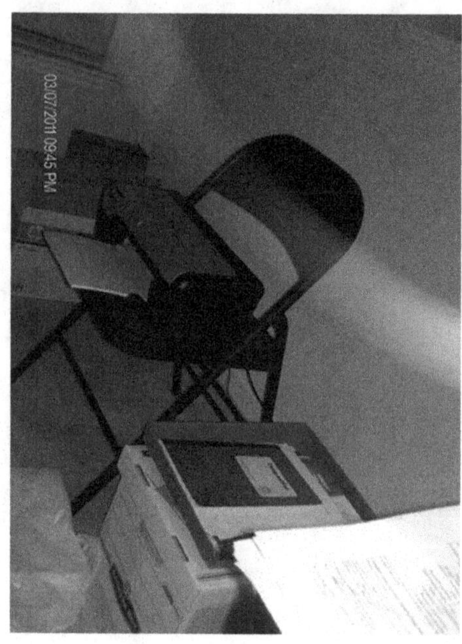

March 7, 2011 9:45 PM (3)

March 7, 2011 9:46 (4)

They were patiently shot to Phiem's ear with the time proved it on the pictures.

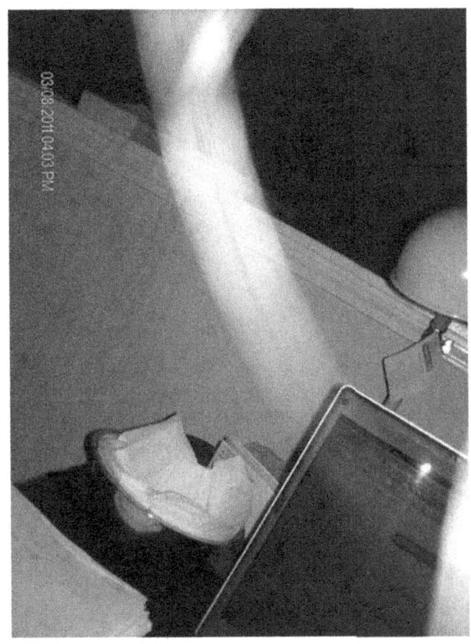

March 8, 2011 4:03 PM (1)

They beamed to Phhiem's ear during the time she was at her computer.

March 8, 2011 4:03 PM (2)

March 8, 2011 4:03 PM (3)

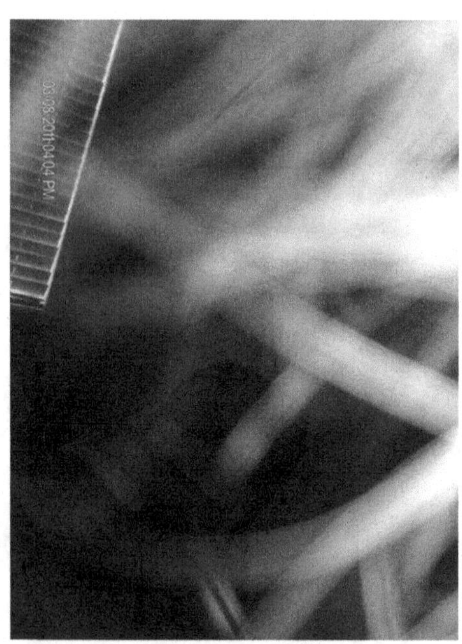

March 8, 2011 4:04 PM (4)

March 8, 2011 4:05 PM (5)

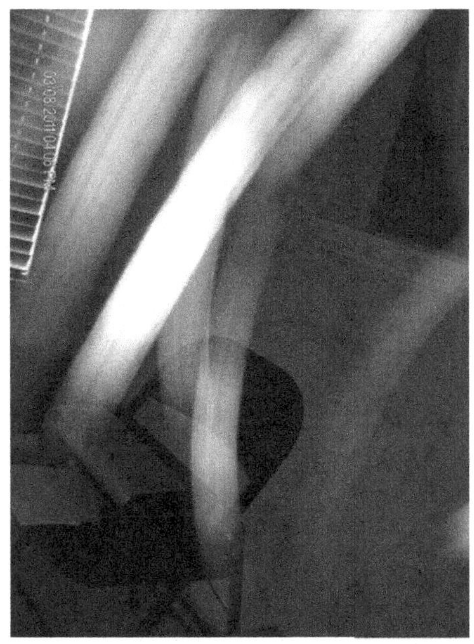

March 8, 2011 4:06 PM (6)

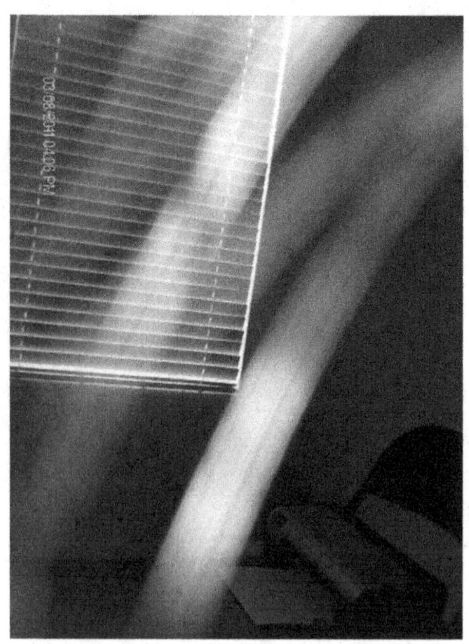

March 8, 2011 4:06 PM (7)

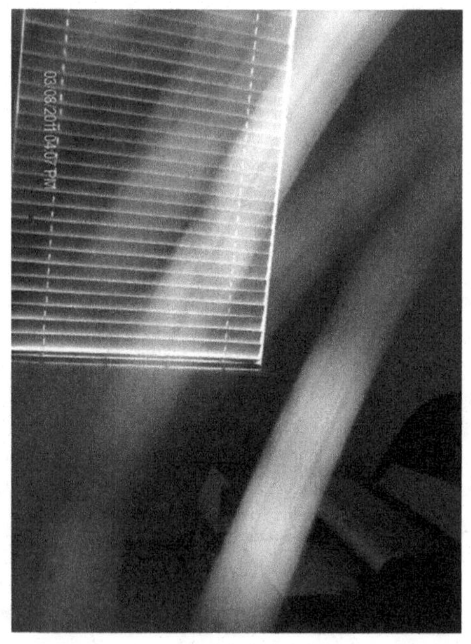

March 8, 2011 4:07 PM (8)

March 8, 2011 4:08 PM (9)

March 8, 2011 4:08 PM (10)

March 9, 2011 4:09 PM (11)

All the series pictures above were proved how many times they change the forces to show the ambitious behavior to prey to Phiem's head through her ear.

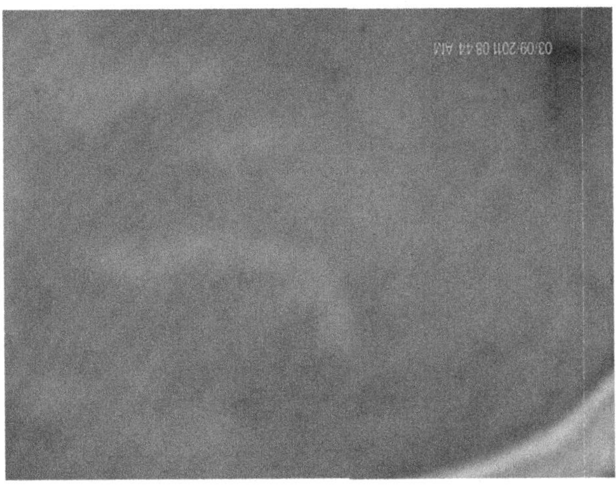

March 9, 2011 8:44 AM (1)

The date on picture was the day Phiem took these pictures but it was happened yesterday evening.

They used Micromagnetic to attack to Phiem stomach side organs as she described it so many times before and they continue doing that to her body so yesterday she applied ices to her stomach at the attacking place then the burning appeared on her stomach skin it's shown the damage to her skin body there. Phiem wondered if it was something doing to damage her body was processing on this case on their assassin actions or it was the method to denounce the secret murder I had to go to the Hospital without health insurance then I have to pay for the Doctor bills and the Hospital bills by my credit cards. They are evils.

Phiem realized this was so terrible savage actions in this civilization society, how can people stop theses atrocious trend toward mental illness. Do you think we need technology at any price like this or you will be pushed back at the time people live with moral without technology development.

March 9, 2011 8:46 AM (2)

Phiem took picture herself to prove that her body they murdered and sabotaged and so on, every victim they did the same.

March 9, 2011 10:55 AM (3)

March 9, 2011 10:57 AM (4)

Phiem took more pictures above to prove the burning skin on her stomach.

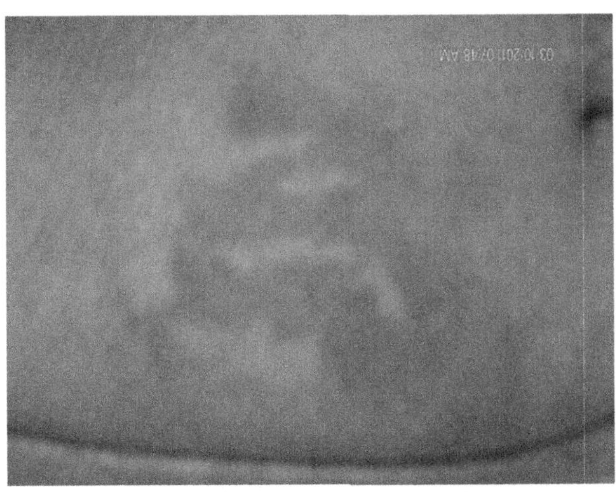

March 10, 2011 7:48 AM (4)

Phiem took this picture today this morning, it showed clearly the burning skin on her stomach and on her lower abdomen.

March 10, 2011 7:50 AM (6)

Phiem presented these pictures to prove the evidences were happened on her body, she took these pictures by herself.

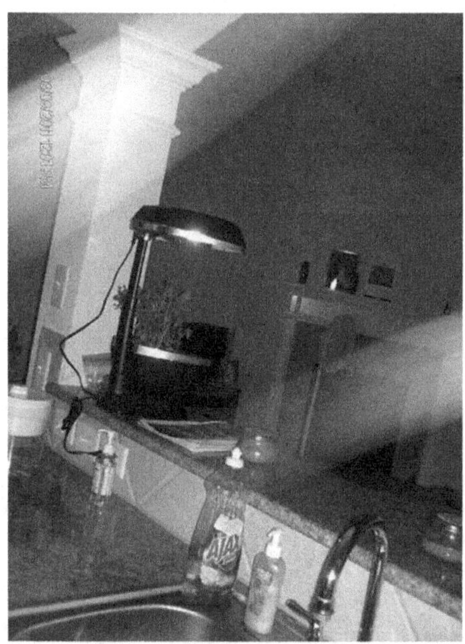

March 9, 2011 12:01 AM (1)

They attacked to Phiem's head through the chip they implanted outside her left ear she mentioned it few days ago.

March 9, 2011 12:02 PM (2)

They attacked to Phiem's head through the chip they implanted outside her left ear she mentioned it few days ago.

March 9, 2011 12:11 PM (3)

They attacked to Phiem's head through the chip they implanted outside her left ear she mentioned it few days ago.

March 9, 2011 12:11 PM (4)

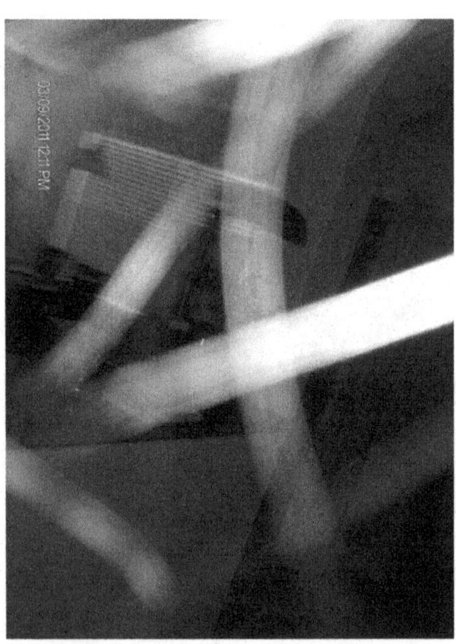

March 9, 2011 12:11 PM (5)

They attacked to Phiem's head through the chip they implanted outside her left ear she mentioned it few days ago, when they attacked the target triggering the whole house the victim had no place to escape as these pictures were proved.

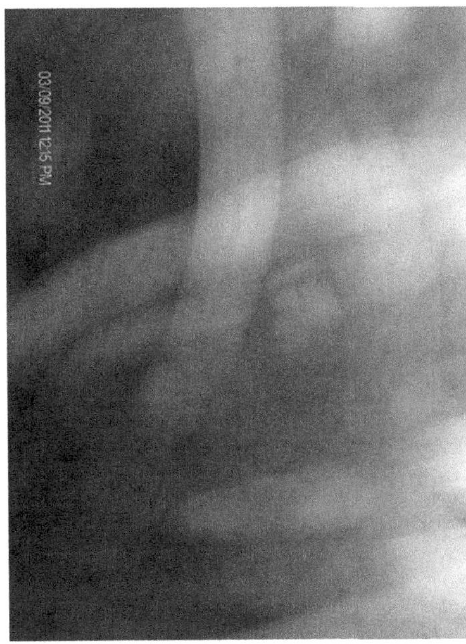

March 9, 2011 12:15 PM

They shot to Phiem's head, they assaulted her head through the implanted chip outside her left ear then to her head on the front, top then back head.

March 9, 2011 12:26 PM (1)

They attacked to Phiem's outside left ear chip it affected to her inside head.

March 9, 2011 12:26 PM (2)

They tortured Phiem's as in the pictures she prepared her lunch, she does dishes, brushed her teeth and typed, her hands were busy she could not shield her body with objects like sponges, ceramic plate or bowl or cup or metal pot lid and she could not take pictures, she had to stop in order to take pictures to enter in this diary book to show the evidences.

Phiem was under tortured 24/7 during the time she was sleeping, working, typing, reading, cooking, eating, and cleaning. She knew these people are sick evils and mental illness also they could think and render that sadistic abuse, ill science and humiliate Phiem like that.

March 9, 2011 2:46 PM (1)

They attacked to Phiem's right ear.

March 9, 2011 2:47 PM (2)

March 9, 2011 2:48 PM (3)

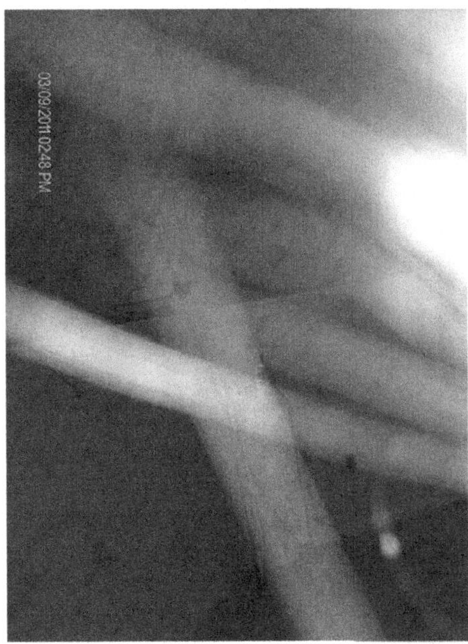

March 9, 2011 2:48 PM (4)

They assaulted to Phiem's right ear they constantly beamed to her ear in order to go to her head through her ear canal.

March 9, 2011 7:25 PM (1)

They assaulted to Phiem's left ear and front head, top then back head when she was in her dinning room.

March 9, 2011 7:25 PM (2)

March 9, 2011 7:25 PM (3)

March 9, 2011 7:26 PM (4)

March 9, 2011 7:30 PM (5)

Phiem saw the plan made 3 or 4 tours surrounding Phiem's neighborhood and passed by her window she took these pictures during the time her cell phone was turned on.

March 9, 2011 7:31 PM (6)

March 9, 2011 7:36 PM (7)

They attacked to Phiem's right ear when she was in her dinning room.

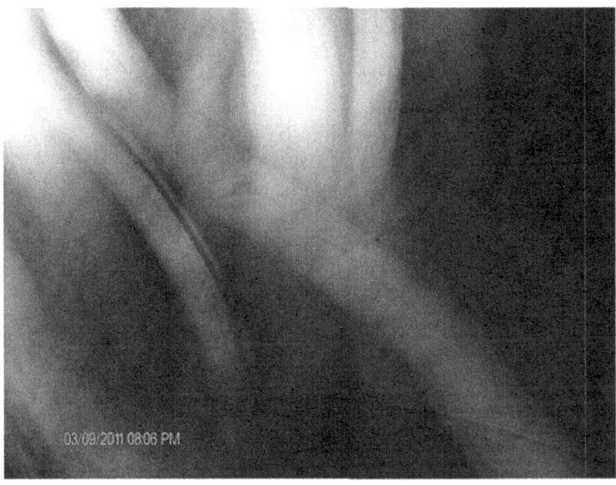

March 9, 2011 8:06 PM (8)

They attacked to Phiem's neck under her ear when she was in her dinning room.

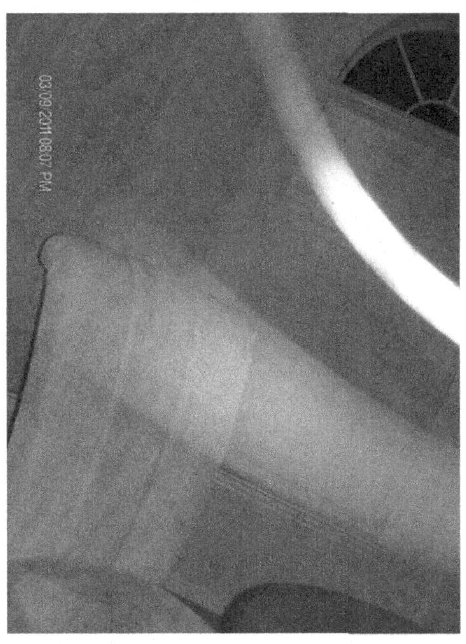

March 9, 2011 8:07 PM (9)

They attacked to Phiem's left ear when she was sitting at her dinning room, they tortured her constantly like that.

March 9, 2011 7:40 PM (10)

They shot and cutting knife to Phiem's head during the time she had dinner she could feel hurt at her back head.

March 9, 2011 7:44 PM (2)

They assaulted to Phiem's head she took these pictures but her camera could not catch the truth image of the Micromagnetic was used to assault on her head, the only images she had on her camera.

March 11, 2011

Yesterday evening Phiem sat at her dinning-room as usually she have dinner at that place, she did not see the plan but she felt she shot first then the plan past by her window, the plan passed by her window 4 tours this evening, they shot at her back side at the kidney, she took these pictures of her back but she could not upload her photos to her computer; she could not present the pictures here to prove.

Good News!!!

Phiem uploaded her pictures to her computer today, she copied it here to show the evidence on the picture, yesterday when she took shower they shot at that place again.
The date on the picture is the date and time she took the picture it was not the exactly date and time when they attacked her back. Phiem took the pictures by herself, it was not easy to take picture of her back, this was by luck to have pictures after a series of pictures were taken her back fell into strange images.

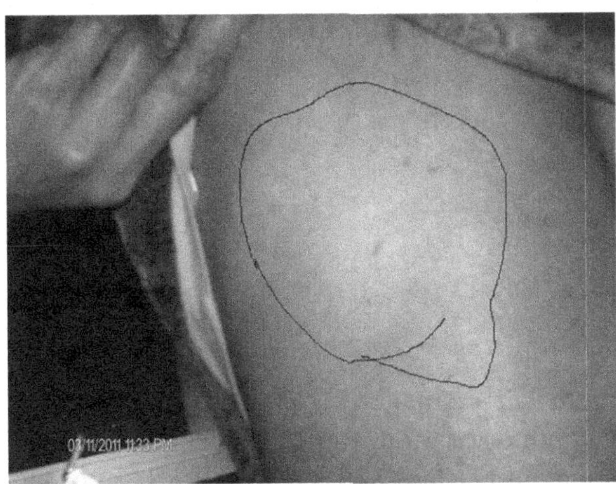

March 12, 2011 12:33 AM

March 13, 2011 8:21 AM (1)

They attacked to Phiem's ear when she was at her computer. They also used harmful chemical busted to her nose then she felt her mouth dried out then her lips, her skin turned aging. Every time Phiem ate food or used the cream her face skin turned back her normal they immediately used the micro heat or harmful chemical to keep down the degrade stage her beauty to deprive. The chemical was organic smelt they used, it was Corn chip or Doritos seasoning like today was using, sometime the garlic, Asian food, bake bean, French dish, and sewer. Phiem did not know what they put in the water ask them.

March 13, 2011 8:22 AM (2)

They attacked to Phiem's ear when she was at her computer.

March 13, 2011 8:22 AM (3)

They attacked to Phiem's ear when she was at her computer, on this picture was showing a bunch of Nanowiremicromagnetic weapons to beam to Phiem'ear in order through her brain to control her mind, that was the classic one and modern way to do various function to harm her health and her body.

March 13, 2011 9:55 AM (1)

They attacked to Phiem's ear when she was sitting at her computer, she was in their target setting, these following pictures will prove how long they constantly assaulted to her head through her ear canal by Nanomicromagnetic weapons to control her mind and to damage her brain and physical body and made affected to her health.

March 13, 2011 9:56 AM (2)

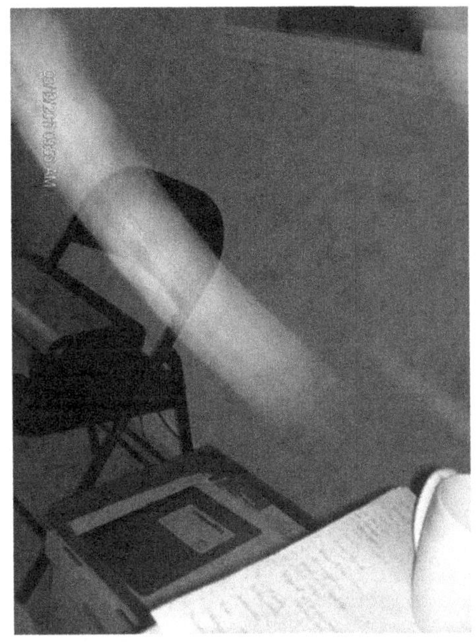

March 13, 2011 9:56 AM (3)

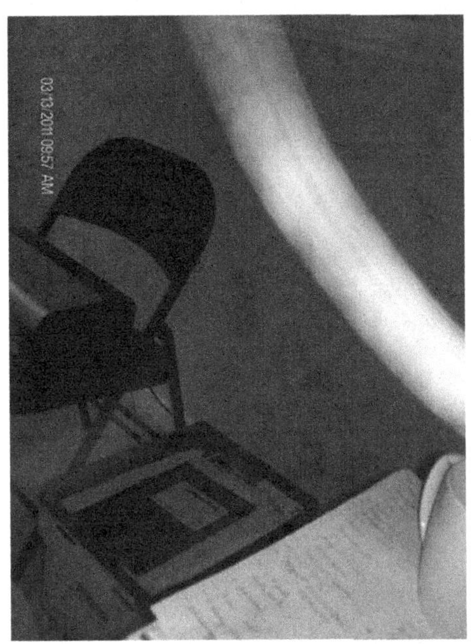

March 13, 2011 9:57 AM (5)

March 13, 2011 9:58 AM (6)

March 13, 2011 9:59 AM (7)

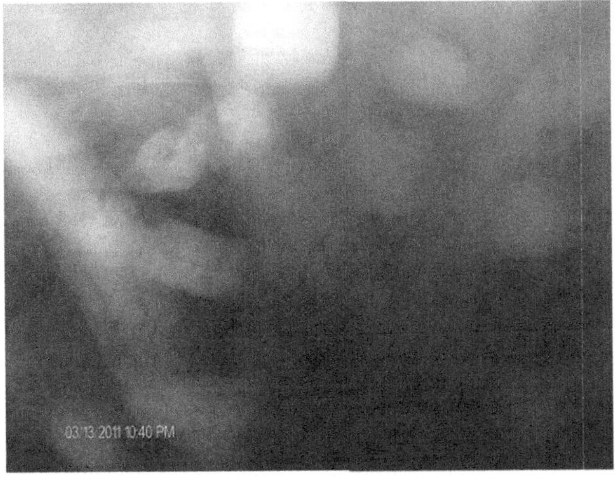

March 13, 2011 10:40 AM (1)

March 13, 2011 10:40 AM (2)

They bombarded NanoMicromagnetic to Phiem's head all the time she was in their attacking asked them how these weapons affected to her head skull, her
brain and her health and what they took out from her head and then they pressed dented in her skull to change her head shape.

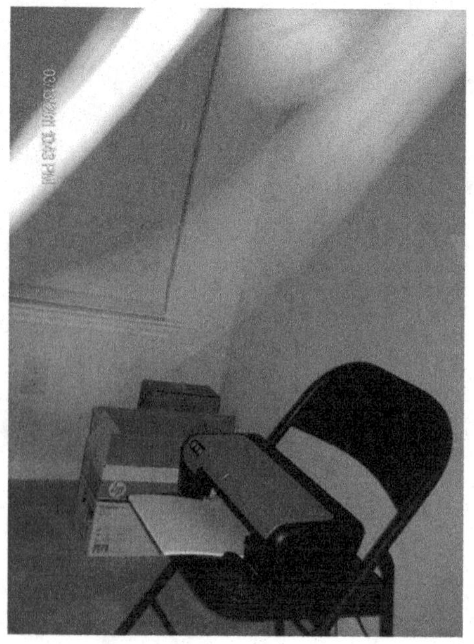

March 13, 2011 10:43 AM (1)

These pictures showed the time they assaulted to Phiem's ear when she was sitting at her computer.

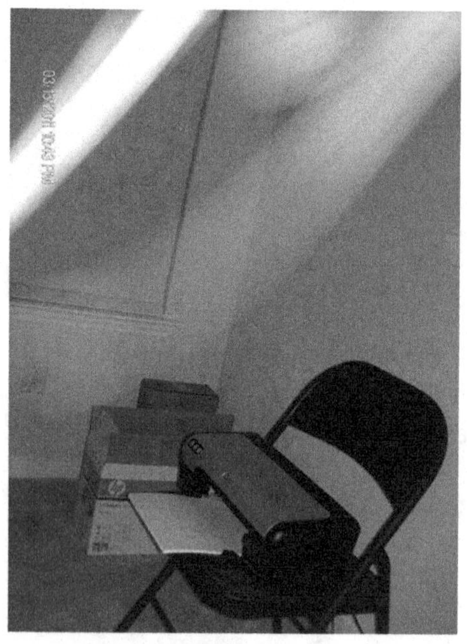

March 13, 2011 10:44 AM (2)

March 13, 2011 10:45 AM (3)

March 14, 2011 5:41 PM (1)

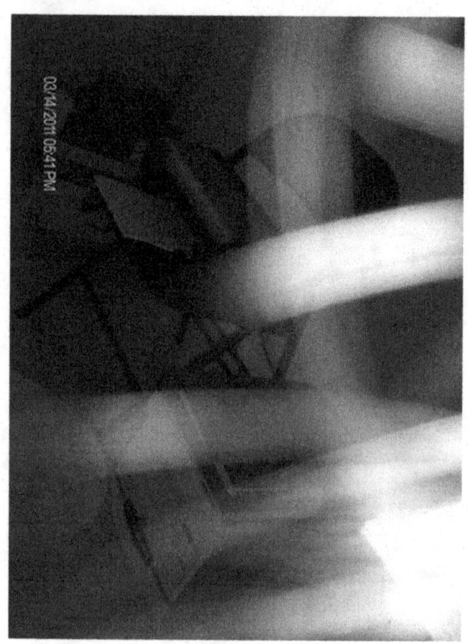

March 14, 2011 5:41 PM (2)

March 14, 2011 (3)

These pictures above were taken when they attacked to Phiem's left ear.

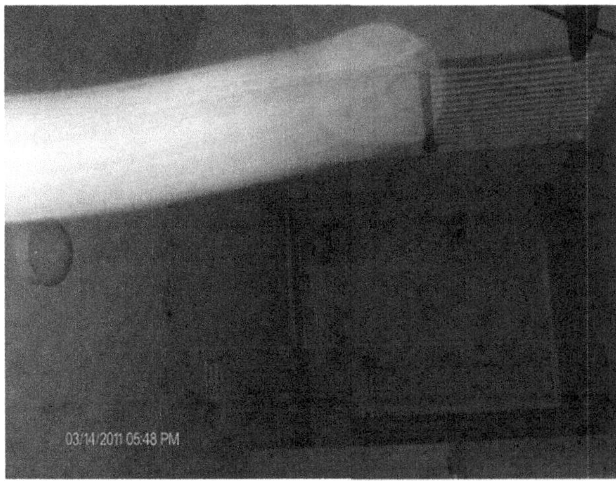

March 14, 2011 5:48 PM (4)

They attacked to Phiem's right ear.

March 14, 2011 5:51 PM (1)

This series of pictures proved that they tried to beam to Phiem's ear canal in order to go through her brain to control her mind action, this time they triggered sex sensation then they were laughing, what they tried to do on her body to rape her, this afternoon when she was taking nape they invaded in her subconscious to do the sick sex they wanted her to say when they wok her up, they constantly to humiliate her day and night like that, when she woke up this afternoon she felt tired in her head it was not like people felt refresh mind after we sleep. Phiem now felt so angry and she wanted these evils should be destroyed. Phiem wanted to revenge.

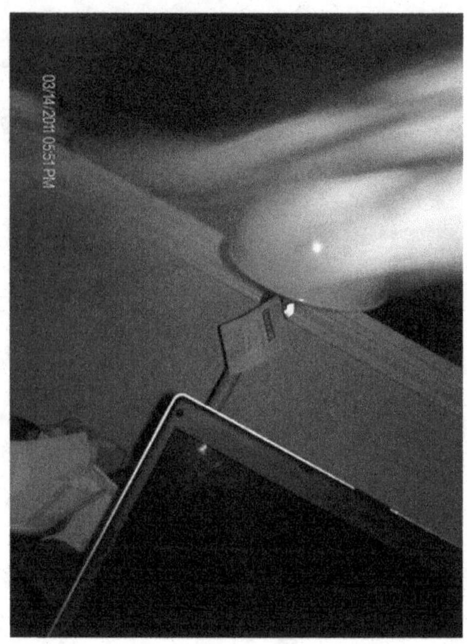

March 14, 2011 5:51 PM (2)

March 14, 2011 5:53 PM (3)

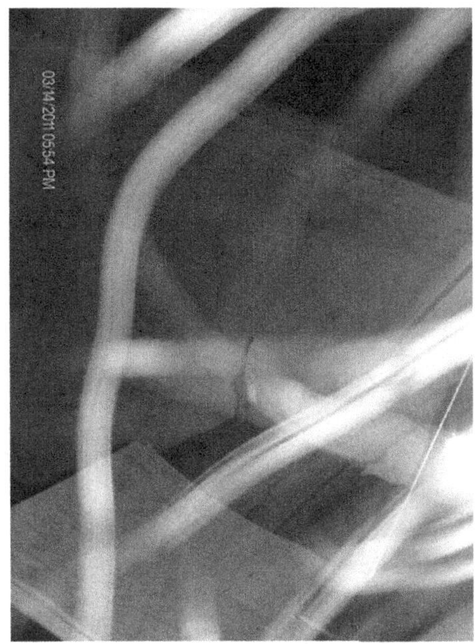

March 14, 2011 10:54 PM (4)

March 14, 2011 10:56 PM (5)

March 14, 2011 6:02 (6)

March 14, 2011 6:02 PM (7)

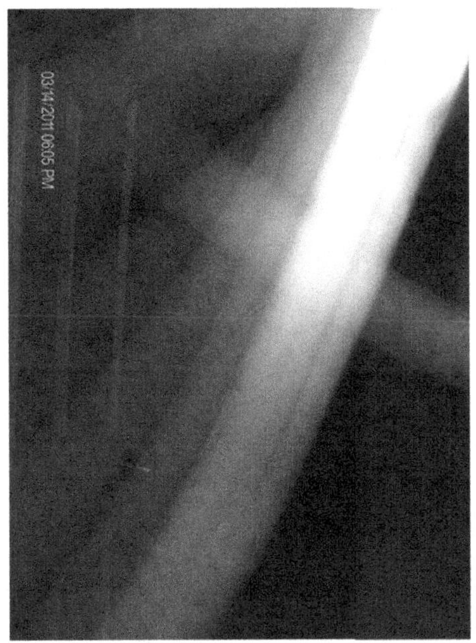

March 14, 2011 6:05 PM (8)

March 14, 2011 6:05 PM (9)

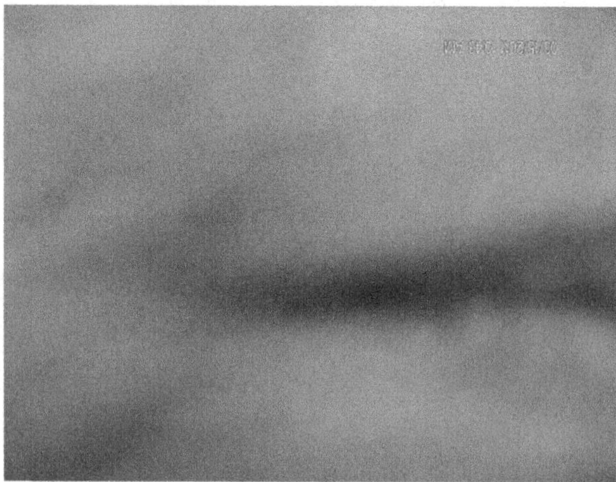

March 15, 2011 10:43 PM

During the time Phiem does dishes and she was sitting at her computer they painted by Nanomicromagnetic ray gun to Phiem's mouth they tried to make beard to her right side upper lip and changed her mouth shape, they tried to make her become a man appearance on her face.

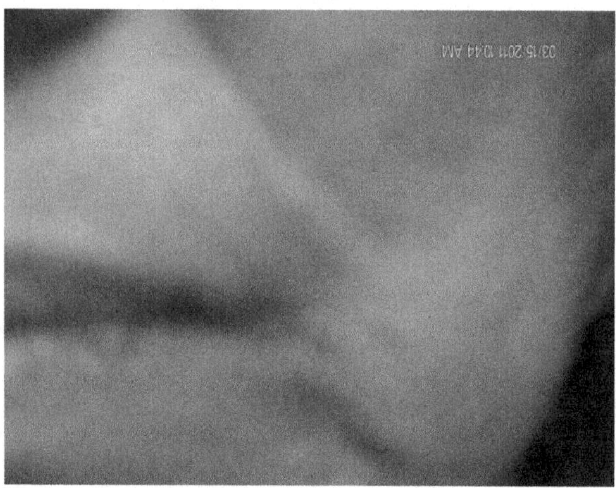

March 15, 2011 10:44 AM

These pictures above proved the evidence they did to her left side upper lip few month ago Phiem presented picture at the time they did it.

March 15, 2011 10:44 AM

Phiem proved she is at the time she took these pictures above and her pictures by herself.

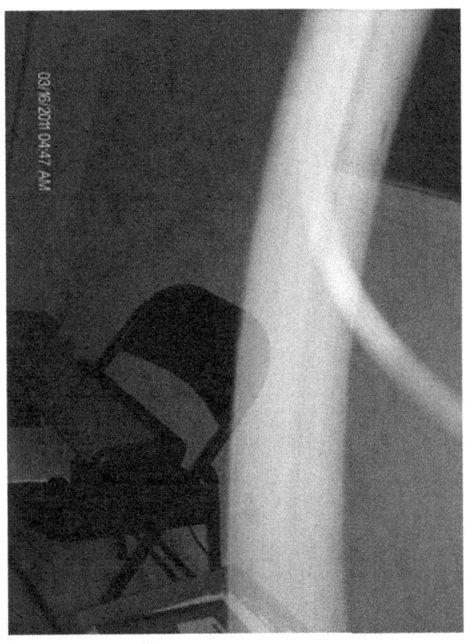

March 16, 2011 4:47 AM (1)

They attacked to Phiem's ear when she was sitting at her computer, she went outside her bed to avoid attacking but she could not prevent their force assaulted to her head or her body wherever she was in her house.

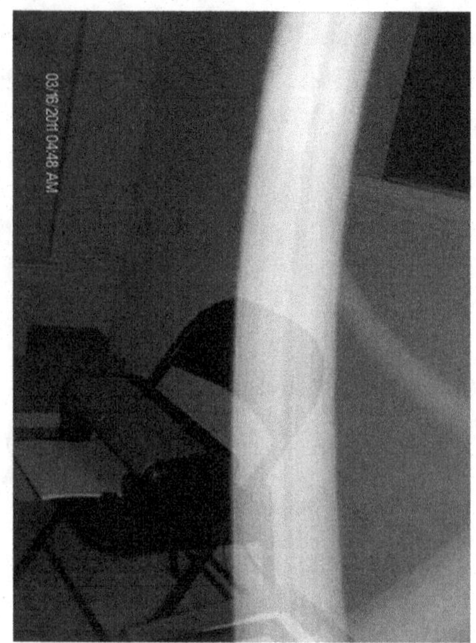

March 16, 2011 4:48 AM (2)

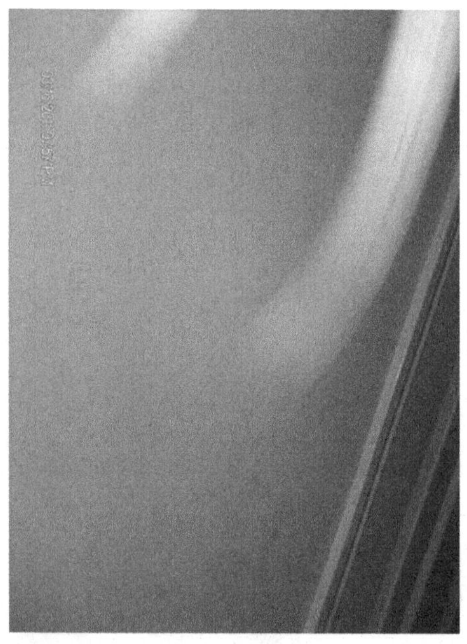

March 16, 2011 7:57 PM (1)

They attacked Phiem when she was walking exercise in her house, these pictures below proved the time continuously following the target.

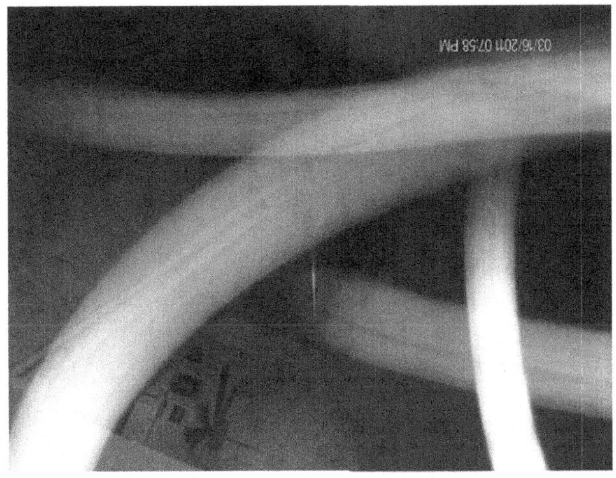

March 16, 2011 7:58 PM (2)

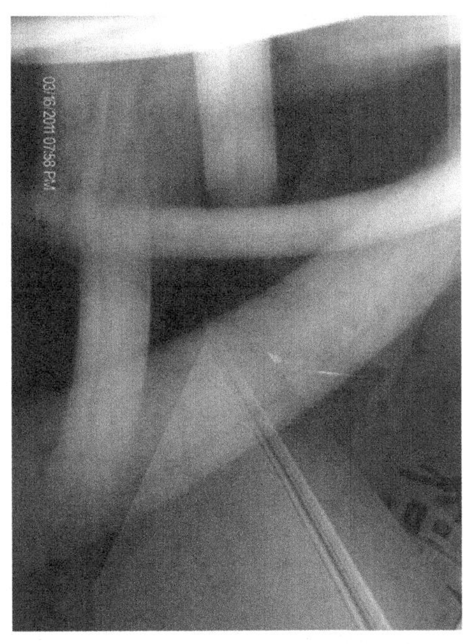

March 16, 2011 7:58 PM (3)

March 16, 2011 7:59 PM (4)

Phiem asked herself why those Perpertrators never tire off their works to abuse, humiliate, harm and murder her.
She was so tired off their mental illness things.

March 18, 2011 4:59 AM

Right they never stop and this picture Phiem's ear was attacking by these perpertrators when she was in her kitchen, they woke her up each one or two hours after they did something in her subconscious and her body so she went outside her bed to prevent controlling her mind during the time she was sleeping but how could human resist sleeping. They worked on Phiem's body 24/7 they noticed immediately where the place was not shield on her body they attacked at it place, it was amazing patiently research manner or murder crime Phiem has learned on her case.

Phiem wanted to know their goals, rape mannequin? We have 7 billions here on this earth, that means not enough for human find human to marry or they wanted to gain money, how much is enough? It seams never be enough.

March 18, 2011 9:52 AM (1)

They are attacked to Phiem's ear when she was sitting at her computer.

March 18, 2011 9:52 AM (2)

This was new image but Phiem did not know what is this, the imperfect image or the shield, she wanted to copy it and displayed it here.

Today is the super full-moon Phiem wished for the ill science be destroyed and the Targeted Individuals will be destroyed too because they are sick evils created the evil things on this planet to make this planet turning into upside down to match the abnormal elements these sciences were created in this universe.

Each night Phiem go to bed is each night slaughters her soul, her dignity, her subconscious. Phiem was so angry to wish for these evils will be destroyed, she is not hypocrite.

March 21, 2011

This morning Phiem woke up she felt that pain her entire body, her stomach, her lower abdomen, she did no know what they did to her body during the time she was sleeping.
Yesterday evening when Phiem does dishes at her kitchen they attacked to her female then they pulled down her uterus, she has 2 hands she could not shield herself with other things during working, she equipped hat to her head, raw silk rope and aluminum foil covered her body and her stomach, sponge covered her female.
Today they pressed and pulled down her uterus again she felt her female heavy down.
Yesterday when Phiem cleaned her bathroom they were attacking to her rectum, her female. They are terrible sick like that, day and night they are sick like that.
Three days ago when Phiem woke up she felt so hurt and soar at her center forefront she could not touch it for three days after, she saw the wrinkle appeared to her forefront, they created aging to her face, degraded her beauty on her face every centimeter and deform her body also and recently her organs to murder her and of-course her mind her brain all of the time day and night from conscious to subconscious.
I do not know exactly who they are they are the coward dinosaurs, I said they have to go to jail and pay my law suit if they appeared but if they are in hidden situation to do this evil thing to me and others they should be destroyed and surrender.
They are so terrible tyrannies but UN did nothing to them, they use weapons to torture human, these weapons are dangerous more than nuclear weapon.
They can create sickness, damage physical body even kill silently and immediately.
Phiem wanted to show this picture her plant was died quickly, she did not know the cause then she heard the strange sound so she turned off the light, the sound went off, Phiem remember each time she does dishes at the kitchen sink for a while she felt her neck strange dried out then hurt, after she turned off the light at her plant she was free this condition. They created cancer tissues.
This afternoon and entire last night then the whole day March 22, 2011 they let Phiem inhaled smoke and attacked on her head it made dizziness and dull to her brain, she could feel pain and the cut on her head then this evening when she was sitting at her computer they let her inhaled smoke and what kind of weapons they used to created cancer tissue, it was from the light or from computer set up or from the chemical smoke, she felt the same as she was at her kitchen sink with her plant light on as she described above.

March 16, 2011 11:10 AM

Phiem showed this picture her plants were died but she did not know the cause she tried to find out then she heard the strange noises then she turn off the light after she unhook the electric she felt free when she does dishes at her kitchen sink.

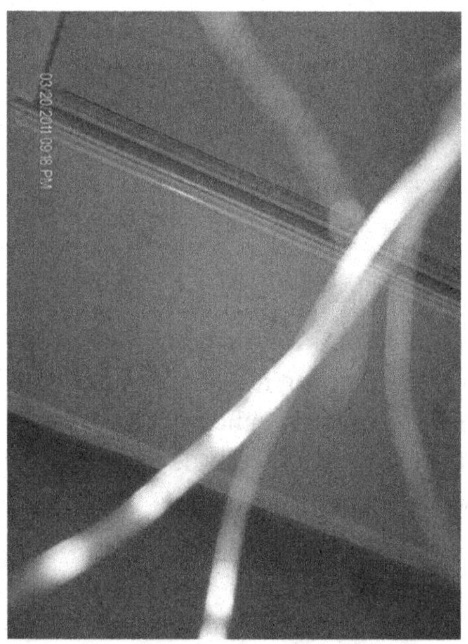

March 20, 2011 9:18 PM

They attacked to Phiem when she was in her bed room.
This is the report pictures of this diary Phiem was so tired of these things but when they stop these terrible things.

March 20, 2011 9:19 PM (2)

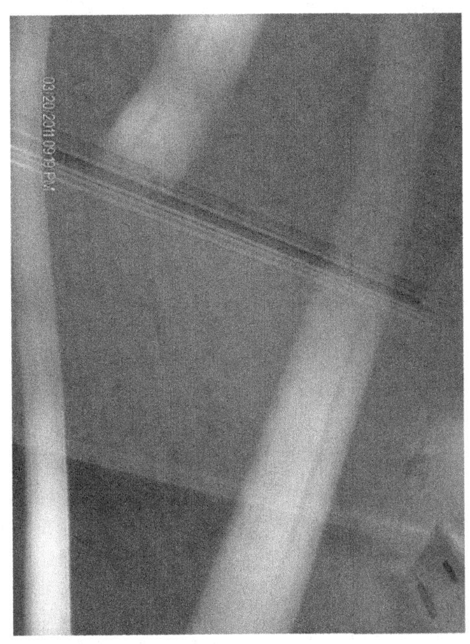

March 20, 2011 9:19 PM (3)

March 21, 2011 11:51 PM (1)

They attacked to Phiem when she was in her bed-room.

March 21, 2011 11:53 PM (2)

March 22, 2011 11:34 AM

They attacked to Phiem's ear when she was in her house.

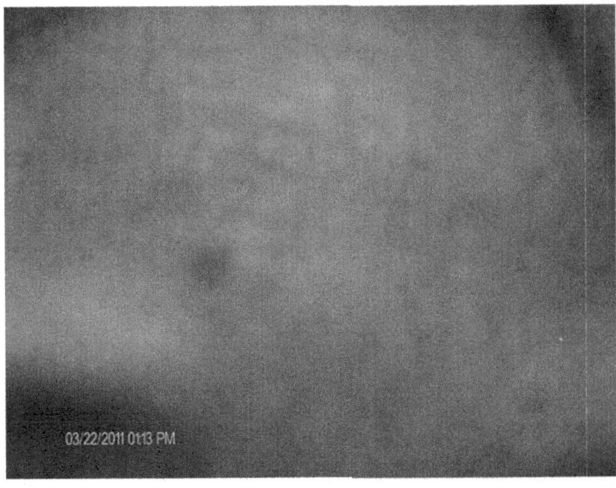

March 22, 2011 1:13 PM

As Phiem noted down the soar and hurtful her forefront, the implanted dot for years near to that place became the acne so Phiem used the needle to open the hole to squeeze it out, it was flatten.

March 22, 2011 1:14 PM

Phiem wanted to prove that is her fore-front.

March 22, 2011 4:39 PM (1)

They attacked to Phiem's left ear when she was sitting at her computer, they constantly doing that to show that they wanted to achieve their goal at any attempted and patiently as I described it.

March 22, 2011 4:46 AM (2)

March 22, 2011 4:47 PM (3)

March 22, 2011 4:52 PM (4)

March 22, 2011 4:59 PM (5)

March 22, 2011 5:00 PM (6)

March 23, 2011 6:11 AM

They attacked to Phiem's head

March 23, 2011 7:13 PM (1)

They attacked to Phiem's ear when she was at her kitchen.

March 23, 2011 7:14 PM (2)

They attacked to Phiem's ear, head, and face when she was at her dinning room.

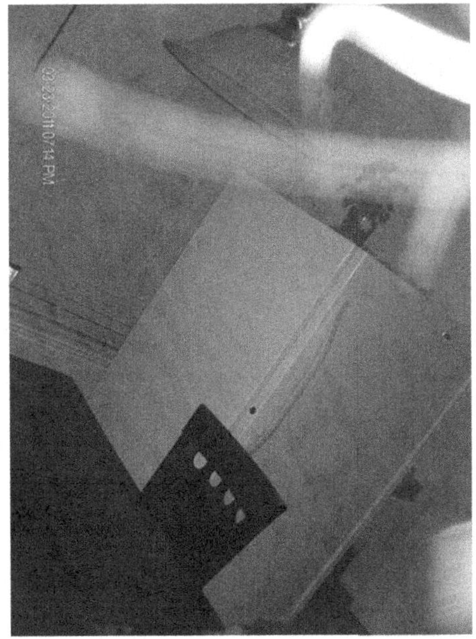

March 23, 2011 7:14 PM (3)

They attacked to Phiem's ear when she was in her kitchen.

March 23, 2011 7:15 PM (4)

They attacked to Phiem's ear when she was in her kitchen.

March 23, 2011 11:43 PM

They attacked to Phiem’s right ear when she was sitting at her computer.

March 26, 2011 11:53 PM (1)

They attacked to Phiem’s left ear when she was sitting at her computer, they were constantly attacking to Phiem’s ear from this series of pictures to prove.

March 23, 2011 11:56 PM (2)

March 23, 2011 11:57 PM (3)

March 23, 2011 11:58 PM (1)

They attacked to Phiem's right ear when she was sitting at her computer, the red background it might be the reflection color from her red head because she has to wear hat in her house to cover her head but she could not avoid attacking to her head.

March 23, 2011 11:59 PM (2)

March 24, 2011 12:00 AM (3)

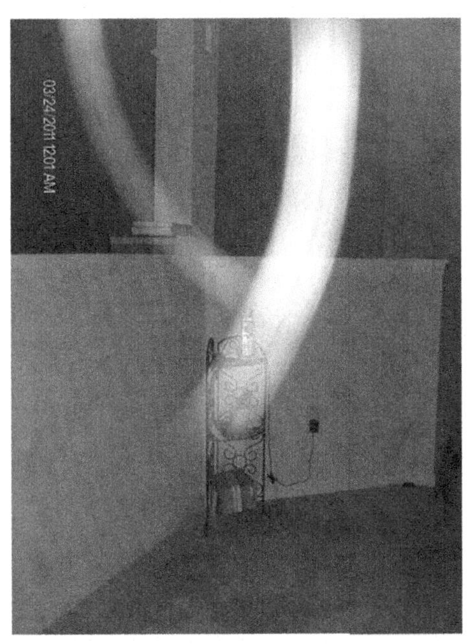

March 24, 2011 12:01 AM (4)

March 24, 2011 2:09 PM

They attacked to Phiem’s head when she was in her bed.

March 24, 2011 2:09 PM

They attacked to Phiem’s ear when she was in her bed.

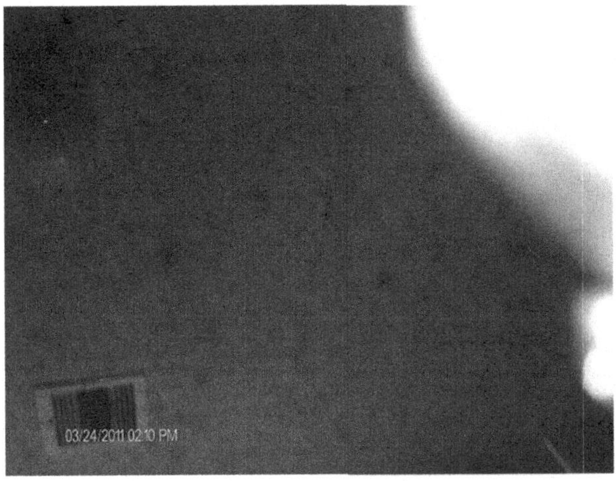

March 24, 2011 2:10 PM (1)

They attacked to Phiem's head she took these pictures with camera face outside from her head.

March 24, 2011 2:10 PM (2)

They attacked to Phiem's head she took these pictures with camera face outside from her head.

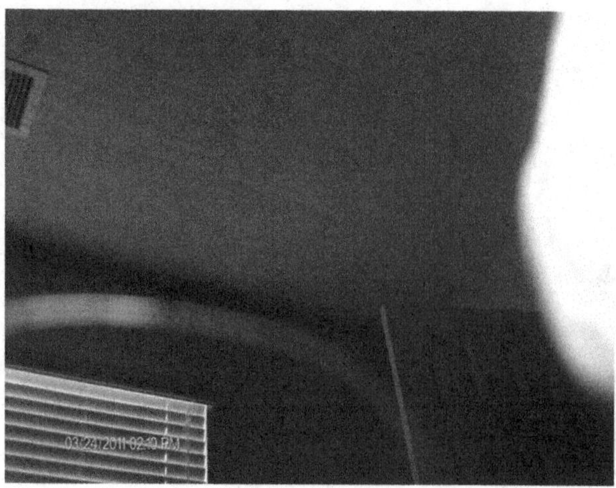

March 24, 2011 2:10 PM (3)

March 24, 2011 2:10 (4)

March 24, 2011 2:12 (1)

They attacked to Phiem’s left ear when she was in her bed.

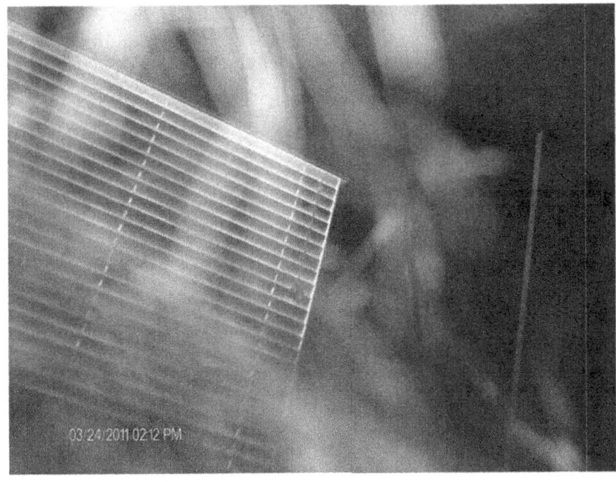

March 24, 2011 2:12 PM (2)

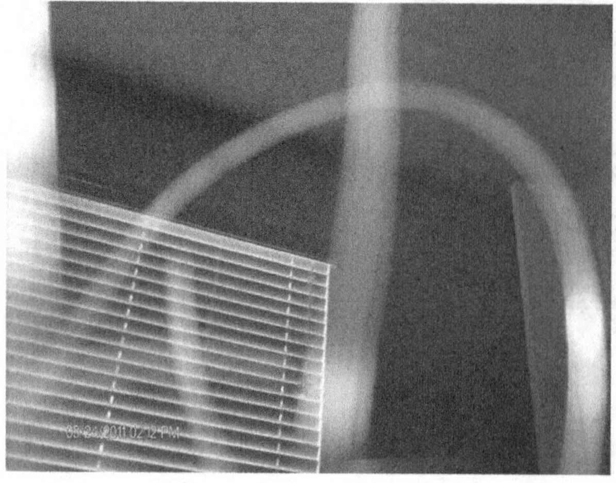

March 24, 2011 2:12 PM (3)

March 25, 2011 12:13 AM

They attacked to Phiem's left ear when she was in her bed.

March 25, 2011 12:20 AM

They attacked to Phiem's head when she was in her bed.

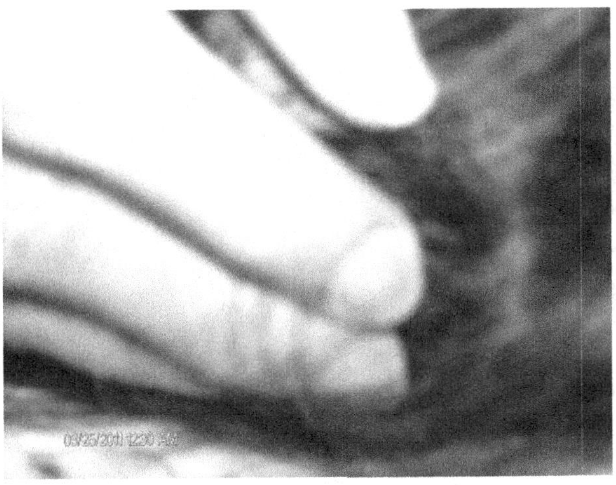

March 26, 2011 12:30 AM

Few days ago they attacked to Phiem's head, it was so hurt her entire top head she could not touch it, she could feel the cut or hole on her head and it was as bruise on that place, today she took picture her head then she tried to take this picture to see how her head injury was but it's hard to take picture her head by herself, to day at that place the bruise was healed. She does not know what they took out from her head and what they injected in her head, she was so angry and wanted to revenge.

As Phiem presented picture of her left knee, now she knew the result that they created handicap to her knee, she saw it changing shape and red veins appearing then hurt her knee each time she sit-down and walking, they damage her body from her veins legs at the ket hang, they attacked her legs they damaged her legs, her body is not free, her finger nails, her finger toes are not free, They used Microwave heated her inside female to damage her female tissues. They have to go out of this earth, the hell is waiting for these evils.

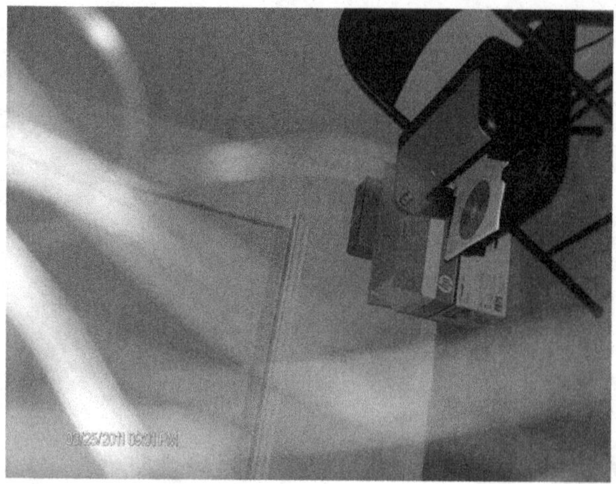

March 25, 2011 9:01 PM (1)

They attacked to Phiem's left ear when she was sitting at her computer.

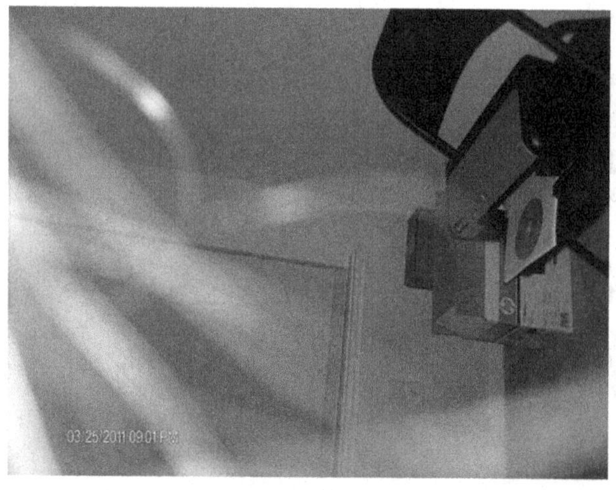

March 25, 2011 9:01 PM (2)

March 27, 2011 12:52 AM (1)

They woke Phiem's up by shooting at her ket hang at her ovary place, it was so hurt after they poured in their conduct dreams to her subconscious. Each week-end they come here in this neighborhood to implanted sex dreams into her subconscious and they wanted to create sick sex life all the time.

Phiem went to bathroom as they created each time they woke her up, ure sex,

Phiem was scare to go back to bed so she was sitting at the chair at her game room then they attacked to Phiem's body and her left's ear she took these pictures to present to prove their evil things 24/7. Phiem wish for all of the evils will be destroyed, she wanted to revenge.

March 27, 2011 12:52 AM. (2)

March 27, 2011 1;00 AM (3)

March 27, 2011 1:01 AM (4)

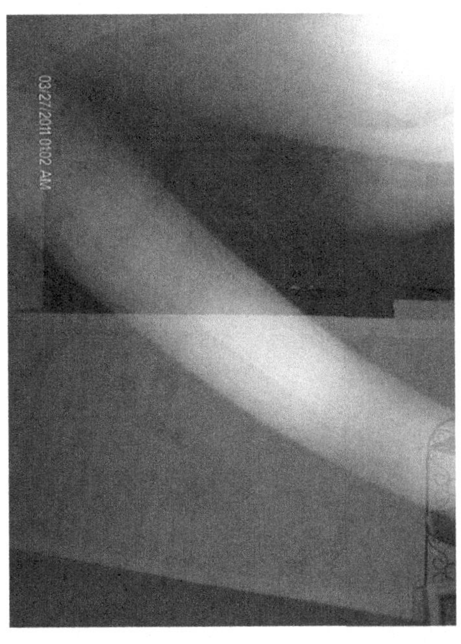

March 27, 2011 1:02 AM (5)

March 27, 2011 1:02 AM (6)

March 27, 2011 1:05 (1)

Phiem was still sitting there in her game room they attacked to Phiem's left ear she took this picture to prove the killing level of Microwave they used to attack to her head through her ear canal, this time she was not wearing her red hat so it was not the reflection color from her red hat.

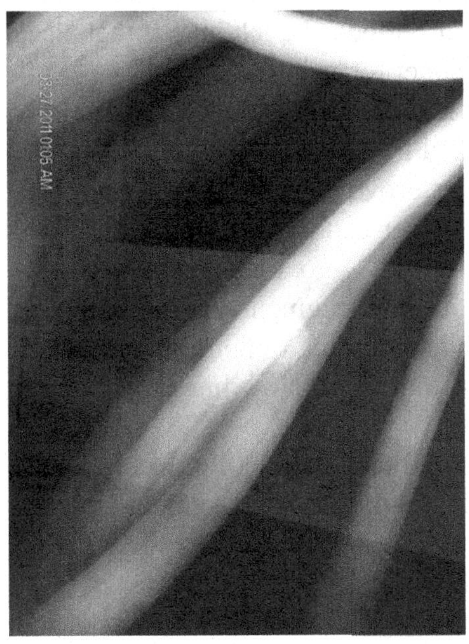

March 27, 2011 1:05 AM (2)

March 27, 2011 1:06 AM (3)

This morning Phiem went to bed at 7:00 AM and she woke up each one or two hours then she brushed teeth during that time they attacked to her as every time she was in her bathroom, they attacked to her female, her thigh, her ket hang, she could smell the burning flesh during the time they attacked to her right thigh and her ket hang.
She feels hurt at her ket hang when they woke her up last night by attacking at that place. Few days ago they attacked to her left back thigh under her buttock she felt hurt at that place when she woke up or they woke her up by the kind of prisoner torturing.
Phiem wondered if some one doing something around her neighborhood before yesterday evening she sat at her dinning room she saw the car parked there then drove to the parking of neighbor house then another car came then another car drove to park there at the place the car parked before then later Phiem felt the vibration to her center forefront at the place Phiem described the painful place at her center forefront few days ago. Phiem does not know what they did to her hairs, they implanted some things or just the fragment made she saw the white hair turning into black hair then the other group did something to her forefront at the evening as she described then she saw the black hairs were turning into white hairs. Phiem wonder if it was true.
Phiem remembered when she was in Irving, Texas she could feel they shot to her forefront head and other parts of her body regularly, people said they killed DNA, Phiem saw her white hairs grew rapidly and she saw her aging face and sagging her under arms when Phiem saw it she was shock her under arms looked like her mother arms.
Here in Houston they used Microwave to attacked Phiem's hang her female her buttocks and now her thighs, they damage tissues to make aging and tissues died out and changing shapes and harm her body will be into handicap body.
They tried to change Phiem's face to look like her mother, she does not know what the reason they were doing that. They want to punish her, she wants to know the reason to punish her, and they did what they want to do on her body, her brain, her subconscious and her conscious, her life, her dignity. The tyrannies, the mafia she could say they are. Phiem wants to revenge.

March 28, 2011

Today the earth will be destroyed to kill all of the sick evils if people wants to know why Phiem noted this please ask them the handlers, the perpetrators, they knew exactly what was happened. People want to know the created sex dreams please read Phiem book she described it in "God Universe and I"
She suggested young people choose the carrier for you remember to avoid the ill science, I am not professional and I am not bring the misery life to people, I always bring the safe and happiness life to people and bring the justice life to people. Please remember that.

March 29, 2011

Phiem was afraid of go to bed last night she's awaken until 7:30 AM then go to bed at that time. She did not know what they will do next, the dream she talk about ill science was applied to her subconscious yesterday they created.

They picked out her subconscious at the time when she was a girl the story she had heard and how she react at that time in her subconscious then they cover their fragment to put it in the created lang loan sex dream then woke her up at the time they wanted her to remember it in her subconscious.

People has to know how the ill science was conduct people behavior, this is the one thing from Mind Control, beamed Psychotronics weapons to head through ear canal, LSD chemical the other thing of Mind Control.

Phiem wanted to pull these ill sciences out of her under bed and out of her under pant but they are evils and they addicted with these things so she could do it, they have lived there so long, now they wanted to transformed her into man or gay, how rude, how cruel they are doing, how evil and sick they are?

Phiem saw the expertise they performed on her body to harm, abuse, deform, degrade, rape, murder and torture process that made her think how many times they did it on victims to become smoothly processing like that in the condition secretly, faceless, handless with no evidences to prove.

Eight millions people here in United States and more than 0ne hundred fifty millions people in China and twenty millions Russian died in Soviet Union time with this Mind Control.

Phiem wanted to revenge to determiner these ill sciences so people have to be wakening to go out of this trend you might were trapped in but never be aware of that. History proved without destruction could not be changed.

March 29, 2011 9:24 PM (1)

Phiem felt soar at her in the eye so she took these pictures to show they might attack her when she was at her computer or she was in her kitchen, then two days later she was in her bathroom she felt the microwave heat at her both end the eye then she saw it burn to the red and died out it places, Phiem applied sunburn cream then it reduced dried out then she was in bathroom they heated that places again then she saw at that places became wrinkle appearance.

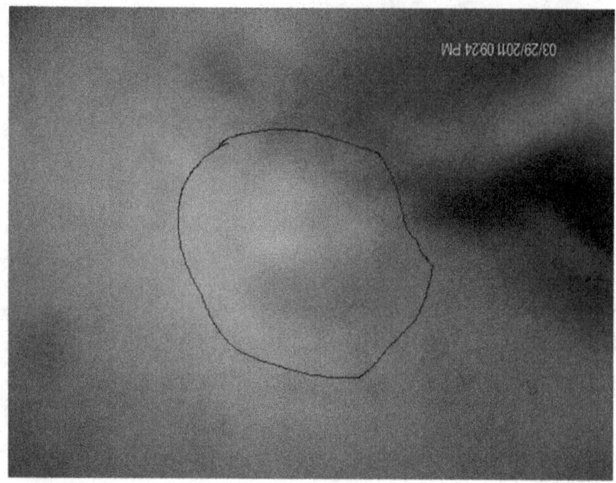

March 29, 2011 9:24 PM (2)

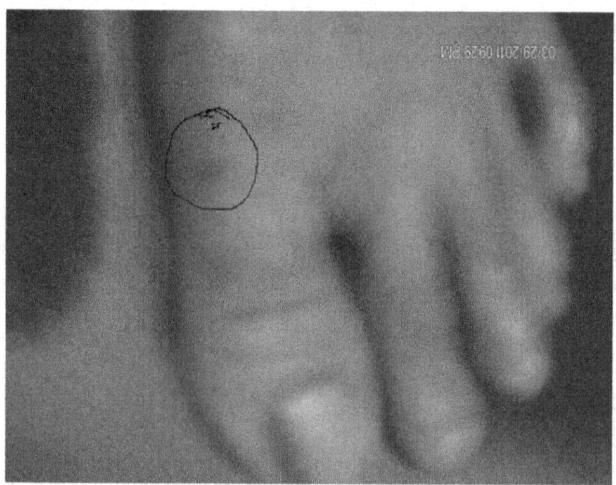

March 29, 2011 9:29 PM (1)

The time and date on this picture was not the date it was happened but it few days ago they shot or they implanted to Phieim's foot at her toe in this picture, they did it then they activated their chips to make her physical feet pain and twisted veins to created the strange muscles and legs scram to torture her to deform her physical feet.

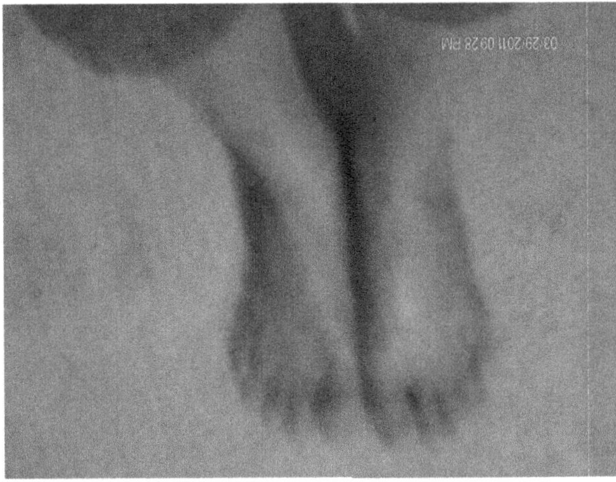

March 29, 2011 9:28 PM (2)

Phiem displayed how her feet under their scheme in this picture.

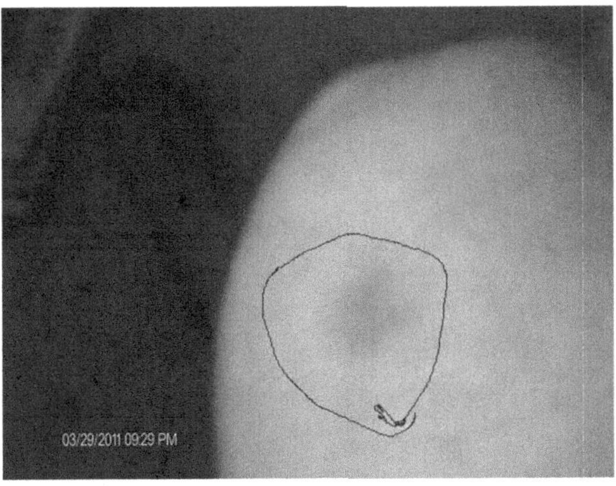

March 29, 2011 9:30 PM (1)

Few days ago they attacked to Phiem's right knee when she was sitting at her computer, she felt pain at that place then it turned to gray color then it hurt when walked or when they activated it hurt.

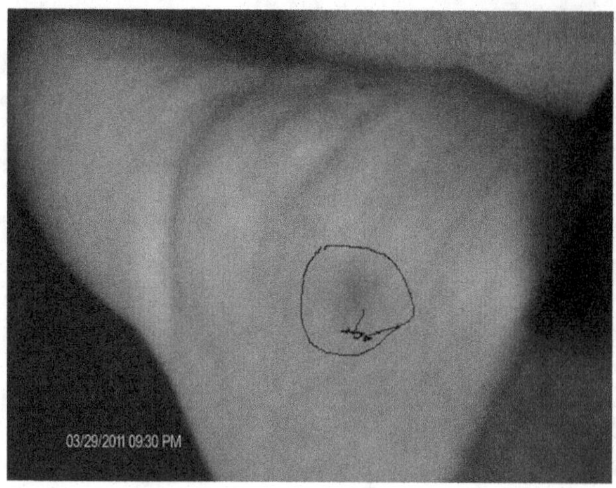

March 29 9:30 PM (2)

Phiem's right knee appeared with the gray color attacking.

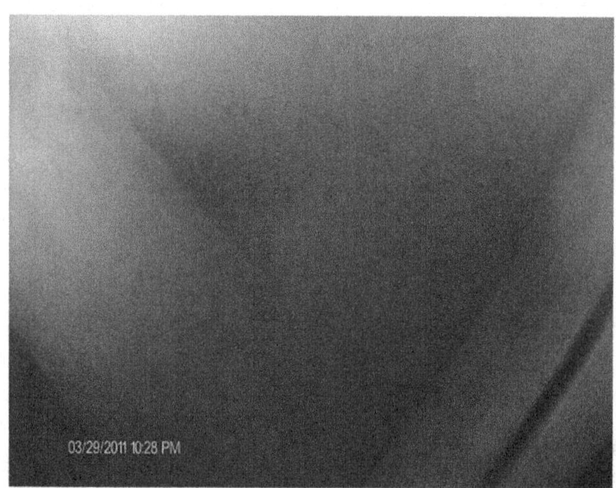

March 29, 2011 9:28 PM (1)

They attacked to Phiem's head.

March 29, 2011 10:29 PM (2)

They attacked to Phiem's head.

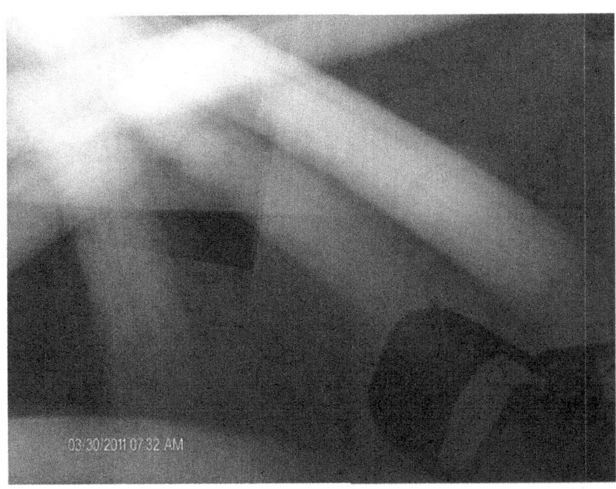

March 30, 2011 7:32 AM (1)

Phiem was awakening until this time she was sitting at her computer desk they attacked to her left ear canal in order to her head.

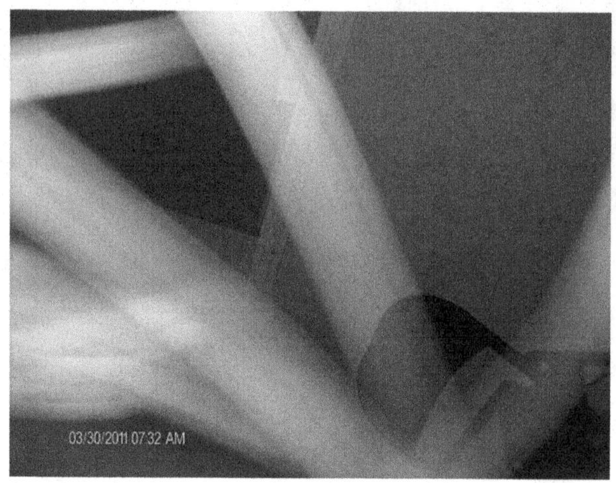

March 30, 2011 7:32 AM (2)

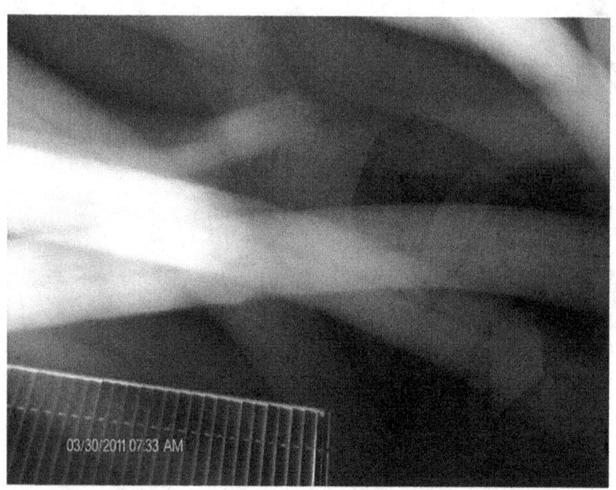

March 30, 2011 7:33 AM (3)

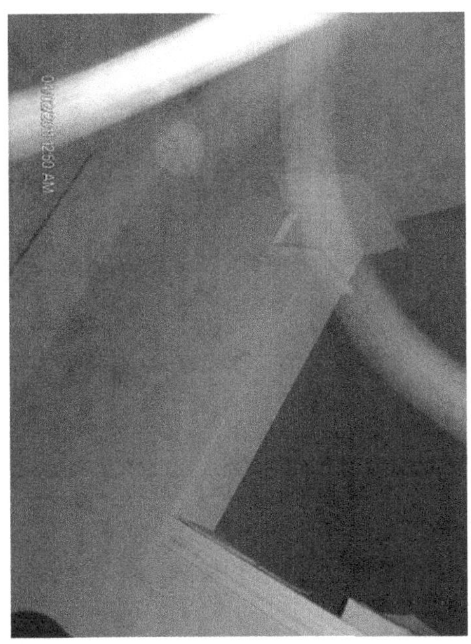

April 2, 2011 12:51 AM (1)

They attacked to Phiem's left ear when she was sitting at her computer.

April 2, 2011 12:51 AM (2)

April 2, 2011 12:51 AM (3)

Reader could imagine how strongest force they wanted to attack to Phiem's left ear in order to go to her brain.

April 2, 2011 8:51 AM

They attacked to Phiem's left ear when she was sitting at her computer.

April 2, 2011 4:56 PM (1)

They attacked to Phiem's left ear when she was sitting at her computer.

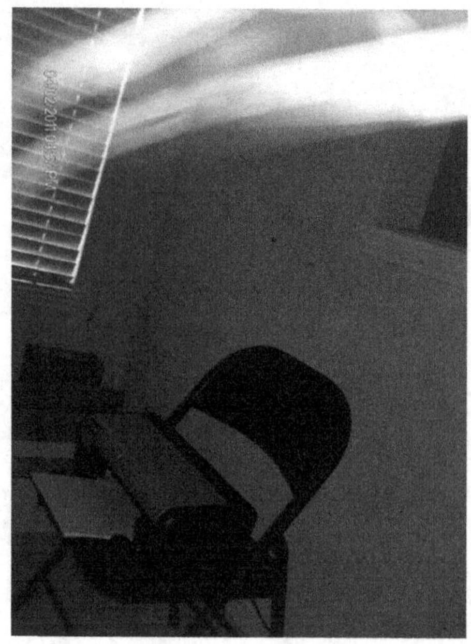

April 2, 2011 4:57 PM (2)

They attacked to Phiem's left ear when she was sitting at her computer, this is the series of picture to prove the time they were attacking to her ear canal in order to her brain to control to damage her brain and to take out her brain what they wanted to take out and what they wanted to inject into her brain.

April 32, 2011 5:01 PM (3)

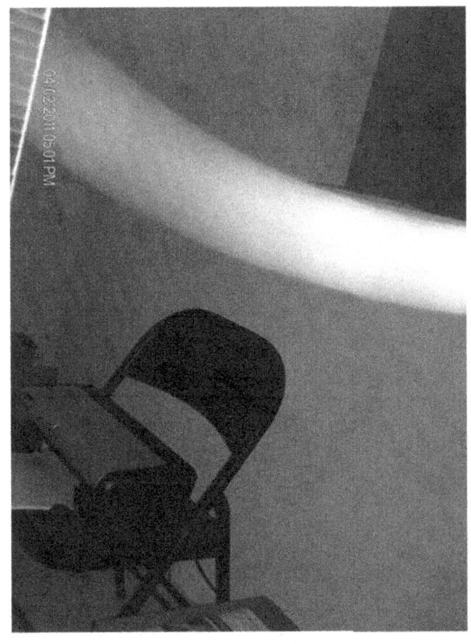

April 3, 2011 5:01 PM (4)

April 2, 2011 5:44 PM (5)

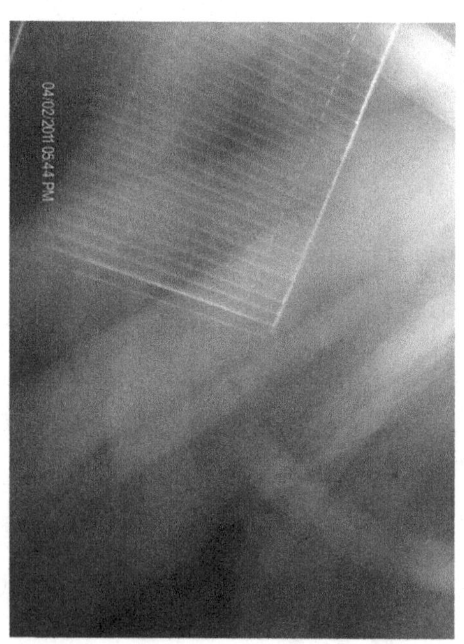

April 2, 2011 5:44 PM (6)

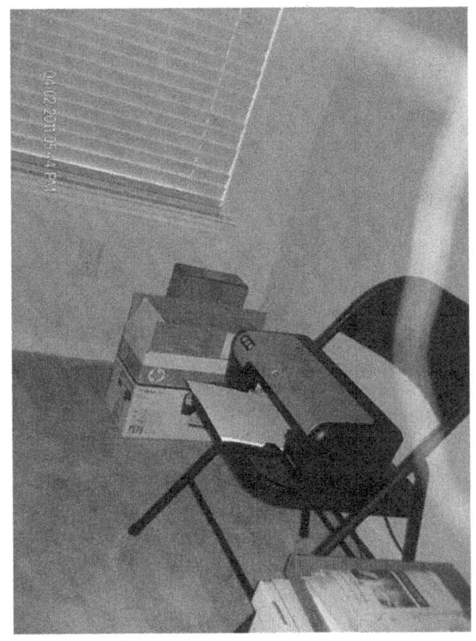

April 2, 2011 5:44 PM (7)

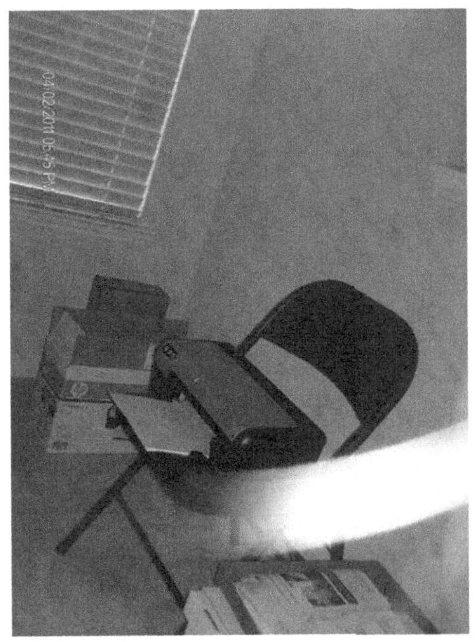

April 2, 2011 5:45 PM (8)

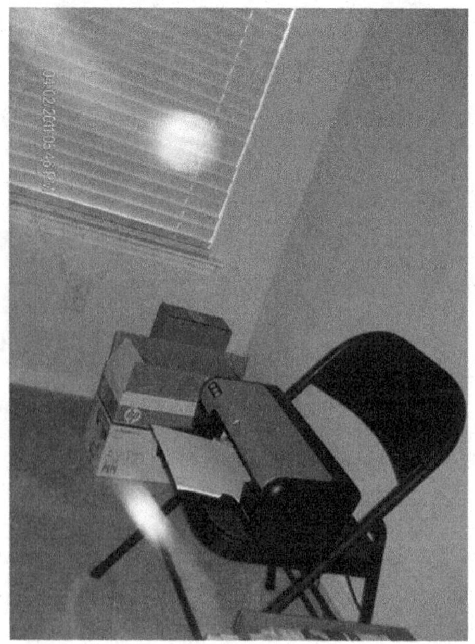

April 2, 2011 5:46 PM (9)

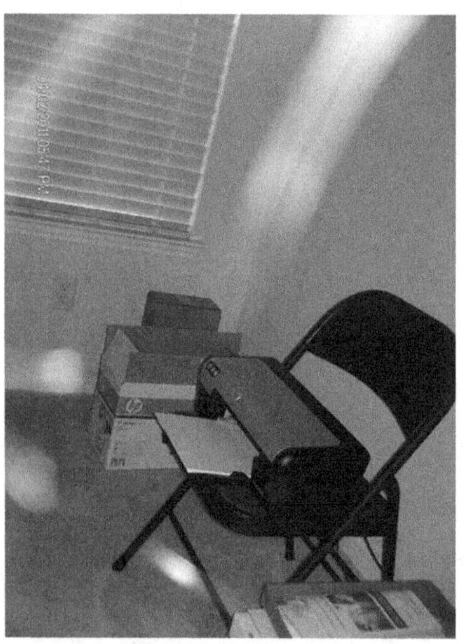

April 2, 2011 5:47 PM (10)

These pictures above in the series of attacking to Phiem's ear canal, this is important for investigation and for studying.

April 3, 2011 7:21 AM (1)

They attacked to Phiem's left ear canal when she was sitting at her front door, she opened her door for the fresh air, and reader can see their attacking 24/7/365 whenever and wherever she was.

April 3, 2011 7:22 AM (2)

April 3, 2011 7:22 AM (3)

Reader can see the attacking was proved at this moment to the hackers or the invaders into her computer to see the truth at this time she enter this information.

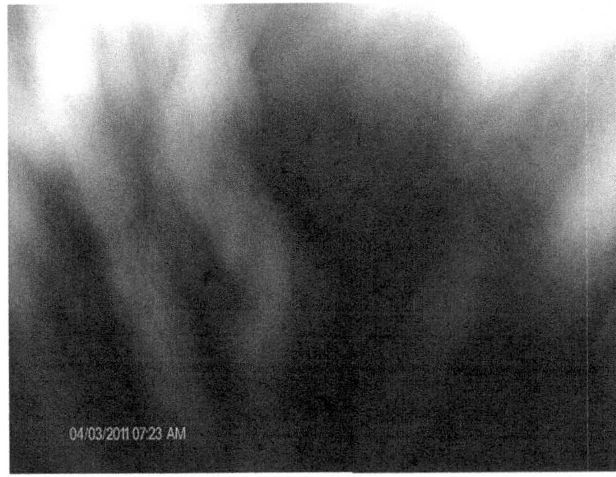

April 3, 2011 7:23 AM (1)

They attacked to Phiem's head during the time she was sitting at her front door for fresh air.

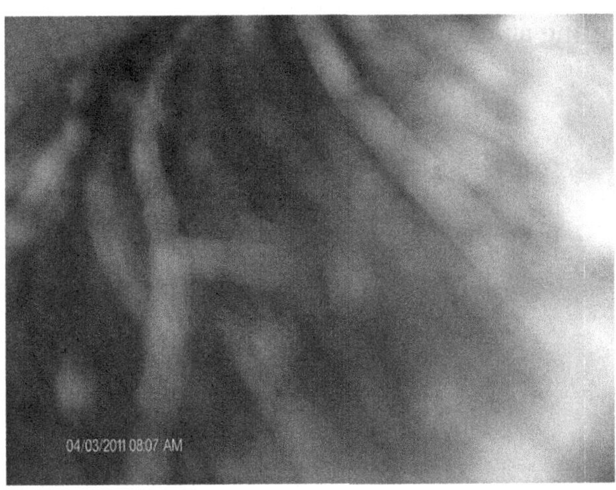

April 3, 2011 8:07 AM (2)

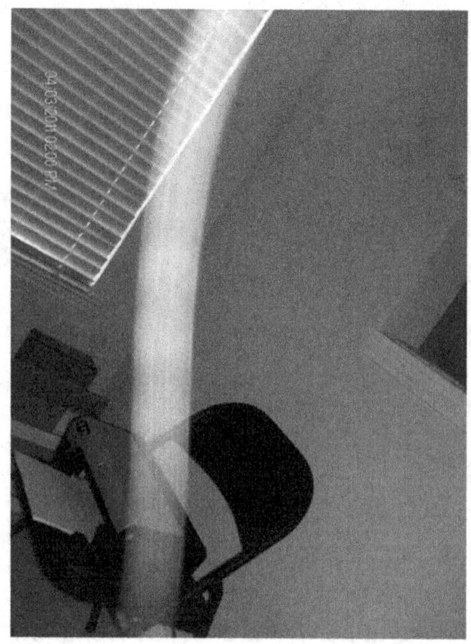

April 3, 2011 2:01 PM (1)

They attacked to Phiem's ear when she was sitting at her computer.

April 3, 2011 2:03 PM (2)

April 3, 2011 2:05 PM (3)

They attacked to Phiem's forehead at tempo.

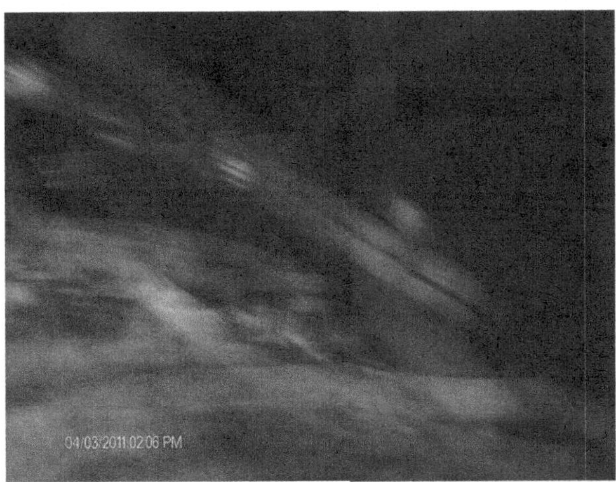

April 3, 2011 2:06 PM (4)

They attacked to Phiem's tempo when she was sitting at her computer.

April 3, 2011 2:07 PM (5)

They attacked to Phhiem's right ear when she was sitting at her computer.

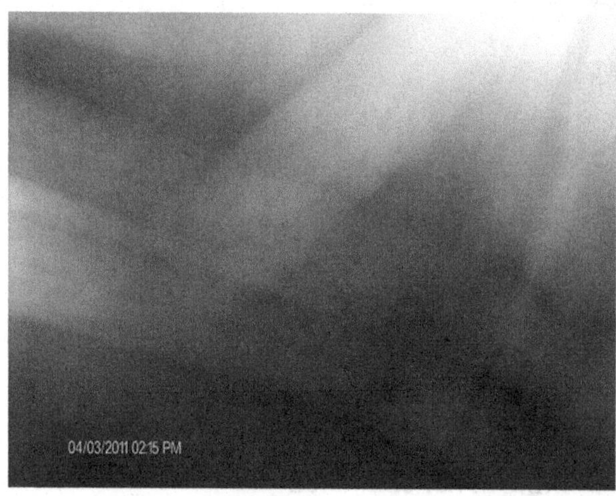

April 3, 2011 2:15 PM (6)

They attacked to Phiem's ot back head at her back neck.

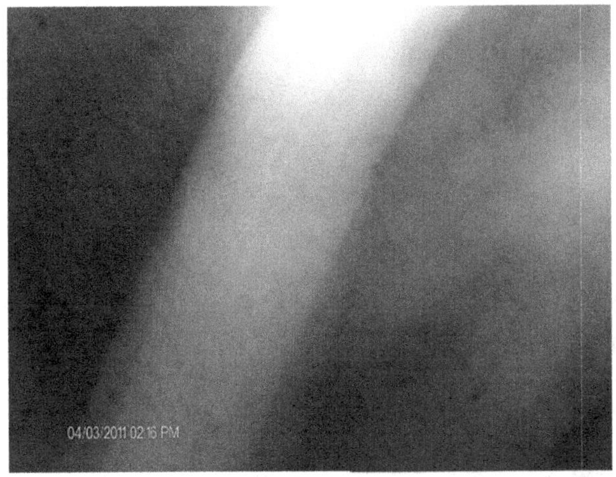

April 3, 2011 2:16 PM (7)

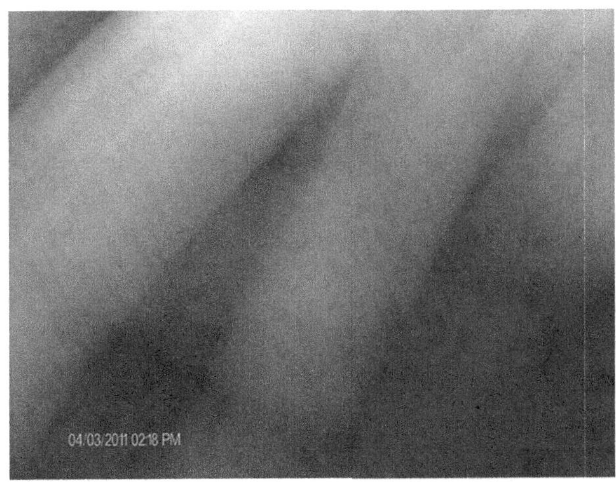

April 3, 2011 2:18 PM (8)

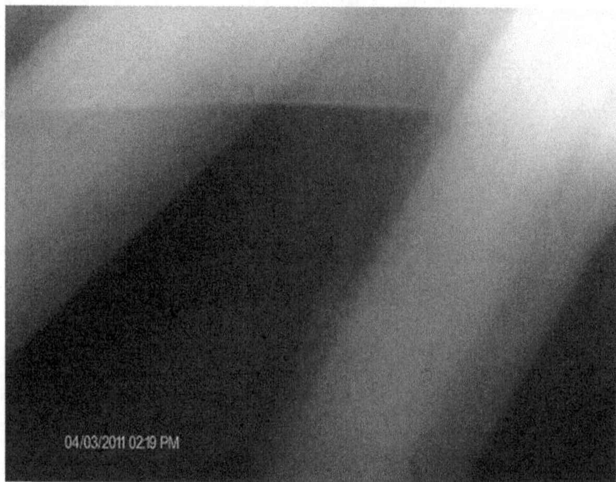

April 3, 2011 2:19 PM (9)

They attacked to Phiem back neck from 2:15 PM to 2:19 PM the time on the pictures proved what her evidences were saying.

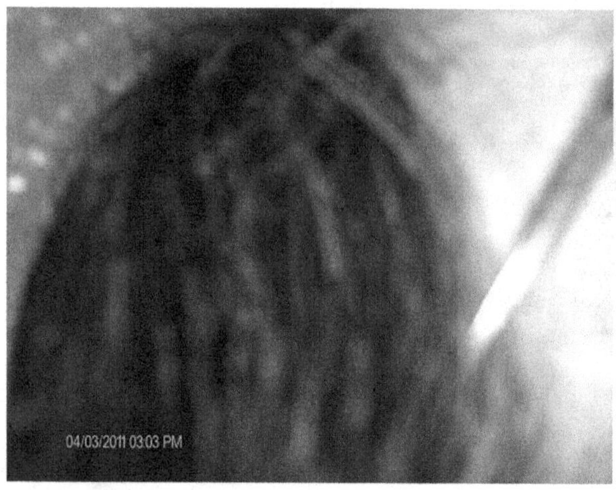

April 3, 2011 3:03 PM (10)

This time they attacked to Phiem's back ear and her ear frame then her inner ear.

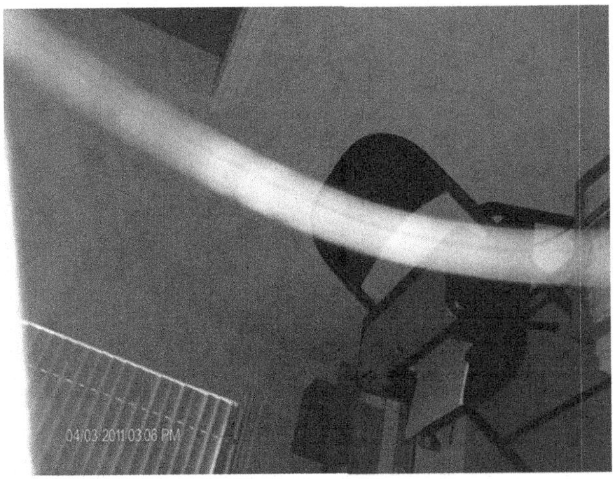

April 3, 2011 3:06 PM (11)

They attacked to Phiem's left ear canal.

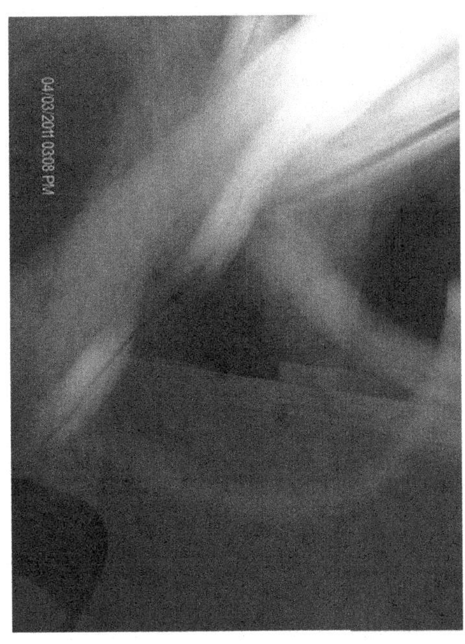

April 3, 2011 3:08 (12)

They turned to Phiem's neck then forefront head.

April 3, 2011 3:09 PM (13)

They attacked to Phiem's left ear.

April 3, 2011 6:07 PM (1)

They attacked Phiem when she was in her bathroom, they attacked from head to toes, at this time she went outside to take camera to take these pictures.

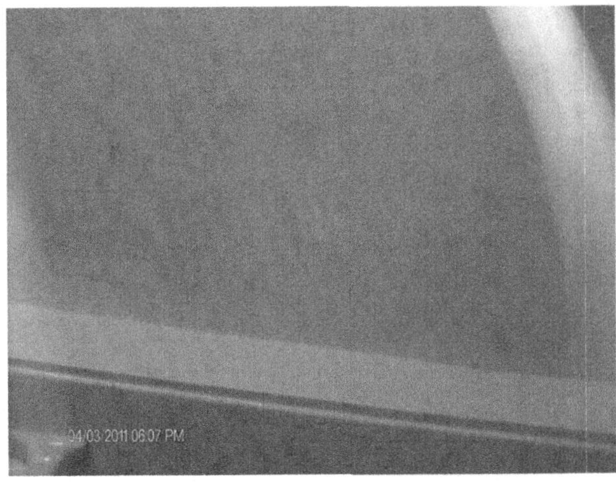

April 3, 2011 6:07 PM (2)

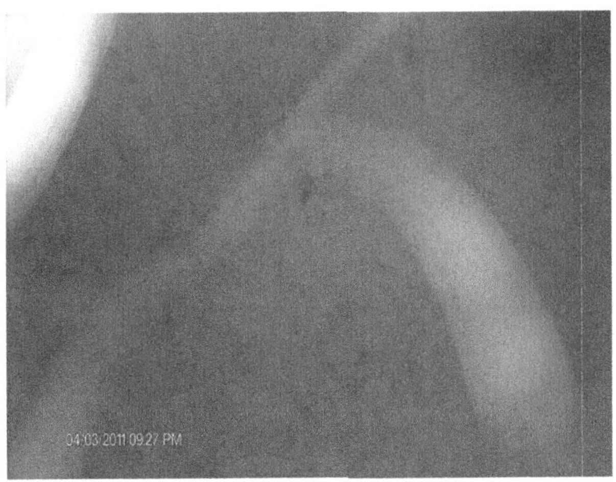

April 3, 2011 9:27 PM

Phiem was in her bed they shot to her head she took this picture. Phiem go to bed each night she shield her body with sponges, she was tired of doing this so she bought shield overcoat and under clothe shield suit but it was not protected her body with their weapons were attacking on her body, she returned those items few days ago.

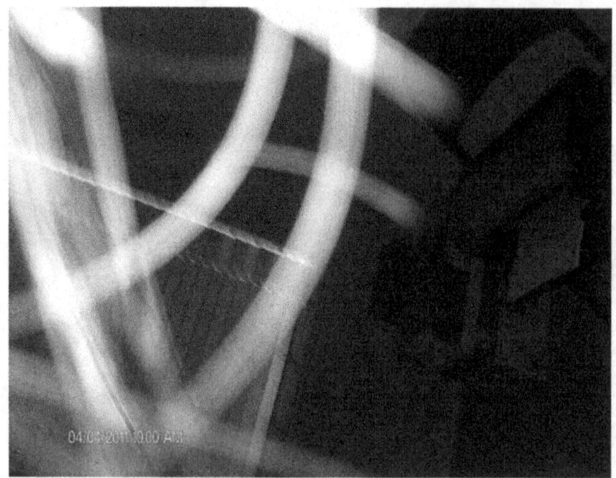

April 4, 2011 10:00 AM (1)

They attacked to Phiem's left ear when she was sitting at her computer.

April 4, 2011 10:03 AM (2)

April 4, 2011 10:04 AM (3)

They continued attacking to Phiem's left ear 3 more minutes later in the weakening power.

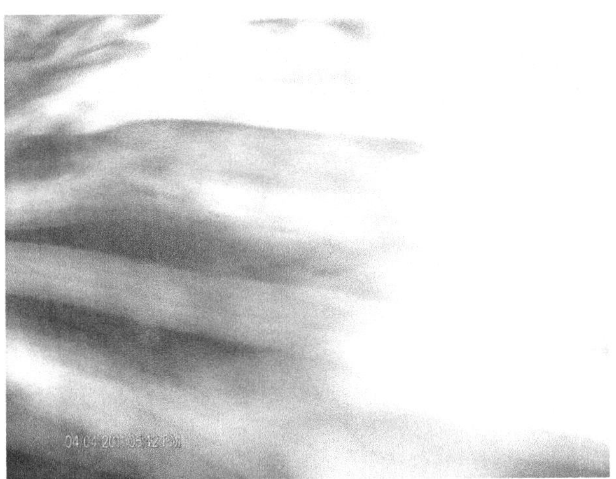

April 4, 2011 5:43 PM

They attacked to Phiem's head.

April 5, 2011 4:13 PM

They attacked to Phiem's right ear when she was in her bed to take nap.

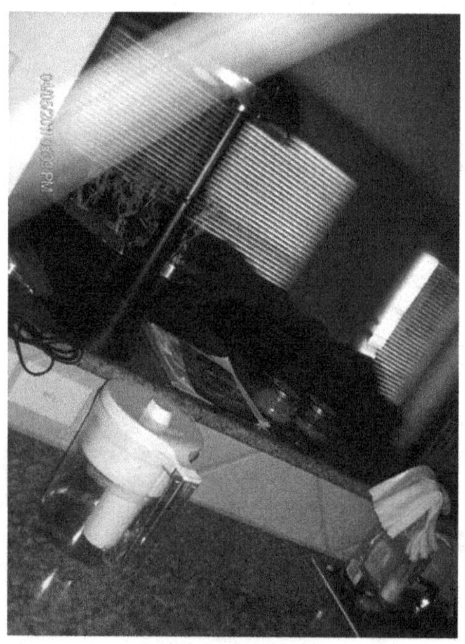

April 5, 2011 5:09 PM

They attacked to Phiem's left earring when she was in her kitchen.

April 5, 2011 8:21 PM

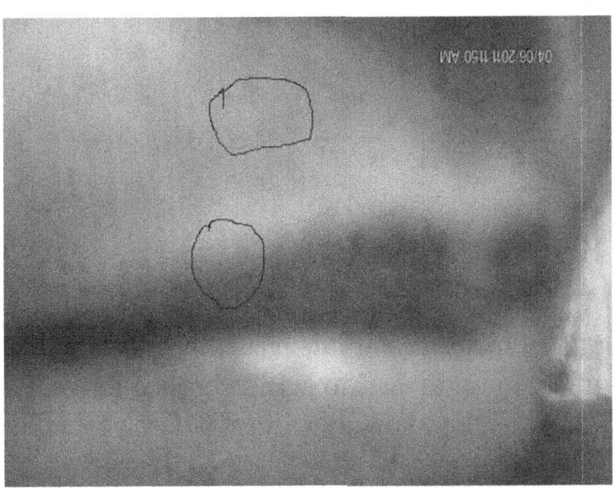

April 6, 2011 11:50 AM

Few days ago they implanted the white tissue micro chip to Phiem's right upper lip then 2 days ago they implanted another white tissue micro chip into her upper lip liner, they tried to sabotage her beauty, she tried to pull it out but she could not.

They implanted micro chips all over her face to degrade, to sabotage, and to damage her face, her beauty then they activated it to be painful or twisted it whenever they wanted to be. They attacked to her female in order to sabotage her female and her female organ constantly day and night and mad sensation with high tech rape.

Yesterday evening when Phiem was sitting at her computer they shot to her stomach to make stomach upset then went to bathroom and last night Phiem was in bed she was sleeping about one hour they were surely did it again during the time she was sleeping then they woke her up to go to bathroom. She was waiting outside her bathroom to turn off the exhausted fan then went back her bed then they did the same as they did to make her stomach upset again but this time she took her cell phone guarded at her stomach she felt the force they used was neutralized so she could sleep well until 6:00 AM.

Phiem said they are evils, they are human misery, how people were turning themselves into evil like that, Phiem wanted them adapt God Universe and Me self help, the reason is moral intolerable in human life.

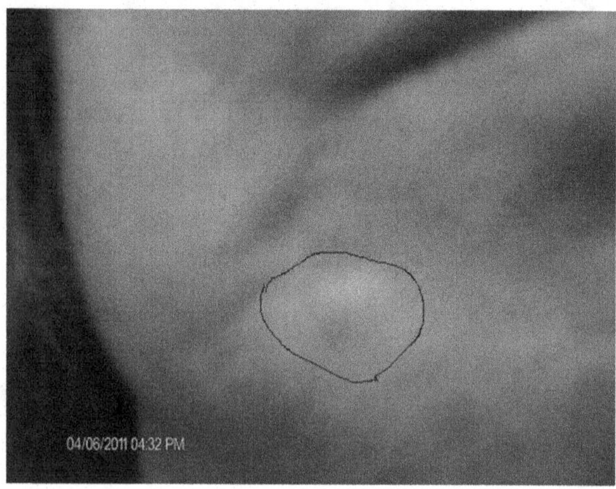

April 6, 2011 4:32 PM (1)

They shot or implanted or injected something into Phiem face at this place, they usually did it to her face so many times to deform, to degrade, to saggy and to aging her face for years, yesterday she took these pictures but she did not when and how they did it before yesterday but she forgot to take pictures to show.

They intended to damage her chin because the Chinese believed if the chin was in that shape made people misery life in old age life, Phiem wrote it in her book to describe why they tried to do it. They tried to block everything, to deprive her life. Another thing they believed if woman urine with the sound of whistle that person is rich and people has the short mouth are rich so they tried to change her urine line and they tried to pull her mouth, they pull her teeth then down her nose, they pin down her eye lid, they pressed in her head to change her head shape. They did what they wanted to do to her beauty and to her body, damage her body, her breast, her female. Control her subconscious mind the whole night, injected what they wanted to injected into her subconscious, outcome dream what they wanted her to dream.

Last night they made Phiem smell the horrible male part, how they did it please ask them. Phiem notice the microchip they implanted inside her nose that they might trigger the smell or pain or sneeze or something else.

This morning Phiem woke up they shot or laser knife cut inside her female, it was so painful, she did not know what they tried to do to her female, to change into male or what they tried to do to her female day and night 24/7.

Phiem said they are sick evils, savage evils.

Phiem wish for all of them the evils will be destroyed.

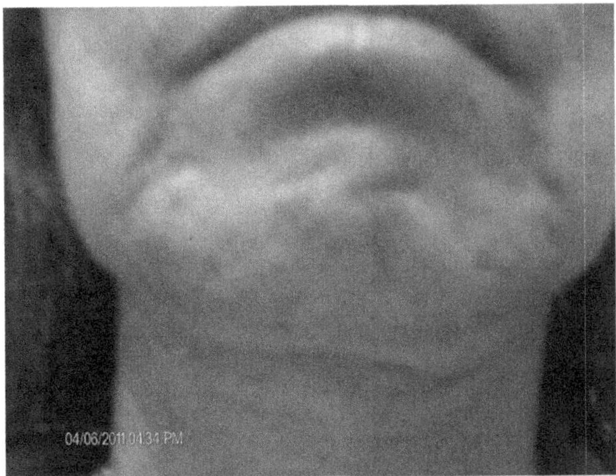

April 6, 2011 4:34 PM (2)
Reader could see Phiem's chin and her neck, they attacked to it too.

April 6, 2011 4:34 PM (3)

Phiem proved she is and she took those pictures above by herself.

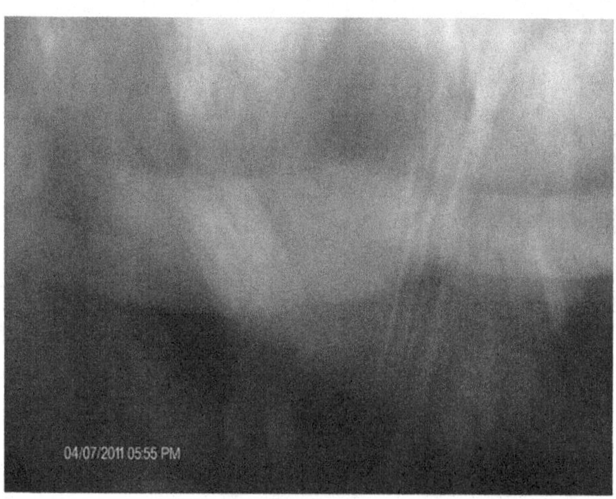

April 7, 2011 4:55 PM

This picture was captured the force of NanoMicromagnetic attacked to Phiem's head, it was separated her hairs that the force went through and under it, it was hard to take picture the Nanomagnetic attacked to Phiem's head but this is the one can prove how different between Phiem's hairs and the Nanomagnetic force on her head.

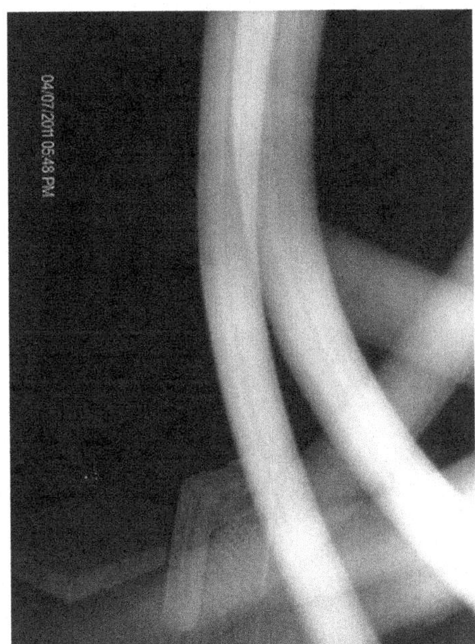

April 7, 2011 5:48 PM (1)

Phiem was at her dinning room they attacked to her ear.

April 7, 2011 5:48 PM (2)

It proved that was true they set up device to surveillant her so it was at any time they can attack her to torture her.

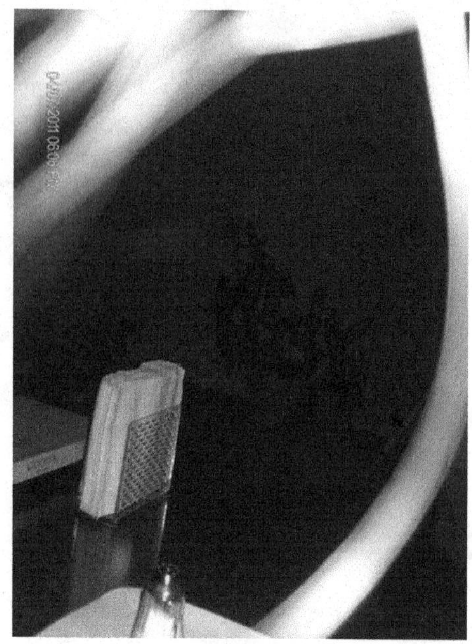

April 7, 2011 6:07 PM (3)

They were continuing attack to Phiem.

April 8, 2011 6:14 PM (4)

They attacked to Phiem's forefront so this picture were taken, she did not know what it was she wanted to show this is the other shape of NanoMicromagnetic force to attack to human body.

April 7, 2011 6:19 PM (5)

They attacked to Phiem's neck when she was at her dinning room.

April 7, 2011 6:19 PM (6)

They attacked to Phiem's neck.

April 7, 2011 6:19 PM (7)

They attacked to Phiem's neck when she was at her dinning room.

April 7, 2011 8:01 PM

They attacked to Phiem's when she was working into her bedroom to change her clothe she took this picture. Surveillant her in her house 24/7 and 365/Y.

April 8, 2011

Last night they shot to her female place like the place of ovary and the bladder, it was so painful she had to take her camera to place at that place to shield then they attacked to her buttock born, it was so painful she had to place the camera to shield that place then they used Microwave heated her ket hang at the side of female and leg she took her cell phone to cover that place.

This morning Phiem woke up at 5:00AM she is still feeling hurt at her attacking part last night.

Phiem said these evils will be destroyed that bring to end these evil things on earth.

Phiem said they are Gods they do not have limit so the place for Gods at the heaven and ghosts do not have limit so the place for ghosts at the Hell. We are the human we have limit we have lived here on this earth.

Human do not need the Destruction, the Plague, the Misery, the Mental Illness.

Human we needed harmony, love, and peace, happy, safe.

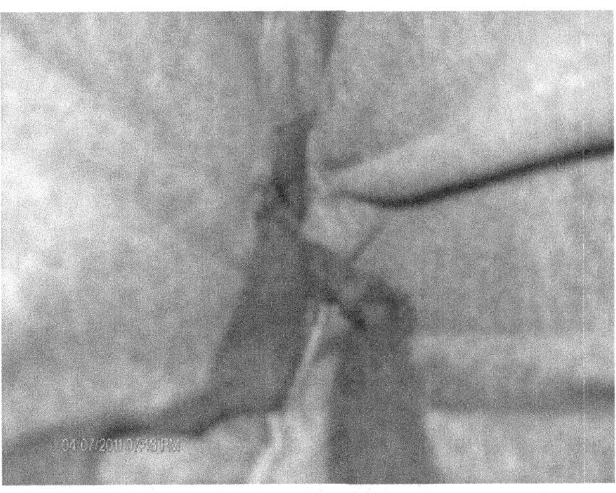

April 7, 2011 7:48 PM (1)

Yesterday Phiem was not sure what it was when she took these pictures with camera facing to her pant during the time they were attacking to her female, she thought it was her pant but today April 9, 2011 she took the others pictures when they were attacking to her female she wanted to enter these pictures to proved what they did to her body and to her female. They were not only make sensation her female but they do surgery to cut to change shape, to damage and to make water running she could feel at her female too.

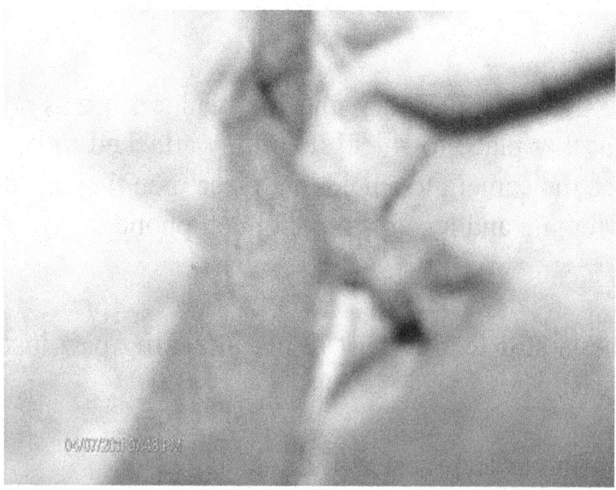

April 7, 2011 7:48 PM (2)

April 9, 2011 8:57 AM (3)

This morning Phiem stood at her kitchen to eat breakfast they were attacking to her female they did it all the time when she was sitting at her computer as the pictures 1&2 and she was in her bathroom, in her bedroom, at her kitchen sink, she wanted to entry these picture to prove that was doing the evil science and the abnormal notion on this planet. What the technology was doing to this mankind, they do not care what they were doing things for their sick sex, nature needed balancing.

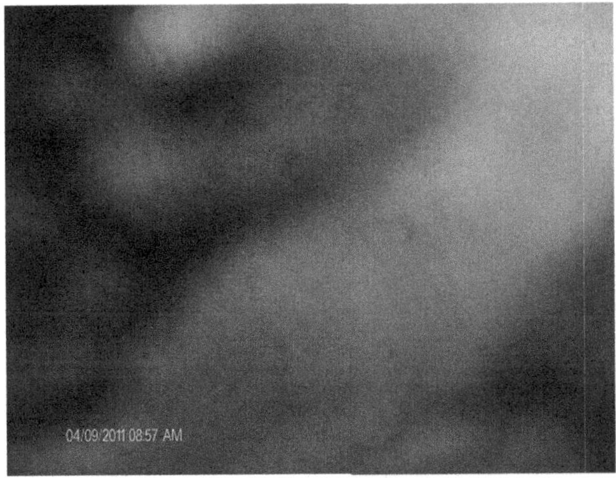

April 9, 2011 8:57 AM (4)

April 8, 2011 7:38 AM (1)

They attacked Phiem's ear when she was in her kitchen to entry evidences to diary to prove it is continuing day and night 24/4 and 365/year torture, murder, abuse, humiliate, rape, high-tech rape day and night and deprive.

April 8, 2011 8:23 AM (2)

Phiem took this picture with camera was facing to her ear during the time they were attacking to her ear.

April 8, 2011 8:24 AM (3)

Phiem took this picture with camera was facing to her ear during the time they were attacking to her ear.

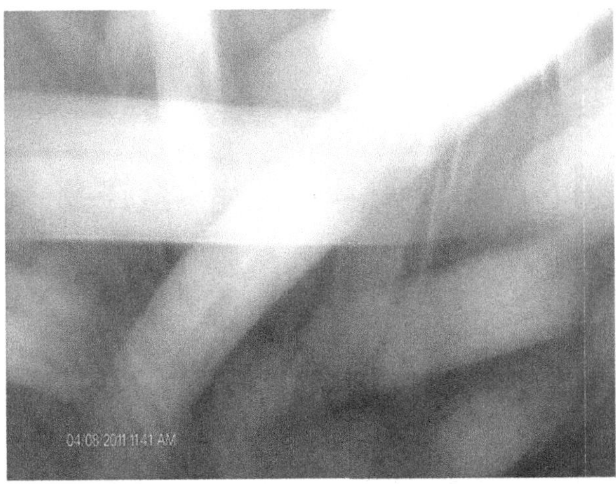

April 8, 2011 11:41 AM (1)

They attacked to Phiem's head, she took these pictures by herself, Phiem saw on face book one friend on face book displayed his picture was taken by another proved the Nanomagnetic rays were attacking to his head with shield clothes and cap.

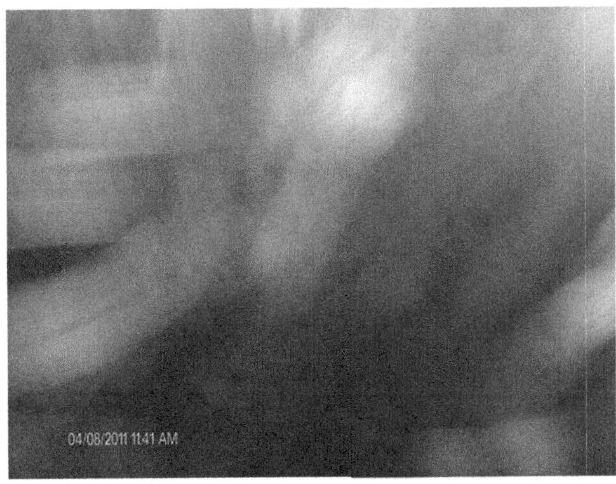

April 8, 2011 7:41 AM (2)

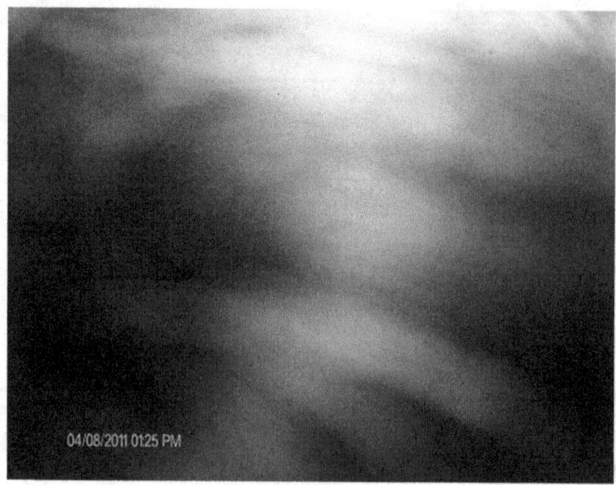

April 8, 2011 1:25 PM (3)

They attacked to Phiem's head when she was sitting at her computer.

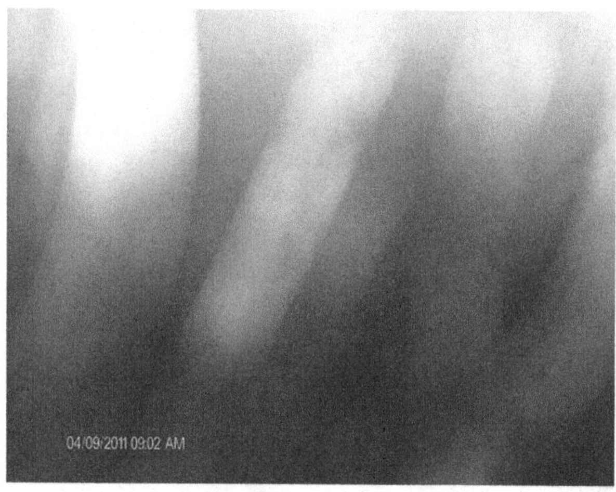

April 9, 2011 9:02 AM (1)

They attacked to Phiem's head when she was in her kitchen to have breakfast.

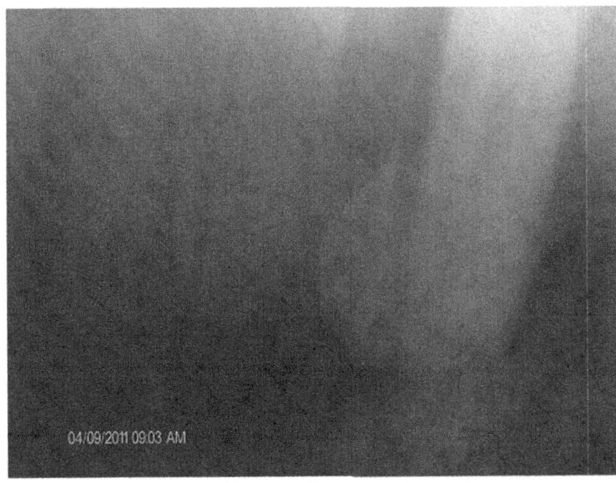

April 9, 2011 9:03 AM (2)

They attacked to Phiem's forefront head at the tempo.

April 9, 2011 10:51 AM (1)

Phiem was sitting at her computer to entry her Criminal Psychotronic Weapons pictures diary they attacked her left ear she took these picture to prove the time constantly bombarded to her ear.

April 9, 2011 10:52 AM (2)

April 9, 2011 10:53 AM (3)

April 9, 2011 10:54 AM (4)

April 9, 2011 10:55 AM (6)

April 9, 2011 10:56 AM (7)

April 9, 2011 10:57 AM (8)

April 9, 2011 10:58 AM (9)

April 9, 2011 10:59 AM (10)

April 9, 2011 11:00 AM (11)

April 9, 2011 11:01 (12)

April 9, 2011 11:02 AM (13)

April 9, 2011 11:04 AM (14)

April 9, 2011 11:05 AM (15)

April 9, 2011 11:06 AM (16)

The above a series of picture they bombarded to Phiem's ear constantly from 10:51 AM to 11:06 AM it was 16 minutes.

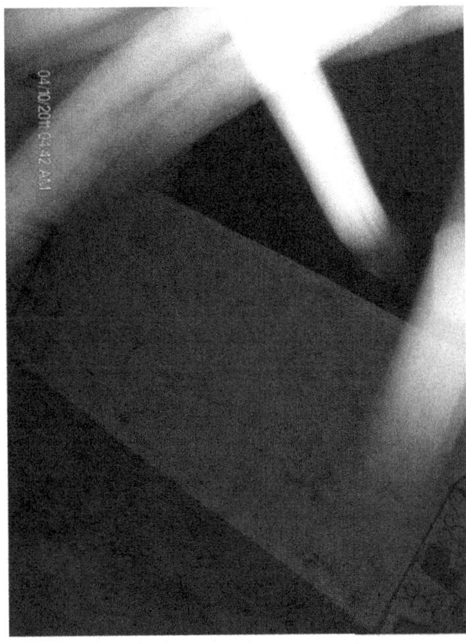

April 10, 2011 4:42 AM

Phiem was scared to go to bed she did not know what they did to her body so she tried to be awaking all night, they attacked to her head through her ear canal at this time.

Phiem went to bed at 6:00 AM then they busted smell something forcing her smell it but she did not know what it was, they used to do it she had to cover her nose with Kleenex or handkerchip or hold her breath. She was so tired then was fallen in sleeping easily then they woke her up about one hour later by attacking her lower abdomen so painful and they cut or pin or tear at her female to make her wake up then to go to bathroom. Phiem said that she can not live like that, these evils should die quickly.

They attacked to Phiem's heart when she was at her kitchen it was painful that they tried to kill her, she knew that they kill people immediately they claimed it heart attacked, she wanted this will open to public to barn this ill science, it was developed for spy agents now using on civil.

April 10, 2011 3:38 PM (1)

They attacked to Phiem's ear canal when she was sitting at her computer.

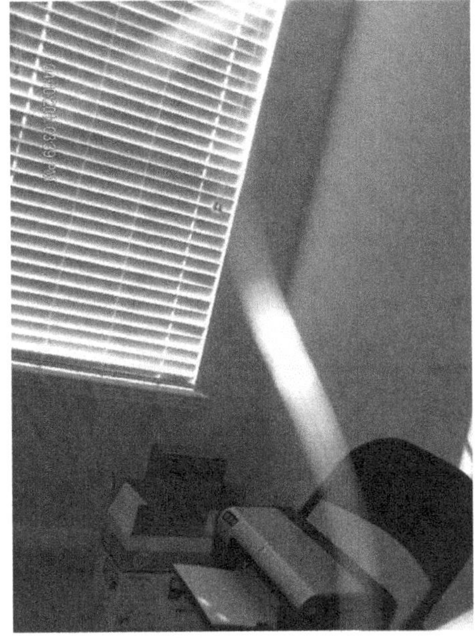

April 10, 2011 3:39 PM (2)

They attacked to Phiem's ear canal when she was sitting at her computer.

April 11, 2011 5:53 PM (1)

They attacked to Phiem's head when she was at her dinning room.

April 11, 2011 5:53 PM (2)

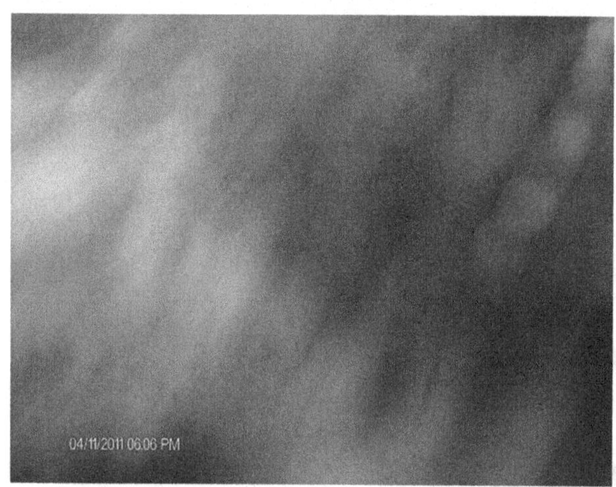

April 11, 2011 6:06 PM (3)

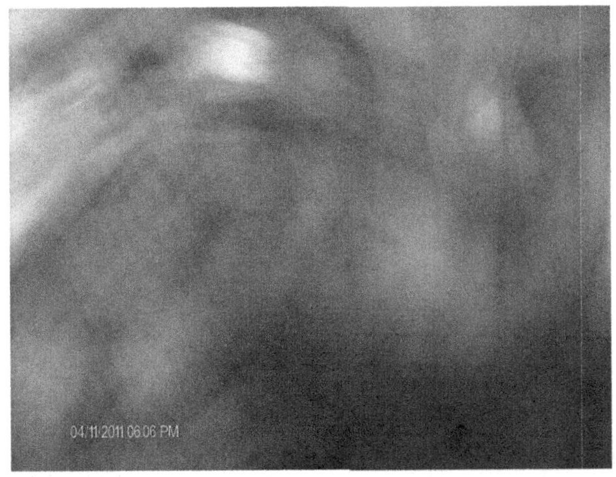

April 11, 2011 6:06 PM (4)

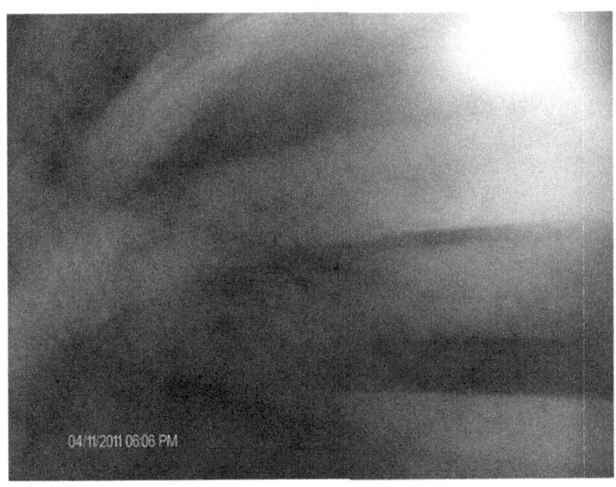

April 11, 2011 6:06 PM (5)

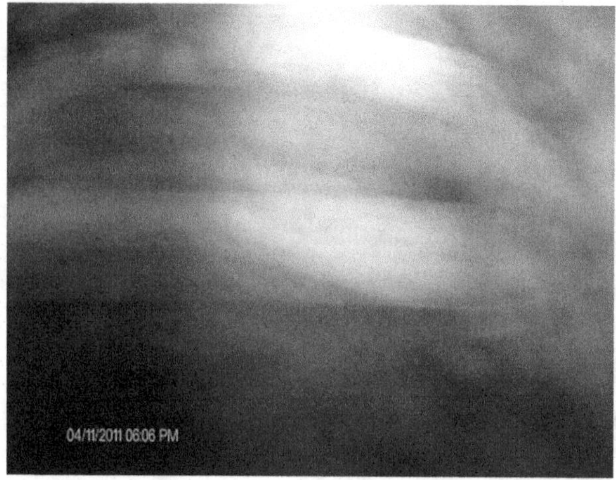

April 11 2011 6:06 PM (7)

During the time she was eating they attacked to Phiem as these pictures above were presented.

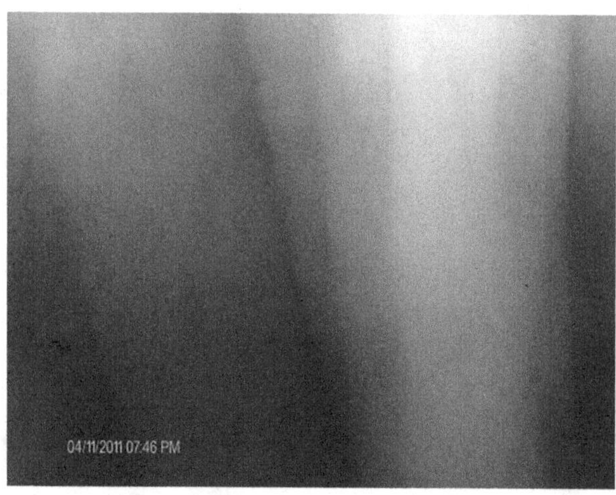

April 11, 2011 7:46 PM (1)

They attacked to Phiem's head when she was sitting at her computer.

April 11, 2011 7:46 PM (2)

April 11, 2011 7:47 PM (3)

They attacked to Phiem's head when she was sitting at her computer, this will prove that they are constantly surveillant and attacking her wherever she was in her house.

April 11, 2011 7:48 PM (1)

They turned to attacked Phiem's stomach side organs when she was sitting at her computer, she took these pictures this is the few she captured it in the pictures while hundred or thousand times she could not capture it to show. Another part of her body like her face, her lungs, her heart, her stomach, her back, her legs and her feet she could not take picture to present her in her diary.

April 11, 2011 7:48 PM (2)

April 12, 2011 5:36 PM (1)

They attacked to Phiem's head when she was at her dinning room.

April 12, 2011 5:39 PM (2)

April 12, 2011 5:40 PM (3)

These three pictures above proved the attacking to Phiem was perform outside her house, it proved that but it was a crime executed on her body inside her house. Sometime they also attacked to Phiem female and her rectum when she was outside her house at her front yard, back yard, few times on the street.

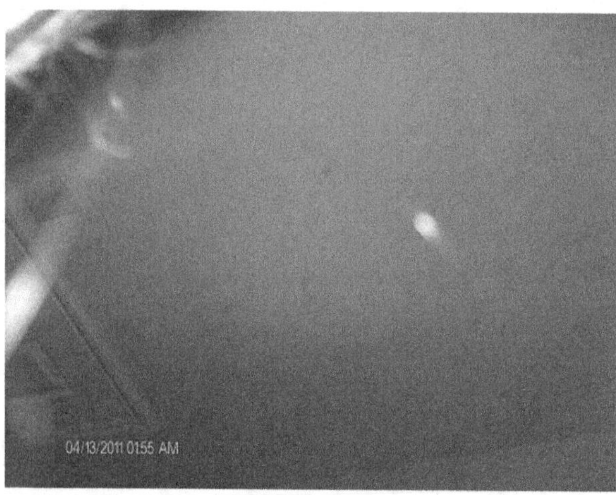

April 13, 2011 1:55 AM

They attacked to Phiem's right ear when she was in her bed.

April 14, 2011 4:52 AM (1)

They attacked to Phiem's head through her ear canal when she was in her bed.

April 14, 2011 4:52 AM (2)

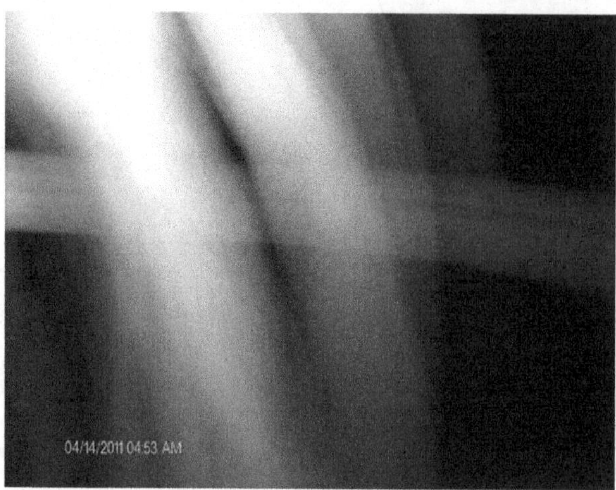

April 14, 2011 4:53 AM (3)

They attacked so hard to Phiem's head through her ear canal when she was in her bed.

Few days ago they used laser to make shape her chin when she was at her kitchen sink then yesterday they used the ray gun or special Nanomagnetic pincers for surgery to go into my chin to make shape to change the out look her chin, after she finished doing dishes she saw her chin look larger than her original chin that they tried to damage her face on what face they wanted it to be.

They also pulled her cheek born grew bigger and higher, they did it to her cheek bone, Phiem felt pain inside her cheek born then it was gray color at her left cheek born.

They implanted or injected material into her end eye, she saw it was swollen at that place at the place they pinned down her eye led. They also made change Phiem's eye shape into what shape they wanted for pleasure, her eye brows they cut then they grew the shape that they wanted to sabotage her beauty for joking.

April 16, 2011 12:45 AM

They attacked to Phiem's ear when she was sitting at her computer.

April 17, 2011

They busted smoke forcing Phiem inhaled for 3 days and nights until now they still doing this, they forcing her to smell it until she got cancer in her lungs and her glands and her oral. They shot to Phiem sole, toe, heel, thigh that made her leg pain then yesterday they shot to her left leg vain at the ankle when she stood at the kitchen sink, her left feet was pain for walking then they shot to her right feet sole. They attacked to Phiem right shoulder, her left back shoulder, her spine cord, her female all the time. Phiem does not need to note down the head, the ears, neck, stomach and her entire body but it was daily they constantly attacking her body 24/7 and 365/year but they tried damaging Phiem body since 2004 when Phiem came back USA from Viet Nam.

April 19, 2011

They did something to my right neck vein, it was so tighten and hurt when I woke up, then afternoon when I took shower they did something to my back at the lungs that mad me felt so tighten and heavy on my back, it look like they did something to prevent from working my both hands as they did it to my left hand, I could not rise my left hand straight and could not do the thing my left hand does for years, now they wanted to do it to my right hand. My legs they shot veins, born, joins, it made me to hard to walk with my tennis shoes then they used Microwave to heat my veins and my born to inflame it and to strengthen the muscles in both my ankles and feet. I had trouble walking these days. I did not know if they did something to my shoes or not.

April 19, 2011 1:23 PM

They attacked to Phiem's ear when she was sitting at her computer.

April 19, 2011 11:42 PM (1)

They attacked to Phiem's ear when she was in her bed room, she took this picture camera was facing to her ear.

April 19, 2011 12:44 PM (2)

They attacked to Phiem's ear when she was in her bed room, she took this picture camera was facing to her ear.

April 21, 2011 7:17 AM (1)

Phiem proved how she took pictures when they attacking to her right ear but this time she could not capture the images of Nanomicromagnetic outside so she turned camera to her ear to take picture, these following picture will show how Nano technology and Micromagnetic on these pictures.

April 21, 2011 7:18 AM (2)

They attacked to Phiem's ear when she was in her bathroom camera faced to her ear.

April 21, 2011 7:18 AM (3)

April 21, 2011 7:18 AM (4)

These pictures were shown the Nanomicromagnetic attacked to Phiem's ear when she was in her bathroom camera faced to her ear.

April 21, 2011 9:16 AM (1)

They attacked to Phiem's ear when she was sitting at her computer to enter data into her diary book.

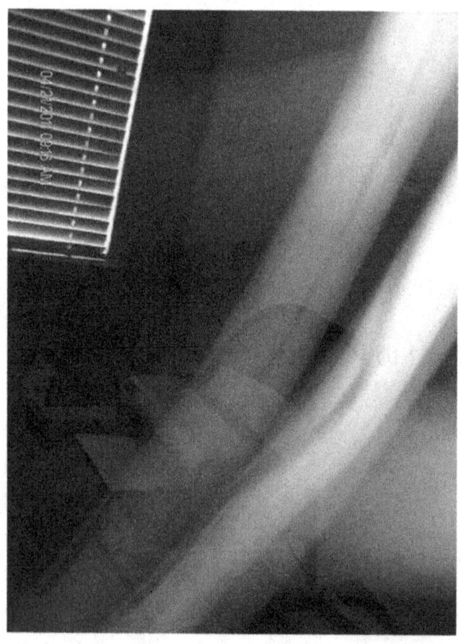

April 21, 2011 9:16 AM (2)

They attacked to Phiem's left ear when she was working on her diary.

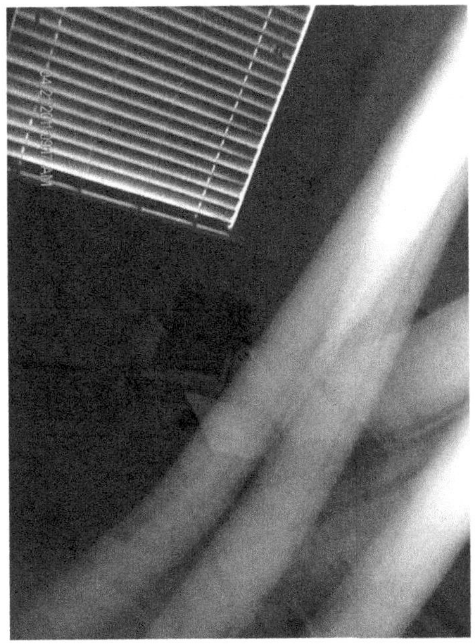

April 21, 2011 9:17 AM (3)

They were constantly beamed Nanomicromagnetic rays to Phiem's left ear when she was sitting at her computer to enter data into this Criminal Psychotronic Weapons diary.

April 21, 2011 9:47 AM (1)

They beamed Nanomicromagnetic rays to Phiem's right ear when she was sitting at her computer.

April 21, 2011 9:47 AM (2)

They beamed Nanomicromagnetic rays to Phiem's head through her right ear canal when she was sitting at her computer.

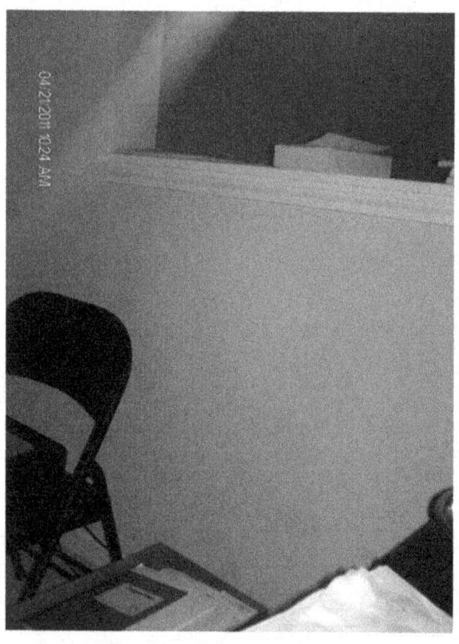

April 21, 2011 10:24 AM

They beamed Nanomicromagnetic rays to Phiem' left ear when she was sitting at her computer.

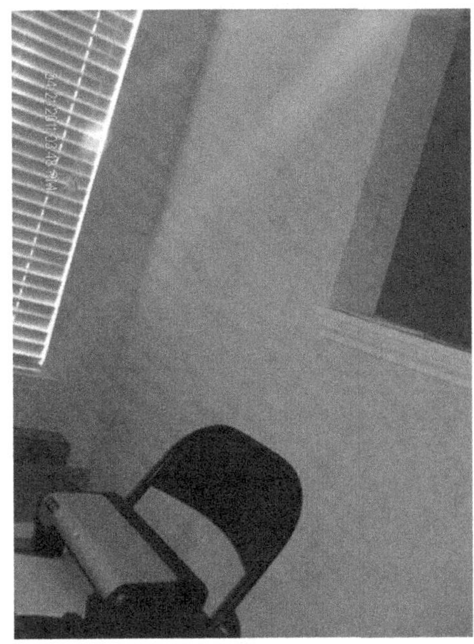

April 21, 2011 3:48 PM (1)

They keft beaming Nanomicromagnetic rays to Phiem's head through her left ear canal.

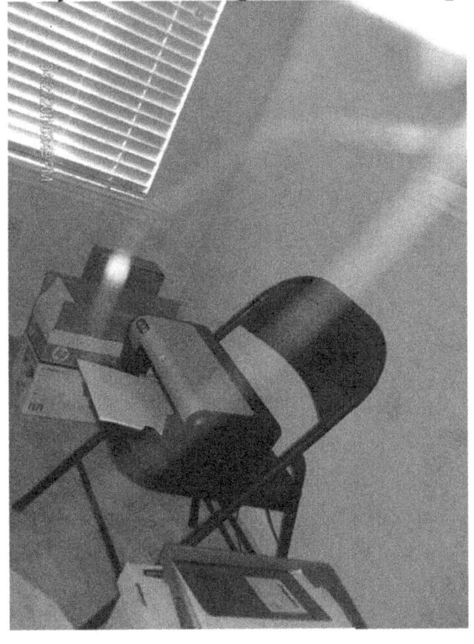

April 21, 2011 3:49 PM (2)

April 21, 2011 3:49 PM (3)

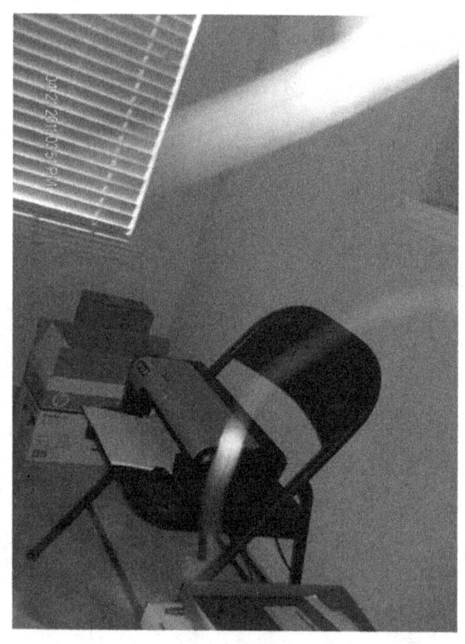

April 21, 2011 3:50PM (4)

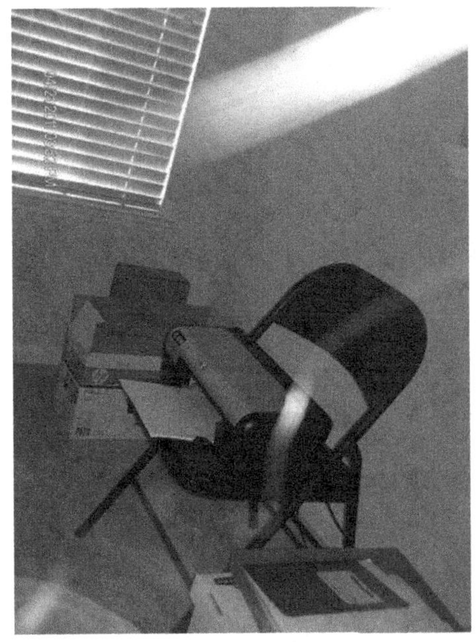

April 21, 2011 3:51PM (5)

April 21, 2011 3:52 PM (6)

April 21, 2011 3:53 PM (7)

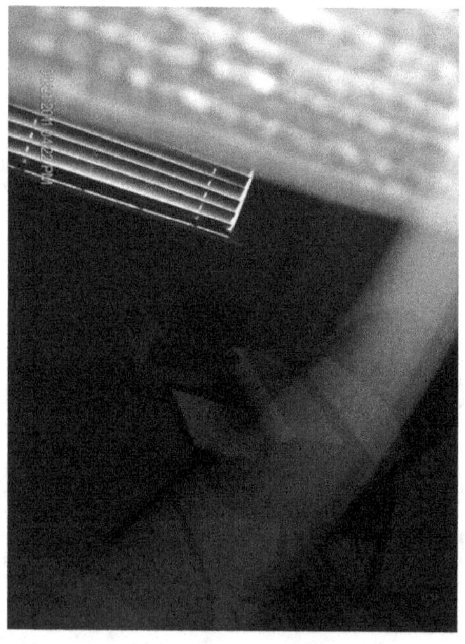

April 21. 2011 4:22 PM (8)

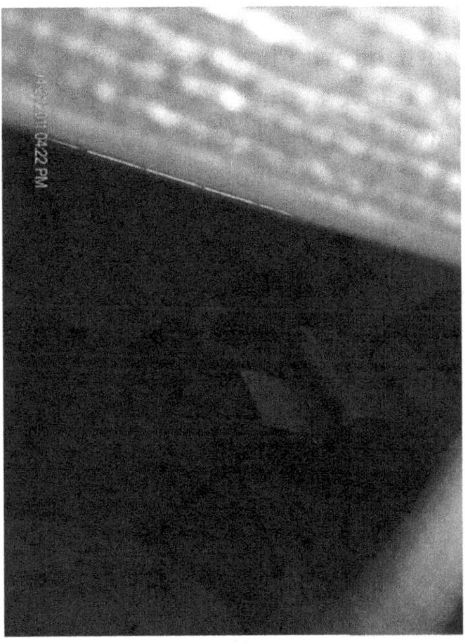

April 22, 2011 4:23 PM (8)

Phiem's hat is red color, she has to wear it to cover her head, they attacked to Phiem's head as the time in the pictures proved it how long they patiently to tried to do it.

April 22, 2011 10:07 AM

This is the time Phiem took this picture but it was happened yesterday but she forgot to take picture to show, they shot to the place they burned her stomach organs, she did not know what they tried to do.

Last night they made the injustice sex dream with the voice sang to her right ear and made the New Age imagining flew on the air and to public. They are sick. Phiem wanted to know who did it, she needed the answer.

Recently Phiem wanted to remarry because she needed husband who has the condition she said in 2005 because they humiliated her life. Of course who love her at heart, care for her, respect her and protect her, sex she prefer normal sex but it will be not the sick and evil sex. She is naïve so she needed husband naïve like her, she can not deal or handle the trouble, and she needed safe.

Phiem asked how she protect herself, her house with security system, front door and back door with rod blocks then her bedroom with door knob clock then rod block also, this is dangerous situation but she has to do it to secure herself but she did not know how they get into her house to do everything they wanted to do even the ring she wore at her finger they change the crystal when she was in New Orleans, Louisiana, she noticed it was losing she can turn the crystal around, she did not know how they did it but she continue wearing it until tow days ago she found out that the crystal was changed, it was not the lose one she could circle it, this morning she took it off her finger.

History of the ring Phiem bought it when she travel to Thailand, she like diamond but do not have money to buy diamond then jeweler invited her to buy American diamond, it was chip like crystal so she bought it to enjoy to wear it because she is Vietnamese she accustoms to buy jewelry for herself, it was not engage ring. At that time in Thailand Phiem went to fortune teller he said Phiem remarry but she does not want that she said no, no, no then he said marry is very good. At that time she did not see but recently she went to Hospital and when she was ill, she needed husband to care for her, her children could not abundant their family to take care her. Specially she was blocked from financial and even her brother stole her money like animal did, she had to go to security office to applied for benefit sharing from her ex-husband because she did not have enough credits, it forced her to decide what to do.

April 22, 2011 7:33 PM (1)

They attacked to Phiem's head when she was in her dinning-room, she did not know who and where it was executed, Phiem saw the light at her front home she opened her window to see and opened the light too.

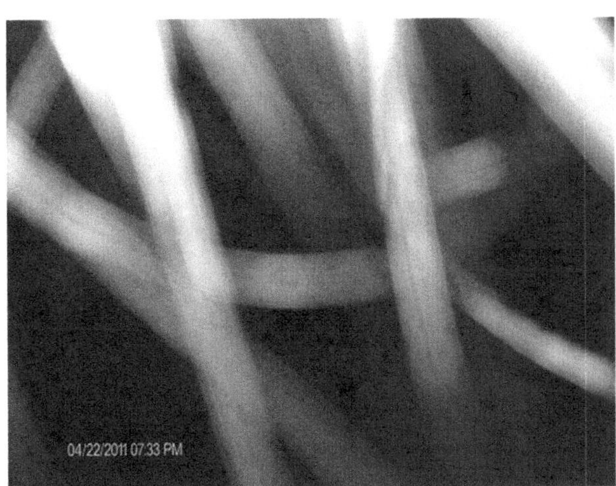

April 22, 2011 7:33 PM (2)

Phiem was at her dinning-room they attacked to her head.

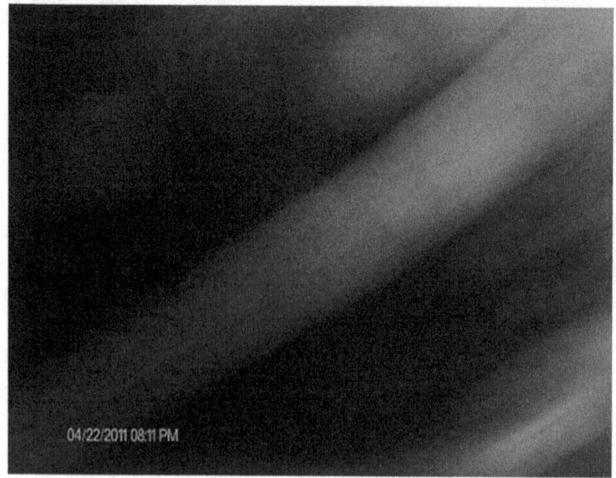

April 22, 2011 8:11 PM (3)

Phiem was at her dinning-room they attacked to her head.

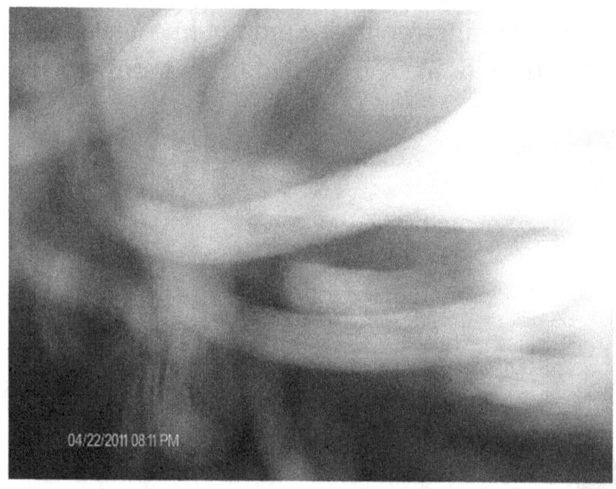

April 23, 2011 8:11 PM (4)

Phiem was at her dinning-room they attacked to her head.

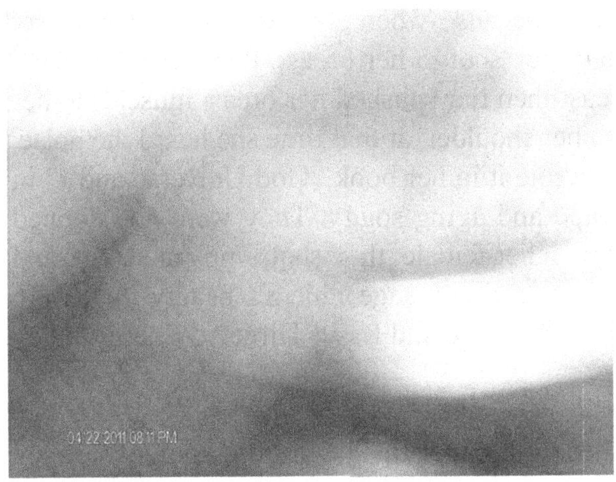

April 23, 2011 8:11 PM (5)

Phiem was at her dinning-room they attacked to her head.

April 23, 2011 5:47 PM

Phiem took pictures they shot to her left breast because when she takes shower she saw the big red dot at her left breast, few years ago they shot to her breast, they pulled, pushed behind her left's arm, lungs and under her breast then they pushed her breast muscles to her underarm, they formed man muscle looking to her shoulder, at that time she heard the noise, she thought they tried to opened her wall, she wrote it in her book "God Universe and I" in 2007, her breast became smaller, changed shape and aging soggy. They were not stopped there, they continued to harm her right breast then her female, they shot, implanted, cut, and pliered it they attempted to change gender, meanwhile damage Phiem's beauty they were going on to harm her body, her organ with Nanomagnetic and Laser Directed Energy. They are savage!

Few days ago she saw the dot of implant on her right upper lip she did not know what they tried to do to her lip, on the left side she took picture and presented in this diary book then later they activated by moving her left side upper lip, that mean they control it as they did it to Phiem's female and they activated by moving the place at her cua minh in 1980 at that time Phiem could not understand what it was until now she remembered that was that kind.

Two days ago she woke up brush her teeth she felt soar at her gum at the center gum and the lower lip, she saw red at that place and it still red and soar now, she does not know what they tried to do to her.

April 23, 2011 5:50 PM

Phiem proved she took picture above by herself to prove.

April 24, 2011 2:33 PM (1)

Today is Easter Phiem just wrote on face book hope that they will let her friends and Phiem free from their attacking then public can see what was going on.

They attacked to Phiem's left ear when she was sitting at her computer. The series of pictures below proved how they were patiently and eager to do what they wanted to do, to kill, to torture, to rape, to prevent and etc.

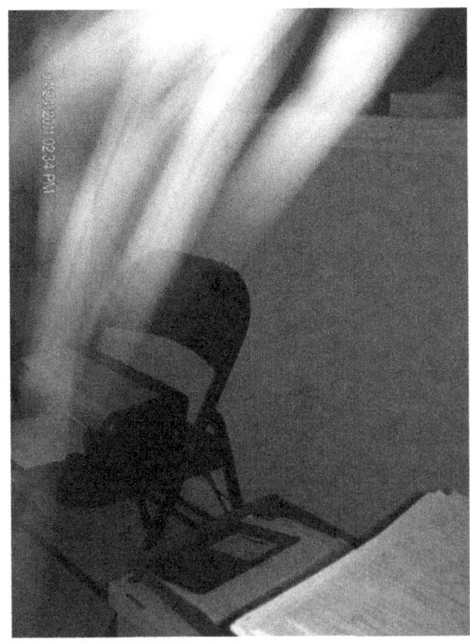

April 24, 2011 2:34 PM (2)

April 25, 2011 2:35 PM (3)

April 24, 2011 2:36 PM (4)

April 24, 2011 2:36 PM (6)

April 24, 2011 2:37 PM (7)

April 24, 2011 4:32 PM (8)

April 24, 2011 4:32 PM (9)

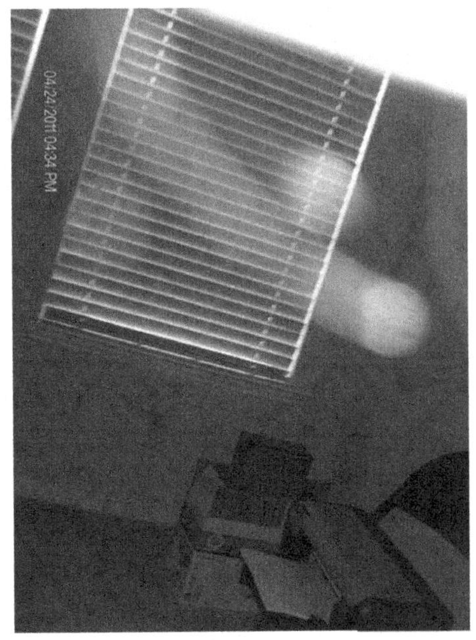

April 24, 2011 4:34 PM (10)

April 24, 2011 4:36 PM (11)

April 24, 2011 4:40 PM (12)

They turned to Phiem's right ear to beam to her ear canal.

April 24, 2011 4:41 PM (13)

April 25, 2011 7:00 AM

Phiem exercise in the morning they kept attacking her she had to move to avoid hit but that was not help as she proved it the target could not avoid it when it was trigger to attack to the victim, after she finished exercise she took pictures. This picture they beamed to her right ear canal.

April 25, 2011 7:01 AM

Phiem took pictures her left ear was attacking during the time she was doing exercise but after she finished exercise she took pictures what was left at the end of their attacking.

April 27, 2011

They are still attacking Phiem took pictures but she could not upload in computer because some of them were Phiem. privacy she took her shoulders with her breast pictures to prove so she had to wait after her card full she will change new Memory card.

April 28, 2011

Yesterday evening they attacked to Phiem's back head at her left neck, she felt head ache and they did something to her head during the time she was sleeping when she woke up she felt heavy and head ache then at lunch time they attacked to her head, she felt head ache and vomit too.

More than week they smoked or they busted smoked inside Phiem's house they forced her inhaled smock all day and night then gasoil, they tried to make her lung cancer, coughing she had this evening. Devil must be destroyed.

Yesterday Phiem placed and advertisement for help and donation for victims of Targeted Individuals, Directed Energy and Psychotronic Weapons because they needed help. Phiem does not want to involve in money as she stated at the beginning on her face book but she could not keep stand still to know victims suffering silently and slowly die but do nothing. Phiem hope that the rich and poor who can help, please help victims, they are sorrow all aspects human life have experience. Phiem wrote agents who penetrated all of societies on this world may know who she was, she meant the victim, the innocence, her character and she can handle money.

May 3, 2011

Phiem did not enter any information because her memory card is not full so she describes the situation here with limited images, the other camera was hard to take picture for herself.

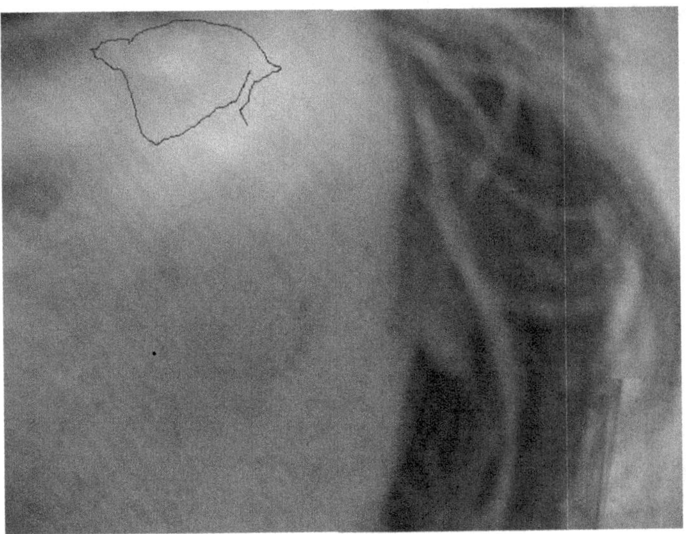

May 2, 2011 7:04 PM (1)

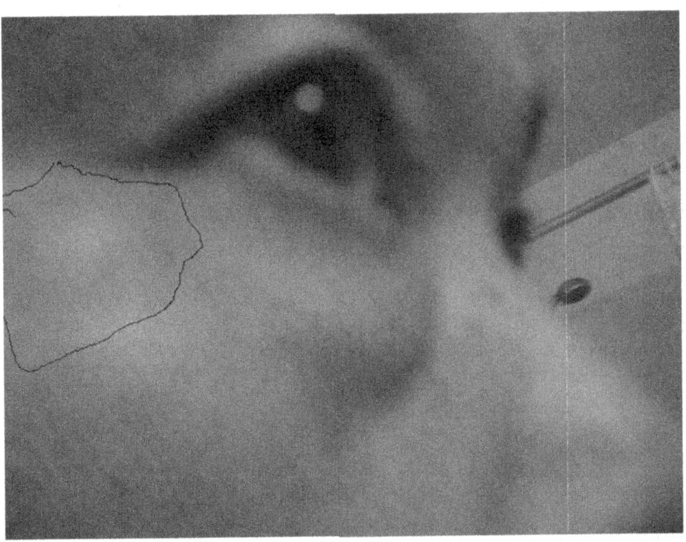

May 2, 2011 7:05 PM (2)

They attacked to Phiem's eyes, her both eyes, she thought she was sitting at her computer then she felt the shot to her both eyes, she saw it in mirror then she took pictures to show, they beamed then they heated it, Phiem does not know what they tried to do.

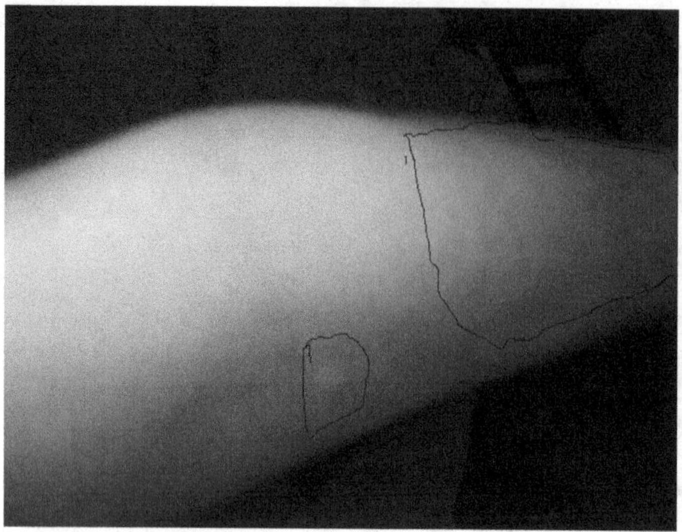

May 3, 2011 9:48 AM

This is the time Phiem took this picture but it was not the time they attacked to Phiem's hand, few days ago, Phiem went outside to water her flower in back and front yards, they attacked to her left hand and her neck, at that time she just felt itchy then she just washed it when she washed her hand, 2 or 3 days after she saw the stranger feeling like orange skin at that place and the skin was turned red. Today when she does dishes they activated to her left hand she was feeling num, she took magnetic metal to hold it in her left hand.

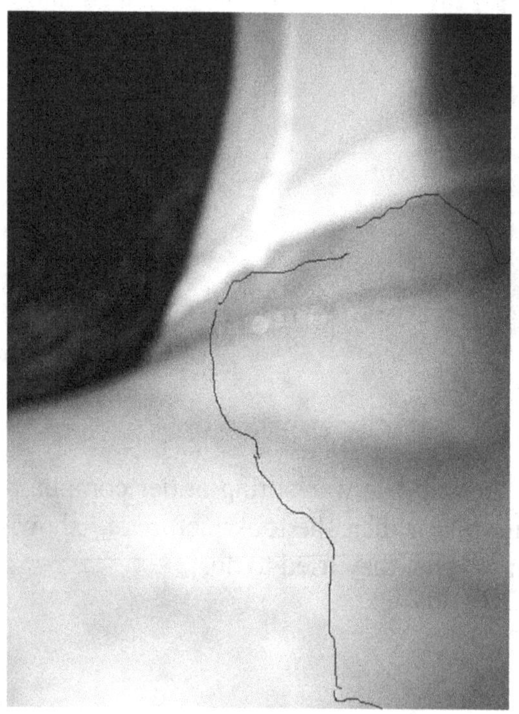

May 3, 2011 9:50 AM (2)

The date and time when she took this picture but it was happened as Phiem described above, she took picture her neck. This camera it's hard to take picture for herself.

They constantly attacking her day and night, it was their routine attacked to her ears canal, head, neck, stomach, organs, hands, legs, feet, veins, buttock, thigh and her female.

Phiem launch the campaign on face book to ask for donation, yesterday she went to bank to make deposit check her son gave her each month to support her living expensive, she asked bank official bank account for the fund she created. She ask him if he know about Psychotropic Weapons, Targeted Individual, Directed Energy, he never know about that, Phiem thought she needed the bill boards to educate public what it was, you are the next victim.

We are victims, we are in the same condition, we could not do anything, we gather on face book, posting, giving comment, exchange news, singing petitions, that is it, we knew victims needed help but do nothing more than that. The handlers control to keep victims in situations suffering and wanted to continue their power to control more people.

I said if nobody makes a donation then I will do it, only I help victims.
That is the other element adds to the list I needed to marry, I needed my future husband will love me, protect me, care for me, bring me out of this situation, provide me financial need to do my project to help victims.

May 4, 2011

The smoke Phiem inhaled weeks constantly it was real and fake combine to harm her health and to make her be addicted drug, Phiem found out it yesterday during the time she was taking shower, they busted smoke as it was in the water then they lead her feeling like that smell, Phiem immediately cursed back to them, now she knew how people was harmful in that way. They also busted the real smoke in her house it made Phiem coughing and stagnant in her throat, when Phiem opened her doors they spayed to cover that illegal drug or smoke in her house escaped to the air outside.

Yesterday Phiem saw the Quantum Leap science video, it was not Quantum Mind, she wondered why they clone her body in order to make Quantum Leap why they destroyed her original body, she love her flesh, her born, her skin, her organs, her brain, her unique, her beauty, her real own body. Give her back her own body.

Phiem heard people said that the fake was giving out but the real was in hiding, is that the true or made her thought to soften her grievance. Recently, Phiem believe the camouflage technique in advance they can fake her in temporary or they can fake her for life, she believe it.

May 6, 2011

I took pictures in both cameras but the one I uploaded to my computer was not reading they might locked it so I could not show the cut at my back right hand shoulder, I did not know what it was just want to show. I felt it strange there this morning then I observed it in mirror, I took pictures then at noon they performed the test at that place it made me feel painful the whole right hand and down whole my back. People can see what they tried to do to people, harm, abuse and kill people with their technology. This is mass destruction weapons!

The thing I wanted people should let the whole world know the war people are facing now the Ecology war and Nonlethal weapons war, the powers should let people know it, please do not blame on the innocent victim or God, do you know if God is murderer they should be kill first, I urge powers have courage to do those things please reveal this war to the whole world.

May 9, 2011

Today Phiem took shower when she washed her female she found out it was hurt and a lot hairs dropped out at the place they made sensation all days and nights, they use Nanomicrochips implanted into that place, it were working itself inside then her side female shape was misshaped, damage then they remote it to be itchy then trigger the sensation not at that place alone but the thought but she always refuse it by placing the things to prevent it ill itchy. Four years ago they began implanted to Phiem's two side female then year or more from now they began implanted Nanomicrochips on top at the center of two side females then the process was the same they did to her two side female then they remote itchy it place then sensation. They cut to change shape or change gander, they heat to make her female cells died to become aging. They are sick evils. Phiem wanted them will be destroyed. She was so angry at their savage actions.

Now I knew they made my stomach looked like Jesus, long time ago when I saw my stomach like that I thought it might be the cause I was hungry so I told myself I must eat more food then later I saw it develop more I wondered then I thought it might be from I bore my children but I said I did not see my stomach like that because I did not know their secret duties to harm, to destroyed people body like that until now I understood that it was.

They shot and cut inside Phiem head yesterday and the day before, it made her dizziness, unbalance.

Today at noon they attacked to Phiem's rectum then she had lunch they attacked to her stomach, she felt pain then she had to go to bathroom right away.

Today when Phiem take shower they attacked to her right wrist, she felt hurt then she cover her right wrist. Few days ago Phiem felt on ground, she got hurt at her right hand, she could not do anything.

They attacked to Phiem's legs and whole her body every day and every night, each time she is in bed they attack to her legs all the time, they want her to be handicap.

May 10, 2011

Last night Phiem was afraid of going to bed because she knew that they will do something on her body but she was so tired to death so she went to bed at that condition, they are sick evils and they created sex dream, I wanted them to be destroyed.

During the day they attacked to Phiem' head then hands, legs, to create pain to her hand and her leg, when they attacked to her stomach side and center her stomach that made Phiem's diarrhea.

May 11, 2011

Phiem saw her body she was shock they deform her stomach to create the ugly body, everyday she was so angry to curse them to be get kill and to be destroyed, they are the sick evils and savage evils, I pray for them will be destroyed. Phiem took pictures her body buy she can not show her privacy here.

May 13, 2011

Phiem went to bed last night she thought they will do something but she had to do it because she has work to do today she could not stay awake for the whole night as usually she did it when she was afraid of going to bed. That was exactly the same they did it, they let her sniff the air busted in chemical or drug to created sex dream, last night was rape sex dream.

Phiem said her subconscious does not have the fire wall, it does not have the door lock, the rod lock, security system and the motion detector as she secures for herself at her home in the dangerous way, they invaded into her subconscious then they did everything they wanted to do. This processing who will be condemned on, the victims or the Controllers, she wishes for the sick and rude savage evils will be destroyed.

Afternoon, Phiem took shower she felt and she saw the different to her female, they changed the female sensitive part to smaller or what she did to that part for what reason she does not know. How they rude, crude, savage and sick evils?
May 14, 2011

Yesterday Phiem copied the May 13, 2011 entry diary to her face book to prove how the Controllers, Handler, Perpetrators did and how the victim was, who should be condemned.

Phiem said the investigation was on and their tactic were amazing to Phiem, she said they, the Controllers were scammers, manipulated people to do things for theirs government interest, their government had responsibility to pay the law suit at their part as the others did.

Phiem reputation, her life, her health, her income, they have to pay by money. Phiem dignity they can not pay by money but they have to bring her dignity back then they have to stop, to end, to get rid, to abandon what they were doing to her and others. She summit her case to the Rule of Law that included the case from 2004-today 2011, this she sue for her beauty, her body, her health, her brain, her reputation, her life, her dignity and her liberty.

May 6, 2011

I took pictures in both cameras but the one I uploaded to my computer was not reading they might locked it so I could not show the cut at my back right hand shoulder, I did not know what it was just want to show. I felt it strange there this morning then I observed it in mirror, I took pictures then at noon they performed the test at that place it made me feel painful the whole right hand and down whole my back. People can see what they tried to do to people, harm, abuse and kill people with their technology. This is mass destruction weapons!
The thing I wanted people should let the whole world know the war people are facing now the Ecology war and Nonlethal weapons war, the powers should let people know it, please do not blame on the innocent victim or God, do you know if God is murderer they should be kill first, I urge powers have courage to do those things please reveal this war to the whole world.

May 9, 2011

Today Phiem took shower when she washed her female she found out it was hurt and a lot hairs dropped out at the place they made sensation all days and nights, they use Nanomicrochips implanted into that place, it were working itself inside then her side female shape was misshaped, damage then they remote it to be itchy then trigger the sensation not at that place alone but the thought but she always refuse it by placing the things to prevent it ill itchy. Four years ago they began implanted to Phiem's two side female then year or more from now they began implanted Nanomicrochips on top at the center of two side females then the process was the same they did to her two side female then they remote itchy it place then sensation. They cut to change shape or change gander, they heat to make her female cells died to become aging. They are sick evils. Phiem wanted them will be destroyed. She was so angry at their savage actions.

Now I knew they made my stomach looked like Jesus, long time ago when I saw my stomach like that I thought it might be the cause I was hungry so I told myself I must eat more food then later I saw it develop more I wondered then I thought it might be from I bore my children but I said I did not see my stomach like that because I did not know their secret duties to harm, to destroyed people body like that until now I understood that it was.

They shot and cut inside Phiem head yesterday and the day before, it made her dizziness, unbalance.

Today at noon they attacked to Phiem's rectum then she had lunch they attacked to her stomach, she felt pain then she had to go to bathroom right away.
Today when Phiem take shower they attacked to her right wrist, she felt hurt then she cover her right wrist. Few days ago Phiem felt on ground, she got hurt at her right hand, she could not do anything.
They attacked to Phiem's legs and whole her body every day and every night, each time she is in bed they attack to her legs all the time, they want her to be handicap.

May 10, 2011

Last night Phiem was afraid of going to bed because she knew that they will do something on her body but she was so tired to death so she went to bed at that condition, they are sick evils and they created sex dream, I wanted them to be destroyed.
During the day they attacked to Phiem' head then hands, legs, to create pain to her hand and her leg, when they attacked to her stomach side and center her stomach that made Phiem's diarrhea.

May 11, 2011

Phiem was shock when she saw her body they deformed her stomach to create the ugly body, everyday she was so angry to curse them to be get kill and to be destroyed, they are the sick evils and savage evils, I pray for them will be destroyed. Phiem took pictures her body but she can not show her privacy here.

May 13, 2011

Phiem went to bed last night she thought they will do something but she had to do it because she has work to do today she could not stay awake for the whole night as usually she did it when she was afraid of going to bed. That was exactly the same they did it, they let her sniff the air busted in chemical or drug to created sex dream, last night was rape sex dream.

Phiem said her subconscious does not have the fire wall, it does not have the door lock, the rod lock, security system and the motion detector as she secures for herself at her home in the dangerous way, they invaded into her subconscious then they did everything they wanted to do. This processing who will be condemned on, the victims or the Controllers, she wishes for the sick and rude savage evils will be destroyed.
Afternoon, Phiem took shower she felt and she saw the different to her female, they changed the female sensitive part to smaller or what she did to that part for what reason she does not know. How they rude, crude, savage and sick evils?

May 14, 2011

Yesterday Phiem copied the May 13, 2011 entry diary to her face book to prove how the Controllers, Handler, Perpetrators did and how the victim was, who should be condemned. Phiem said the investigation was on and their tactic were amazing to Phiem, she said they, the Controllers were scammers, manipulated people to do things for theirs government interest, their government had responsibility to pay the law suit at their part as the others did. Phiem reputation, her life, her health, her income, they have to pay by money. Phiem dignity they can not pay by money but they have to bring her dignity back then they have to stop, to end, to get rid, to abandon what they were doing to her and others. She summit her case to the Rule of Law that included the case from 2004-today 2011, this she sue for her beauty, her body, her health, her brain, her reputation, her life, her dignity and her liberty.

May 15, 2011

Phiem was in attacking to her left top head yesterday evening and this lunch time too, she took pictures but can not upload her pictures here but these were the same as she took it before.

Phiem was afraid of going to bed last night she thought they will do something so she tried to keep her in awakening until 6:00 AM then she woke up at around 10:00 AM. She went to bathroom then came back her bed they attacked at her ket hang at the place between her leg and female, it was so hot, laser burned, she took pictures and she saw the thin brown line on the picture has date on it, they tried to burn her thighs with laser during the time she was in her bed, in her kitchen and all the time, they also brace her ankle, and paralyze leg and hand veins.

Phiem's female they used Nanotechnology and laser attacked, they cut, they implanted, they shot, they remote, they activated all the time days and nights for years, she has to cover her female with ice or sponges with metal, ceramic bowl and aluminum sheet, that why she went out without that things covered she felt light, free at the stage she was shock at that freedom for her female.

May 16, 2011

Phiem took pictures prove how they used camouflage technique to transform her upper lip into her father lip then they created bear on it by using Nanomicromagnetic gun to inserted tissues bear to grow. They did it when she was at her kitchen sink, in her bathroom and at her computer, Phiem just felt like a little itchy at that place and like they painted as doing painting at that place for as long as they wanted to do it, of course Phiem usually prevented it but she said she has two hands and she working with her hands she does not have extra hand to cover that place, if she cover that place she has to stop working, keep doing it when she finish her work. She could not upload pictures to show.

When Phiem was at her dinning room and other places in her house they busted air for her to inhale but she did not what it was Phiem felt it likes smell something strong and dried air.

May 17, 2011

The dried air chemical Phiem inhaled several days ago now it was affected to her health in her body it was appeared through her face, it was like they did it in the past appearing tired, purple gray dried skin, cancer and chemical poisoning.
They were constantly attacked to her head, her thighs, her female, her ket hang, they used laser gun to shot and they might used laser burned or Nanomicromagnetic burned so hard and so long, of course when she had free hands she cover her body with sponges, metal, ceramic bowl, ceramic toothbrush holder.
Phiem wishes for these evils will be destroyed.

May 19, 2011

This morning Phiem went outside from her garage door she felt pain at her heart as the last time she brought out trashcan from her garage door, she felt pain at her heart too like the point shot at that place, she did not know where it came from. Murder people?

This morning Phiem listen to radio from the video friend on face book link to the group site Dr. Julianne McKinney was in interview for almost two hours, she described all the situations victim faced and the technology and the Perperrators, Phiem want this valuable video should be broadcast on the mainstream so public can notice this crime exist and to end this inhumanity abuse.
Yesterday Phiem sent email with excerpt from her Criminal Psychotronic Weapons to the Journalist Investigation Media, she is the one of victims to prove it exist.

May 20, 2011

This morning Phiem woke up she felt something at her left back head like a cut inside her head, she saw her left eye was in obscured harm, she did not know what they did to her body and her head and also her subconscious during the time she was sleeping. Phiem said they are coward dinosaurs. Yesterday evening during the time Phiem took shower she heard the loud noise as if the heavy shipment outside, she had this experience several times before but she could not see anything when she finished and went to look through her window, she said next time when she heard the loud noise outside she has to immediately go out and look. The smell Phiem could not stand the smell they busted it in the air or it was in the water every time she takes shower, they are terrible.

May 23, 2011

They used Nano Micromagnetic gun to vacuumed Phiem's chest tissues or flesh in front of her eyes looked to the mirror, she saw her chest with her skin covered her ribbons.
Weeks ago Phiem notice they did harm to her female during the time she was sleeping, they vacuum the tissues or flesh at the base of her female sensitive place, and she could feel the born at that place when she took shower.
Yesterday Phiem notice they did harm to her female they constantly did years they dua, mai her sensitive place to smaller then smaller then thinner day by day or week by week but the night before yesterday they used high-tech NanoMicromagnetic to change it to smaller and thinner obviously notice it immediately. These sick evils should be destroyed.

Yesterday during the time Phiem was sitting at her computer they attacked to her side stomach, it was through the mouse pat Phiem used to shield her side stomach, it was hurt so she had to take metal to shield that place. They already deformed that place to the fatty gouge she saw her body look different and now they shot to place.
Day and night they were attacking to her body from head to toes, her brain, her organs, and her subconscious and these days she has to smell the recess perfume. What I wish for these evils?

May 31, 2011

Last night Phiem went to bed at midnight they used the force she did not know what kind of this force with strong pushing power to push at her female, her female shield with sponges, metal sheet, magnetic and solid metal, these things of shield against their force, she could feel how strong at that place and the ray gun or laser or Carla attacked to her body outside the shield, she could feel pain, hurt at the whole place at her female and the outside her female, weeks ago Phiem placed magnetic at her female during the time she was sleeping she could feel the place they implanted chips were dead, no feeling like the dead tissues at that place, no nerve tissues then they knew it they implanted new microchips she felt hurt at that place when she took shower as she mention that at the day it was happened in this diary then after that it was in their remote and controlling back again. Then the night later Phiem placed the magnetic at her female when she went to bed they attacked to her female then the vibration was happened, it wave shaken the whole place at that night, they knew it.

June 8, 2011

The day before yesterday when I woke up I saw the dented in on my forefront and it was so hurtful at that place and inside my head then today and yesterday I felt head ache at the stage I felt vomit, it might injury my brain, they did the same to my forefront not to long from now it about week or 10 days ago.

Two day ago when I was using massage mat I did not cover my female they attacked to my female like several pins shot to my female it felt a little pain, then I noticed my flesh was vacuumed out, first I did not know it was from them, they did it, after I had an experience then I used sponge and carton to cover the place they attacked.

June 14, 2011

Today they showed off their Carla force to pump up the cells of my lower leg affronted when I was in kitchen and at my dinning room. They are from my neighbors and on the plane did it I thought so. They twisted my vein left leg, it made my leg cram, they sabotage my legs, they sabotage my body trunk, it looked ugly now. They are so terrible sick science misused, how I can do if I thought they are human and I am human but they did it to me for humiliate me, how I revenge toward this action executed on my body, my life, my honorable life.
They should be destroyed and become the resource for human interest, why they did these sick things to me, because they needed land and resource.

June 16, 2011

Yesterday when Phiem was sitting at her computer they attacked to her right front side head, she lost feeling at that place like it was shut down completely for a while and pain feeling at that place for several hours later, it was the place of moral judgment then they manipulated in sensation nerve sex and thought the wrong doing things like that but Phiem shut it down immediately.
Public knew what they intended to do to people, Phiem made conclusion that Vietnamese popular curse to the bad guys "bait them to Crocodiles" but Phiem will be scare to eat that Crocodiles meat.

June 18, 2011

Before yesterday Phiem ate vegetable dish she just bought from supermarket after that lunch she sat at her computer she felt the shot attacked to her rib so painful and her stomach they attacked to make her stomach upset, then she felt vomit and diarize, she had to stop eating that vegetable. Then yesterday she wanted to find out which one made her sick, none of these vegetable was a culprit.

Phiem saw the red dot at her forefront near to her beginning eye brow, one more red dot at her cheek and one red dot at her right hand shoulder then after lunch Phiem brushed her teeth they attacking to that red dot at her right hand shoulder she saw they pumped up her hand so she took the ceramic brush holder to cover that place.

June 19, 2011

This morning when Phiem bushed her teeth they attacked to her female as everyday they did it then they attacked to her right rib organ she felt usual tired or something die out easily then they attacked to her head like die out her head too, it means unfeeling head, she had to massage her head right away. These evils should be destroyed.

Criminal Psychotronic Weapons VI

June 21, 2011

Today as everyday they attacked to my body, my head it made dizziness, my organs and my female. My female they used Nanomicrochips implanted in then they remote it working to deform my female as they did it since 2007 then they mai, dua my female to deform it as they wanted. I did not know what they did to my mouth I felt hurt at my gum when I brushed my teeth and chewed my food. Cancer cells they injected in everywhere they wanted and they bombarded Micromagnetic to my head, my body everyday since 2005. Aging my face and my body then they said Cancer.
I wanted to go to UN to speak about torture on human at this time but I could not do it because I do not have money to go, they created poverty to victims, they blocked everything on victims like me for my whole life, isolation, they shaped people life, they humiliate, they abuse, they torture, they rape, they deprive, physical high-tech torture and mental high-tech torture.

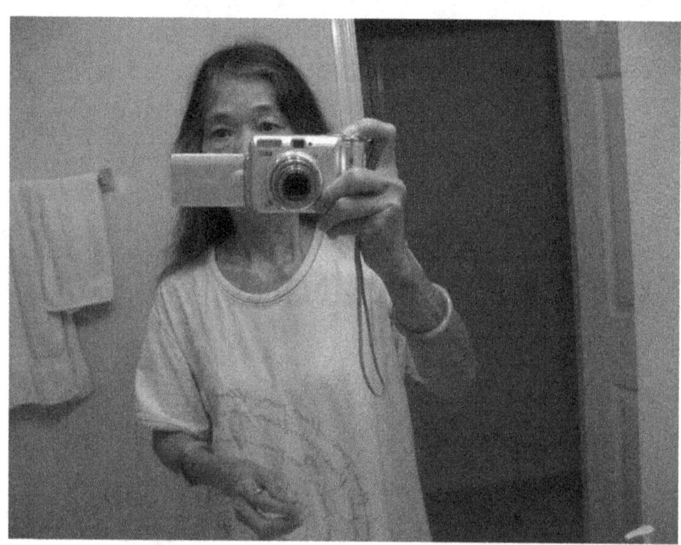

June 23, 2011 3:31 AM (1)

Phiem proved she is and she wore pink night shirt at the time they attacked to her female and she took pictures to show.

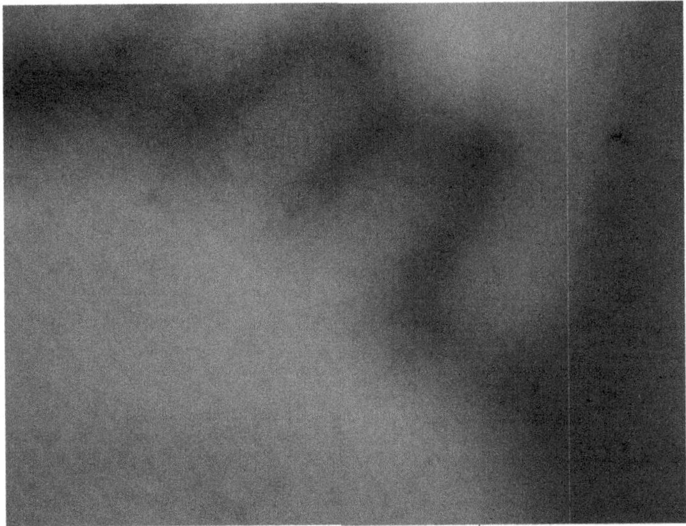

June 23, 2011 3:32 AM

Phiem woke up or they woke her up as they did it to every night which they remote or they shot to her female created urine sex so she rushed to bathroom each time she woke up, this time she brushed her teeth at this time because she was deprived sleeping, they always attacked to her female, her organ and entire her body this time she took picture at the time they attacked to he female, the picture proved above camera face to Phiem outside her nigh shirt at her female.
They shot at her buttock at the place they began to shot at that place since 2001 or 2002 when Phiem was in Plano, Texas.
They bombarded to Phiem's right side head she could feel several cut on her head and feel hurt too.
She woke up at 3:00 AM then she fell in sleeping at around 8:30 AM, during the time she was sleeping she did not know what they did to her subconscious to create sex sensation then they woke her up at around 10:00 AM., day and night, physical and mental abuse constantly.

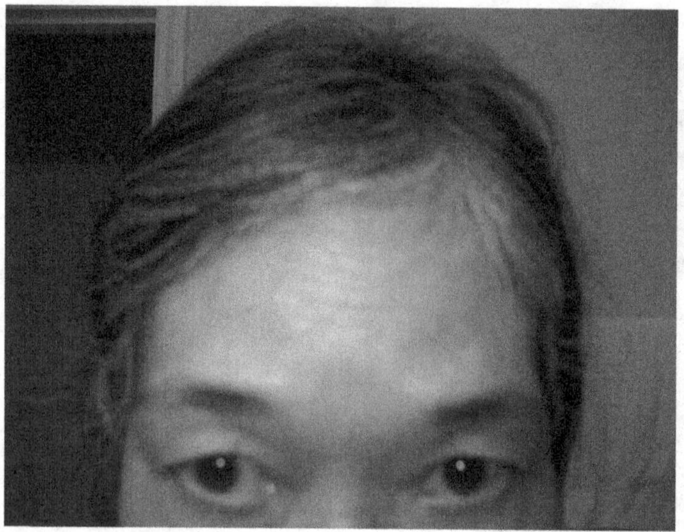

June 24, 2011 6:48 AM (1)

This was the time Phiem took picture this morning but it was occurred during the night she woke up yesterday morning at 3:00 AM, she saw it.
They created her forefront head like tran vo, years ago they created her dented in head at her left side head, they dented her back head too but she could not see it she just felt it then she heard they were laughing.

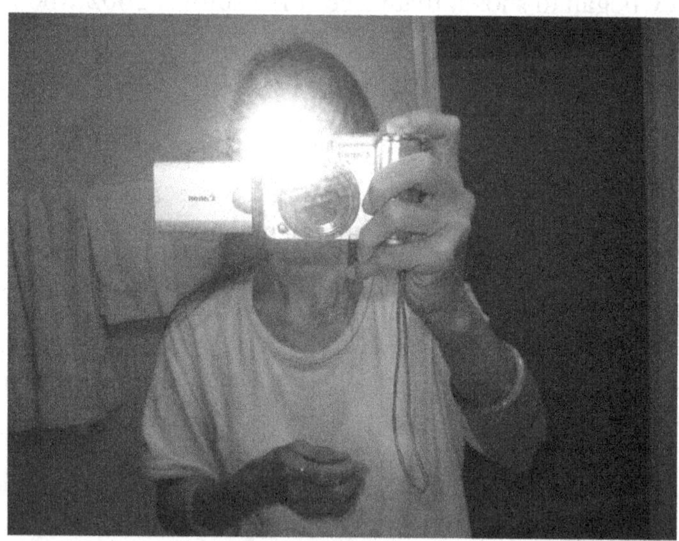

June 24, 2011 6:49 AM (2)

Phiem proved she is and she took these pictures.

June 25, 2011

Yesterday evening Phiem had dinner, the food she ate or the attacking from her head when she just sat down at the dinning room, they were immediately attacking to her head, it made her unbalancing felt from her head and unease then she felt sick at her stomach, cold then she went to bathroom after dinner then she felt tired, she was falling in sleeping until 12.00 AM she went to bathroom then back to her bed, she needed to lay down because she was tired then she was sleeping until 3.00AM under their controlling, she went to bathroom then back her bed sleeping again, she woke up at around 7:00 AM.

It was strange chemical or mind control under attacking Phiem's head.

This morning when she woke up they might did something to her subconscious, they controlled she knew it.

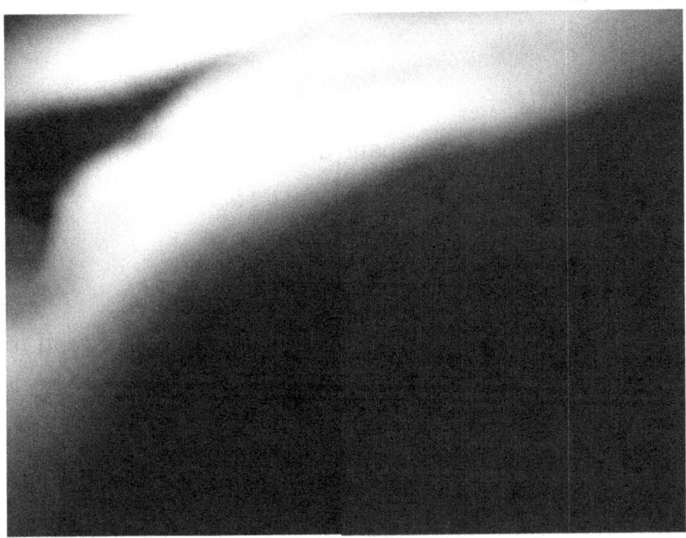

June 25, 2011 7:06 AM (1)

This morning during the time Phiem massaged he face, they attacking to her rectum, she took this picture with camera faced to her pant at her rectum.

June 25, 2011 7:10 AM (2)

This is picture # 2 Phiem took with camera faced to her pant at her rectum when they attacking to her rectum during the time she massage her face.

June 26, 2011

Yesterday I look up from my book mark the Zeitgeist document I might save when I read it from friend posted on face book. I was surprised the document was changed into video so I have to watch it to know what the content because I was so happy I will post it on face book. During the time I watch the video I heard loud music and drum and people voices talking, I thought it loud music from my neighbors but I have to watch the entire video before I post, after video ended, I posted on face book and on twitter because the good idealism with my comment "Good idealism but we are human we needed moderate" after that I walked to the windows to see if they had party there but it was nobody there then I went to my bathroom I heard the drum then I walked outside my bathroom I head only the air-conditioning was running then I stepped back in bathroom I heard the drum playing, I knew it, I cursed, I vented then they stopped it.

I did not know if they hacked into my computer to tape it or if they made change from their original text but I want know who conduct the unhealthy video to harm people who access to the video, I knew it was the same material using I had an experience 1993or 1994 in Austin when I watched my mother house warm up party video. I was wonder at that time after I watched that video then I heard the news when I travelled to Quebec on 1999 the report said a lot of Vietnamese heard the music or video they had the same problem, they remembered everything from their child hood, they missed their families, they were so sad, so depress.

At that time Phiem knew could not understand how they made unhealthy music and video until recently she read document about Mind Control.

Phiem was fallen into the situation as she had an experience when she was in Austin so she deleted the video she posted on face book and twitter.

This evening during the time Phiem had dinner at her dinning room they attacked to her top and back head, she felt dizzy, they murdered her like that everyday, what they say, troke, Phiem could not take picture her back she wanted to see how her back body looks like with the deformed but she knew exactly how it was, they wanted it to be ugly look and further harm with that body woman does not take a good care her husband and her children base on body appearance clairvoyance teller. They always harm people like that but lucky for me, now I needed husband who can take a good care me, my children are grown up and they take good care me every time they came to visit me they did for everything they could for me.

June 27, 2011

Phiem went to bed at around 8:00 AM, she woke up or they did make hurt to her feet so terrible, she had to massage her feet, they tried to handicap her by remote the chip they implanted in her both feet, it turned gray at that places on her feet, they also dented in her left lower leg born, she saw it yesterday.
This afternoon Phiem of course was fallen in sleeping again, the tried to influence her by giving their pictures then manipulate their order, Phiem rejected it.
This evening Phiem found out several cuts on her right side head, she did not know what they did to her head, they vacuum it out or they implanted chips into her head. They are regularly doing it to Phiem's head.
When she was at her chicken sink they did something attacked to Phiem Stomach, when she was at bathroom sink they did remote sensation at the place they implanted Nanomicrochips to her female then it affected to her brain for thinking what they controlled, this is not sex chips only but it was harmful behavior or character of person like they taped the fragments to our brains. Phiem was so angry and she wanted these evils should be destroyed.

June 28, 2011

Phiem sat at her dinning room for lunch after she cut grass they shot to her right side head she could feel the big dot like peas there, they constantly attacked to her head, her right side head, left forefront, right forefront, back head at the neck, behind ears and on the top head.

June 30, 2011

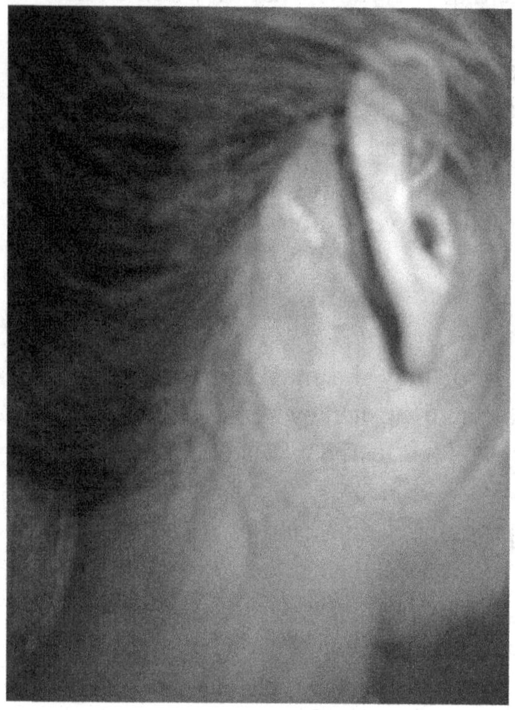

June 29, 2011 10:56 PM

Phiem's left side back ear, she tried to take picture back ear herself it was hard to do it, she wants to know what they did to her ear constantly attacking, I saw the scar there, this is the first time I saw it I do not know how long it was done and what did they do to my head?, controlled my mind? When?

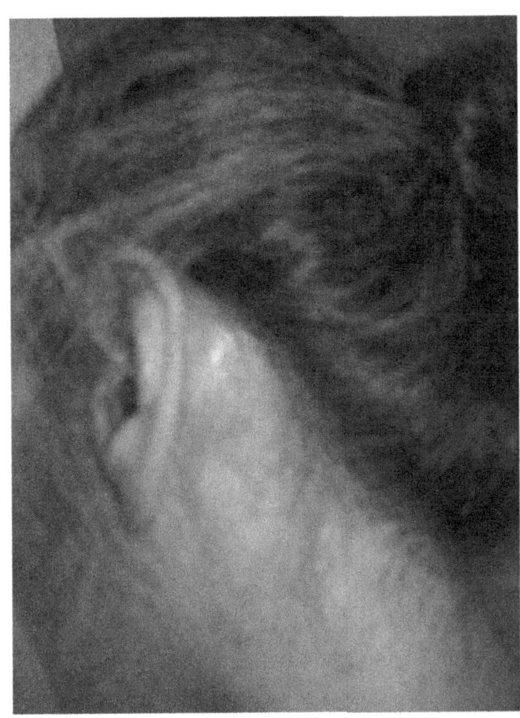

June 29, 2011 10:56 PM

Phiem right back ear they attacked it too, expert will know what it was.

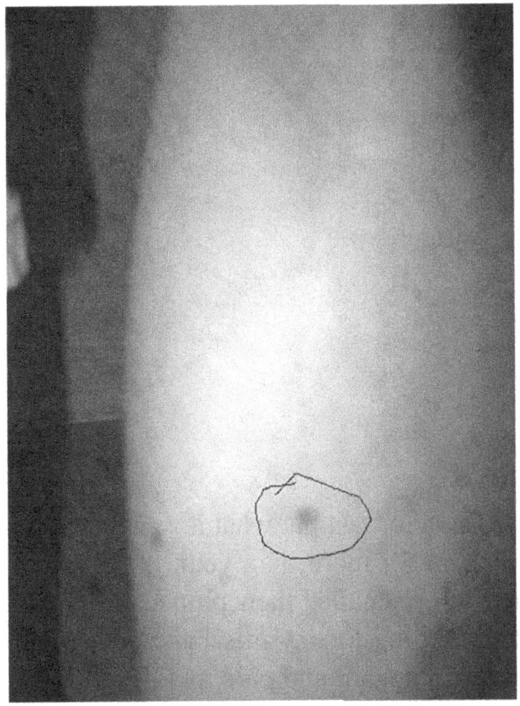

June 29, 2011 11:03 PM

They made new red dot at Phiem's left leg.

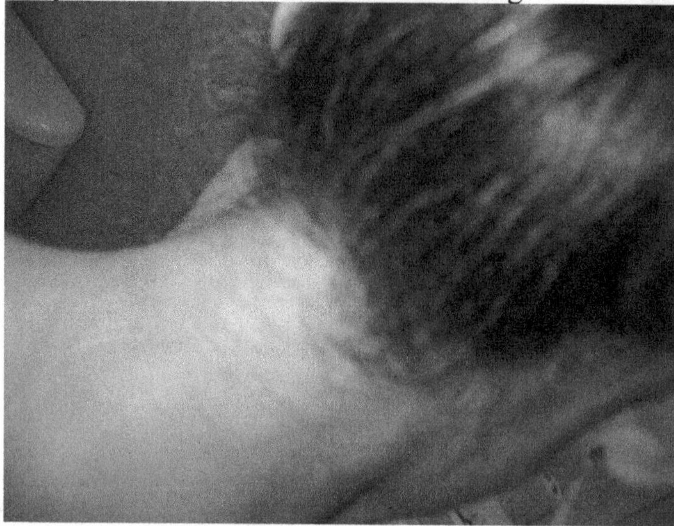

June 29, 2011 10:59 PM

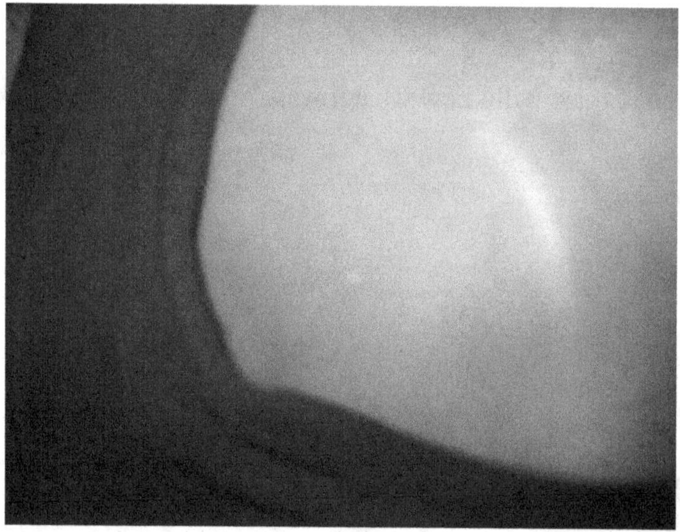

June 29, 2011 10:58 PM

Phiem's back neck, she took pictures herself, it was difficult to do it but what it was the white line? When they locked my arm, I could not rise my arm for more than year, they pulled, pushed my left breast created saggy and small then more smaller then pinned my veins together and placed at my under arm then they were laughing for my misshape breast and hand suffering, my lungs they remote vibration, pressure stagnant and pain as I described it in my book "God Universe and I".

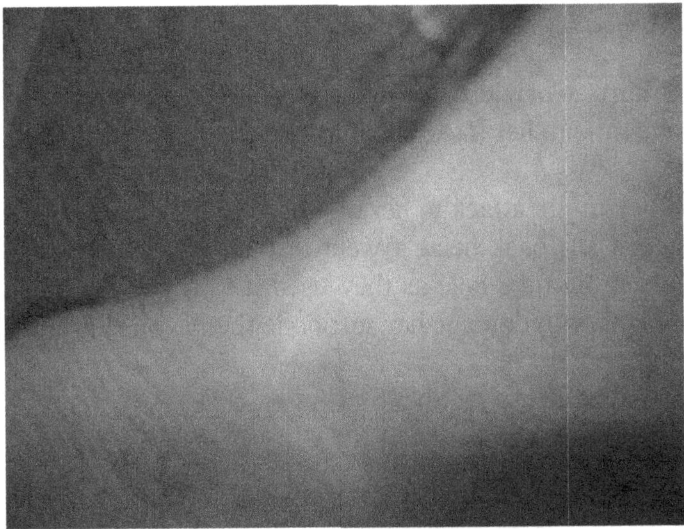

June 29, 2011 10:58 PM

Phiem's back neck, what is the white line?
They used spy technique camouflage and plastic surgery to sabotage her beauty and her body, they tried to make bear on her upper lip. How crude they are, they did what they want to do on her body, her brain, her subconscious and her beauty, the woman beauty.

July 1, 2011

Last night they woke me up at around 1:45 AM, they attacked to Phiem's left side lower abdomen, it was so terrible hurt like my uterus was reshape or shank after my second and third child was delivery. Phiem knew they did something to her woman part or they implanted microchip into her lower abdomen then they activated, they remote it and controlled it pain or sensation which one they like to do, they wanted to kill people by this attempted process, Phiem was so angry she knew they did do this to her stomach and her lower abdomen all the time during the time she was sleeping that made her go to hospital and she is still paying her hospital bills without health Insurance.
From June 29, 2011 they are in her house she guessed or they used technology to set up to create the new attacking or the new level they wanted to achieve on Phiem's body, she heard the small noises in her house she asked if some body is in her house and what you do in her house, she took the long rod to search in her kitchen but nobody answered her and she saw nobody there. Phiem got notice several times after she left her house they might get in to set up things the wanted and Phiem had new kind of attacking from them.
Phiem took pictures at the place they implanted microchips into her lower abdomen and now it was turned into gray color, they remote to control her pain or sensation they wanted whenever they liked but she could not show it here, her privacy but she kept it for evidences.

July 2, 2011

This morning Phiem woke up she felt hurt at her left side intestine they were surely did attacked to that place as they did it all the time to her intestine, that was the cause she had to go to hospital, they are murderers.
They always shot to her rib both sides, they might attack to her organs at that places too.
Yesterday and today they pumped Phiem's left back head it went through to her forefront it was hurt to her forefront head, they used big tube hole as they used it to get through her buttock to reach her buttock bone to implant or to damage her soft bone then it was hurt and they remote to make it feel painful.
What they tried to do to her head? They have to answer. She is so angry, rage.

July 3, 2011

Last night Phiem woke up at around 3:00 AM she noticed them always using their urine sex during the time she was sleeping, she rushed to bathroom and she saw the urine wet her towel which covered aluminum foil sheet to shield her female during the time she was sleeping. She cursed them to death then she went back her bed then she woke up or they made her woke up at the dream they inserted, then they used the big needle with strong force they improve power to shot to Phiem female through the shield she cover her female, the things are aluminum foil, sponge and metal. How they intended to assassin, to harm, to sabotage, to torture, to humiliate, to abuse and to deprive.
What I wanted for these evils?

July 5, 2011

Phiem took pictures her underarm to document evidences what they did to sabotage her breast, years ago they shot, pulled, pushed, pined hers breast tissues to her underarm then they cut the support breast tissues to saggy her breast then they shot or scarla vacuum to make her breast to become smaller then smaller then they laughing.
Phiem can not present her breast picture here, her privacy but for the evidences and the picture her lower abdomen too at the night they attacked to that place during the time she was sleeping, it pain woke her up then continuing attacking for so long, Phiem was under their torture like that terrible pain like the time she born her children. It was the same this afternoon and always like that they remote her leg veins to create the scram to wake her up then they attacked to her female because she vacuum floor then needed to rest, they control like that. Prison in her house for so long!!!
This evening when Phiem was in her dinning room they shot to the left side underarm they shot to her head then Phiem saw the plan past by her window but Phiem does not know where the attacking came from, after dinner she observed her left side underarm she felt it was softer than yesterday and the day before when they shot at that place and made it feel hurt.
Several days ago they stroke at her left side forefront as they constantly did it to her forefront for years.

Few days ago they attacked to her back neck at that time Phiem was feeling it attacked through her borne neck then they attacked two more time later as the same.
Yesterday they injected Nanomicrochip to her back head near at the right ear hair rim, Phiem could feel it like the size of peas, she tried to take picture but she could not do it clearly to show.
Several times few days ago and even today they attacked to her lungs it was pain, she has to cover her lungs with metal object.
Few days ago Phiem sat at her dinning room at lunch time they attacked to her heart, she felt pain so she had to cover her heart with metal object too.
This morning they shot at Phiem's left lung she felt that affect to her left hand for a while.

July 7, 2011

Yesterday they turned on my cellphone to call me and left their message on the phone, it was strange thing to me but I wanted to see who was calling, I read the number: 1-267-592-8355 (this number called me since 2006, it might be before that but I did not pay attention the number) then I hear the message the left there, I heard the sound of eating crunchy food for almost their message then the male voice said Hello then ended the message immediately then I click the number to delete the message, it directed me to call somewhere else but I did not know what number I was calling the operator said that call was not completed I have to dial again then my electric in my house was turned off for a while and I heard the neighbor air conditioner was turned of too, if it was coincident or it was the set up. Phiem did not know that.
Yesterday they shot the big and heavy shot on Phiem left side back head at the place near to the top head, Phiem could not shield herself because her hand with soap she had to wash it, they meticulous watching and know how and when to attacking the target, all day attacking Phiem's ears to her brain, her body, her ugly stomach, her deform body.
They pumped Phiem's intestine both sides her stomach made her felt unease, heavy and hard to move, it made her hard to breath, her stomach looked ugly.

July 8, 2011

This time is 12:01 AM I enter this diary, Phiem is me at the time I do dishes they attacked to my female at the side I could see the big laser gun or electromagnetic gun attacked at that place I felt hurt, this kind is the new kind of attacking I do not know what it was for.
Then at the time I brushed my teeth they attacked to my female at the sensitive place, this is the new kind of attacking I do not know what kind it was for, i did not observed my female to know what they want to do to her female.
I want all of them get kill, period.

They attacked to my head, my left head it made dizziness, they attacked to my shoulder muscles, my neck to make stiff neck, they attacked to my stomach, my side stomach all the time, they pumped up to make ugly look then now they made it saggy, i want all of them get kill, this earth will be safe for a while or long as people want it be safe and peace.

July 9, 2011

Yesterday I went to UPS store to send my package of evidences I wrote down diary and published books and DVDs. To the Rule of Law and I wrote follow up letter I will send too. They attacked on my head, hurt all my head, it was so terrible.
Yesterday afternoon I do dishes they attacked to my female, it hurt through my bone at my female as long as they were attacking, I cursed these evils to be destroyed, when I was in my bed to rest they attacked to my ovary place and my left buttock it was hurt and it was hurt at my sensitive place, I wished for these evils will be destroyed.
Evening when I came to kitchen they immediately attacked to my female to make sensation, I was so angry, and I vented again, I took pictures.
When I was in bathroom they attacked to my female side again ask them what they did to my female, they have to explain it to public I do not know and I do not have experience on this field to explain what they tried to do to my female.
I observe my female I saw it turned into smaller shape, it was not imagining, their technique was using recently in front of my eyes and it was affected immediately when they used scarla force to vacuum my chest, all the flesh was gone after I felt the force attacked to my chest, my chest was shown bone and skin only. The deformed my body like that, the place needed to be tighten muscles they made it saggy and smaller, the second part of my body they pumped up to see ugly body, they destroyed my original body and my beauty completely and my brain my subconscious could not escape these evil hands and minds also.
What I wish for these evils?
After I took shower they attacked to my left side ear then they triggered the mind control nerves to sensation, this sensation from the brain nerves or the nerve microchips they injected in or they past their fragment to my brain nerves then they remote it, to shield my left ear I had to take object to cover my left ear for a while then it was turned off. Please ask them or expertise who can explain that.
Las night I was setting in nightmare that I could not escape the assaulted rap with tighten hands and nobody help I woke up at the time they wanted me to woke up at the heart beat racing, I wanted to know who conducted that dream, they always sick sex procedures all the time.
What I wish for these evils?

July 11, 2011

They remote the microchip they implanted at my blackhead near the back ear which I tried to take picture the trace they injected the microchip but it was difficult to take picture myself, they trigged it I felt paint then severe pain I had to take object to cover it place for a while then they gave up, they came back many times but each time I shield that place, they gave up.

After Phiem take shower they attacked to her female everyday they humiliate her then today they pulled down her uterus again she had to go out to take object to cover her female. They humiliate my human dignity, my reputation, they murder, they harm my health, sabotage my body and my beauty, how Phiem wish for these coward dinosaurs?
This afternoon when I was in supermarket they remote the chip they implanted there at my rectum, it was embarrassing itchy there, I knew immediately they did it then they were laughing, I heard at least two woman voice laughing.

July 12, 2011

This morning I watering my garden they attacked to my female outside my house, this is not first time, they did it so may times outside my house, usually they attacked Phiem inside her home then they expanded the geography tactic to targeted the victims everywhere.
Today Phiem took picture her stomach, the ugly they made to her stomach, they made the wrinkle skin, dented in her stomach, made fatty gouges both her side stomach it effected her breath and they made the deform rib bones at her stomach, how ugly her stomach look.
She could not show it her, her privacy but she documented for investigation and for the legal, every day they created tress, angry on Phiem since 2005.

July 14, 2011

Yesterday Phiem cut grass her front yard they attacked to Phiem's female, this was outside her house, she cursed them at that time, she wondered if they used satellite or handheld device to do it, the expertise will answer that.
Yesterday Phiem took pictures her back and her back bone spine cord too for documented, it was very difficult to take pictures her back by herself.
They injected chip at Phiem's right foot few day ago she saw that trace on her foot skin but she did not mention in this diary then this morning she felt pain to walk.
This morning she felt hurt like cut or injected near her rectum, she does not know what they tried to do to her.

July 15, 2011

They did something to Phiem rectum she felt terrible hurt there and she felt it was grown bigger like they added the other part to it place near her rectum, she did not know what they tried to do to her. Few day ago when Phiem woke up she felt strange to her female like they separated two side of her female, she was hard to work, they did flatten her female about haft side and separated in two part at that day, Phiem wanted and wished for these evils an coward dinosaurs will be destroyed. She was so angry each day for years, have lived under humiliated and abuse for almost her life, now she wanted these evils will be destroyed.
They shot to her eyes several times, attacked from her head to her neck, her lungs, her stomach, her female, her whole body everyday.

This evening they burst the sulfate into her house or they trigger the smell the whole house smelt it, Phiem's physically effected to her nose and her head.

July 18, 2011

Everyday as the same they attacked to Phiem's head, ear, body, heated her thigh when she was sitting at her computer, her chair and under her chairs in her house to attacked her rectum and her female, her hang, it was frivolous sick they are, I vomit each time I remembered how sick they are, they have to go to the labor camp to be regain their normal healthy lives or die.
Laughing for they wanted and eager do everything they could to expand their lives to nurture their sex, how long they have lived on this earth and how much sex they have made that was not enough for them, only covetous hearts and cruel actions, selfish and sex.
They destroyed this earth, harm nature and attempted to destroy human on this planet, they are the sick mind, the sick evils.
Water they change from chemical to detest smell Phiem does not like then now the grass smell they did it to her water when she had lived in Plano, Texas 2001, they continue doing things from water, food, air, my body, my subconscious, my conscious, my mental, my life since 1980 until today and they will be continuing until they died, if I would died will not be finished they continue until nobody left on this planet included them, I want them to be destroyed.

July 19, 2011

Yesterday I took pictures my privacy to save the evidence what they did to my body at the between my rectum and female, few days ago I woke up on the morning I felt like the cut or big pin shot at that place, I felt so much hurt then day later I felt it was grown bigger then grown bigger day by day, they always created misshape, deform, harm and sickness on my health and on my body. I was so angry.
Few days ago they did something to my thigh I saw the big red dot there and a lot of micro chips on my upper lip, they change shape my mouth at my upper lip.
Few days ago they attacked to my eyes but often at the left side eye, I felt unease to read.

July 22, 2011

Every day they attacked to my body from head to toes, I covered my female they attacked my sole, my foot, my stomach, my stomach side, my ears, my back head and my head, I covered my ear they attacked my back, my lungs, my thigh, my ovary place, my uterus place.
Yesterday I took pictures my forefront, and my nose they injected the microchip at that places, I saw the big red dot there.
Yesterday evening I took shower then I saw my skin look tan but the skin at the place my bracelet was lighter I wondered what was that then I understood they dyed my skin, I did not

know when they dyed my skin at the bracelet was turned into tan too. I was so angry, they are sick evils and should go to jail.
Today I read newspaper that hacker hacked into women victims stole their naked photo to place on victims profile pictures who are in the Revenge Club, I read the comment too, people asked these women were crazy why took their naked pictures? I did not write the comment to let people understand why, because they damaged women victim bodies so women had to take picture her bodies to prove then the Controller stole women naked pictures to their properties using. They are expertise and researched on human behavior I could see the processing was the same to any victim.
Everyday they created the new kind, made the new anger, more anger and more ager, victims were under anger burden like that, how people can live the life like that for the whole life as I am. I thought Fema built the camp to prison the evils.
Today and yesterday I ate some mint has grown in my back yard, it was dried out by chemical from the Perpetrators, I tried to water it everyday to keep it alive, I was afraid of eating it but I thought a lot of water and rain might wash that chemical away so I ate some yesterday and some leaves today it created diarrhea and upset stomach; conclusion for the food we got sick from these kind of murder.
During the time I enter this diary they attacked to my head, it looks like they vacuum of blood out of my top head, I got dizziness then I went to bed to sleep.

July 23, 2011

This morning I woke up the dizziness is still on my head I have to cut grass today so I do a little exercise and remember God Universe and Me in this immense universe, I thank God help me to finish my work today, I do not have earn a single penny, people can imagine how victims can handle their jobs, they drove people to the street, they tight people hands then throw them on the street, people can imagine how meticulous processing Targeted and Torture Individuals on any aspect from physical to mental.
Today I want to ask educated people what you want to do to this mankind. Are you sure you will be happy when you discover other planet like our earth, has living things like earth? This planet earth has a lot human living here but you tried every thing you could to destroy them by water, air, food and ammunition that was not enough for you then you develop ill things to degrade nature, to handicap human, to humiliate human dignity and to deprive human life. How it was and will be lead this world into the future to be?
We are now in the front eyes of the Devils and Draculas every one is the victim at any time and at everywhere; we have to protect ourselves by destroying this evil scam!

They attacked to Phiem's thigh by microwave heating to destroy tissues her thighs, they shot to her female like pin though it, what they want to do to her female.

August 2013

I moved to another place, I could not get away from these criminal now I can say Perpetrators, they are continuing attack, we said tortured, humiliated, abused, harass, high-tech raped, harmed, degraded, distracted, damaged, sabotaged my woman body, skin disease, harmed my health, bone, teeth and tried to handicapped my arms and legs.

I stop using computer it interrupted me to enter pictures into diary to present book.
These pictures updated some information

Criminal Psychotronic Weapons part V

Criminal Psychotronic Weapons Part III

Printed in the United States
By Bookmasters